I, RHODA

A Memoir

Valerie Harper

G

GALLERY BOOKS

New York   London   Toronto   Sydney   New Delhi

For Tony and Cristina
and Rhoda Rooters Everywhere

G

Gallery Books
A Division of Simon & Schuster, Inc.
1230 Avenue of the Americas
New York, NY 10020

First Gallery Books trade paperback edition November 2013

GALLERY BOOKS and colophon are registered trademarks of Simon & Schuster, Inc.

For information about special discounts for bulk purchases, please contact Simon & Schuster Special Sales at 1-866-506-1949 or *business@simonandschuster.com*

The Simon & Schuster Speakers Bureau can bring authors to your live event. For more information or to book an event contact the Simon & Schuster Speakers Bureau at 1-866-248-3049 or visit our website at *www.simonspeakers.com*.

Designed by Jaime Putorti

Manufactured in the United States of America

Photo credits appear on pages 317 and 318.

10 9 8 7 6 5 4 3 2 1

Library of Congress Cataloging-in-Publication Data

Harper, Valerie, 1939-
    I, Rhoda / by Valerie Harper.—1st Gallery Books hardcover ed.
       p. cm.
    Includes bibliographical references and index.
1. Harper, Valerie, 1939- 2. Actors—United States—Biography. I. Title.
    PN2287.H244A3 2013
    791.4302'8092—dc23
    [B]
                                    2012037436

ISBN 978-1-4516-9946-3
ISBN 978-1-4516-9947-0 (pbk)
ISBN 978-1-4516-9948-7 (ebook)

PROLOGUE

I first met Rhoda Morgenstern in the spring of 1970 at an old round oak table in the breakfast nook of the small house I was renting in West Hollywood. Through an amazing stroke of luck, CBS had sent me—an unknown actress—an incredible script for the pilot of *The Mary Tyler Moore Show*. Rhoda—free-spirited, funny, and from the Bronx—leaped off the page and grabbed me with her honest and brash humor. This was a woman I liked—no, a woman I loved. This was a woman I wanted to play. And somehow I got the chance.

For nine incredible years I was lucky enough to be Rhoda Morgenstern, who was as funny and as insecure—as downright relatable—as they come. Through Rhoda I met the most supportive, wonderful, and talented television family I could have possibly imagined: Jim Brooks, Allan Burns, Mary Tyler Moore, Ed Asner, Gavin MacLeod, Ted Knight, Cloris Leachman, Betty White, Georgia Engel, Charlotte Brown, Nancy Walker,

Harold Gould, Julie Kavner, and many more. To this day, strangers greet me, their faces lit up with happiness and recognition, as if they are meeting an old friend or relative—one they actually like!

In 2007 I was invited, along with Mary and Ed, to be a presenter at the Screen Actors Guild Awards. A week later, I heard that Cloris would be there as well. I suggested to the show's producers that if they had the four of us, why not invite all seven cast mates, including Gavin, Betty, and Georgia, too. It would be the first time the entire group had reunited in public since 1991.

It was delightful to be with the whole gang again. Backstage was like a company picnic or a family reunion. We schmoozed and dug in to the delicious buffet (always a standout for me at an awards ceremony), and we were quickly lost in our own little world—the same world where we'd all met back in 1970. Nearly forty years later, here were all my friends, the people with whom I loved to work—my very first television family.

Then it was showtime. The announcers called our names, and one by one, we walked single file out on the stage. The applause was thunderous. The star-studded crowd was on their feet: It wasn't a standing ovation, it was a jumping-up-and-down ovation. And suddenly, I remembered how much the show I loved to work on, the television family I was thrilled to spend every day with, meant not just to me but to our peers in the Shrine Auditorium and, most important, to audiences everywhere.

Being and becoming Rhoda Morgenstern has been such a fantastic journey filled with so many hilarious and wonderful people that I wanted to share it with everyone—fans, family, and friends. It has brought such joy into my life, provided so many opportunities, and filled me with so many spectacular memories that I decided to write a book about it. So I did. *I, Rhoda* is a book about me, about Rhoda, and about the people I love.

chapter
ONE

"Valerie, don't overdo." This parental reprimand was the constant refrain of my childhood. One more jump off the diving board when my fingertips were shriveled and my lips blue. One more turn on the swings when my palms were long since shredded by the metal chains as I tried to propel myself higher. One more twirl around the living room to "The Blue Danube," even though my legs were already covered in rug burns. One more. One more.

I was also always looking for something to eat. When I was two years old, I bit the tail of our neighbors' yellow Labrador because it looked delicious. I couldn't help myself—I was drawn to that fluffy golden Twinkie of a tail, and I just had to sink my teeth into it. The dog was not amused; he spun around and bit me right on the lip. (It would be years before I'd overcome my fear of dogs. Though in truth, perhaps they should have feared me . . .)

When I was three years old, while watching my mother get dressed for the evening, I uncorked her beautiful bottle of perfume, Intoxication by d'Orsay. The bottle was so stylish, so alluring. It was in the shape of a cut-glass liquor decanter. How could I resist? I chugged the entire bottle in one gulp. Like the Labrador's tail, the perfume did not taste as good as it looked and boy, did it burn as it went down! Throughout my life I've had no desire to drink anything intoxicating because to me it all tastes like perfume. Talk about aversion therapy!

My mother, Iva Mildred McConnell, was a petite, blue-eyed, blond Canadian. She met my father, the tall, dark, and handsome Howard Donald Harper, through their mutual interest in hockey. Mom played on a women's team in Canada and spotted Dad at a match where he was playing for a visiting team—the Oakland Sheiks, who were named after Rudolph Valentino's famed role.

My mother had always dreamed of becoming a doctor, but her parents insisted that she go into teaching instead. She first taught eight grades, all together in a one-room schoolhouse out on the Saskatchewan prairie, where each row in her classroom was a different grade. After about two years, when she'd saved up enough money, she put herself through nursing school and became a registered nurse, a job she truly loved. As much as she enjoyed nursing, when she met Dad, she obeyed the edict of the day: "No wife of mine goes to work." Throughout most of my childhood, Mom stayed at home with my sister, Leah, my brother, Don, and me, though she always rejected the term housewife. "I'm not married to the house, I'm a home executive," she would say. How true.

My dad was fabulous and charming—a radiantly positive man with a big smile. When his brief professional hockey career came to an end, he became a lighting salesman. One of several companies he worked for did the lighting for New York City's Holland Tunnel—a fact we were reminded of every time we drove into the city from New Jersey. He also dealt in those unflattering lights that used to be in every ladies' room, the fluorescent bulbs that make everyone look like the Cryptkeeper.

Because he was a sales manager and trained new salesmen, my father was often on the road. He also received regular promotions, which meant that my family moved every two or three years as Dad moved up the ladder. Most summers we traveled with my father to work, incorporating family visits to my mom's folks in Vancouver. We had the best times with my Canadian cousins, Michael and Dean—swimming, walking trails, exploring the enormous Stanley Park. Some years we'd go see my dad's relatives in California, where Don and I learned to ride two-wheelers in Canoga Park. Or we packed our things to move to another town and settle in before the school year began. We spent a lot of hours crammed into the back of our Kaiser-Frazer car, traversing the West Coast. During these trips, my little brother, Don, became obsessed with cars and developed the charming habit of naming each and every make and model approaching from the opposite direction, which didn't make the time pass any faster. Leah, a perpetual joker, continually pointed out deer along the side of the road, but when I looked, they were always gone—if they were even there in the first place. Three kids in an unairconditioned vehicle in the height of a California summer must have been a real picnic for my parents.

I was born weeks earlier than expected in Suffern, New York. My parents were on a business trip when my mother went into labor. My father had gone to a tennis match, so my mother lumbered out of the hotel, into a cab, and to the nearest hospital—the Good Samaritan, a fitting name under the circumstances. My mother was so sure she was having a boy, the only name they'd picked was Charles Howard. When my father arrived and learned I was a girl, he was still carrying the program from the tennis tournament. The women's doubles champions were Valerie Scott and Kay Stammers. So Valerie Kathryn Harper was born—and she would never be very good at playing tennis, despite her namesakes.

I came into the world at four in the morning on August 22, 1939, weighing in at a hefty eight pounds, fourteen ounces. I was the middle child—an average, chunky little brunette with a pronounced lisp that I didn't lose until the third grade. My older sister, Leah, was a tall, slender, pretty blonde. When discussing my figure, my mother used to lower her voice, as if imparting a disgraceful secret, and say, "Valerie, you're short-waisted." It seemed that I was cursed indeed to have a waist that was short. At the time, I wasn't at all sure what that meant, but I accepted it because Mom said I'd gotten it from her. How bad could it be? I also harbored the hope that, as I grew, my waist would get longer and my pronunciation of S's would improve.

Despite the difference in our physiques, my mother liked to

dress Leah and me in matching outfits. Leah was able to get her clothes in the regular children's department, whereas my outfits came from the "Chubby" section. Chubby! What a word. It lacked the subterfuge of the boys' equivalent, "Husky." Chubby meant fat or, at any rate, not slim. There was no denying it. I used to cringe when my mother would hold up a dress she thought would look cute on Leah and ask the sales clerk if they stocked the same dress in "chubby" for me.

My younger brother, Don, was born two and a half years after I was, when we were living in Northampton, Massachusetts. My first memory of my brother is of him peeing on my hair as my mother changed his diaper. "Take him back to the hospital," I told my mother. "He pee-peed on my curls." Despite my protests, Don was there to stay. At least he provided Leah and me with a soft (often damp) baby to dress up like a doll and take turns holding.

A few years after my brother's birth, my father was reassigned to the tristate area. We moved from Northampton to South Orange, New Jersey, and our nomadic lifestyle was put on hold. We settled into a house with a huge backyard where Don, Leah, and I frequently played war games, pretending we were the Allies and the Japanese. Leah usually forced me to be a wounded Japanese soldier, which meant I had to lie on the ground while Don and Leah used me as a shield. It wasn't the most exciting role available in our make-believe battlefield. Luckily, when I enrolled in kindergarten at the Mountain View School, I was first introduced to the stage.

I got my first big break playing a snowflake in a school recital. My mother made me a fluffy white costume, and along with the rest of the girls in my class, I tiptoed onto the stage, fluttered around a bit, and then, to portray accumulation, fell as silently as possible to the floor and froze. I guess all my war games with Leah and Don came in handy after all. The next year, I was given the role of a dove in the manger scene of the Christmas pageant. It was my first speaking role. My mother made me a gray costume with wings and a hood with a protruding beak. Leah, a realist and a fashionista, noted, "You look like a pigeon. Aren't doves white?"

"Doves can be gray or white," Mom explained.

I accepted my mom's explanation, although it did seem that a white dove might have been more elegant. At the pageant, after I said my line, "I am the dove who cooed Him to sleep," I cooed a little too loudly and got a laugh—my first laugh! Only, instead of seeing it as a good thing, I was worried that I'd done something wrong and decided to stick with dance to save myself from further embarrassment. And since music was such an important part of our household, dancing seemed only natural to me.

My parents were always trying to open our minds and inspire us to express ourselves. They diligently encouraged us to try new things and be open to a wide variety of experiences. At bath time my mother would switch on the radio, often something dynamic like a Sousa march, and give us what she called "air baths," where we would run, skip, and dance around the house naked until we got in the tub.

Both my parents loved music and turned us on to all kinds

of songs. My mother was a self-taught pianist. She played every-thing—ragtime, honky-tonk, pop standards—everything but classical music, which she appreciated but said made her sad. Some of my fondest childhood memories are of singing around the piano with my parents, sister, and brother, or listening to my father's smooth baritone as he belted out "Stardust," "Deep Pur-ple," and other hits from the 1940s.

It was during this period in South Orange that my parents took me to the ballet for the first time. I was enthralled by the opening ballet—*Interplay,* choreographed by Jerome Robbins and starring Michael Kidd and Ruth Ann Koesun as a stage-hand and a ballerina. Except for a ladder and a work light, the stage was hauntingly empty. The ballerina, in her pink tights and rehearsal leotard, and the stagehand, in his overalls, danced a beautiful pas de deux. I was entranced and inspired. On the way home from the theater, I told my parents that I was going to be a dancer.

This probably didn't come as a surprise to them. Even at six years old, I knew I wanted to be a performer. I just wasn't sure what my outlet would be—dance, ice-skating, roller-skating, gymnastics. I even considered becoming an aerialist. After my parents took me to the circus, I tried to re-create one of the acro-bats' feats by racing my tricycle across our cement basement floor, then standing up on the handlebars. It was harder than it looked; I wound up cross-eyed with a concussion.

To their credit, my parents took my declaration that I was going to be a dancer quite seriously. (They were probably relieved that I'd given up on the circus.) Although we were middle-class, Dad always found the money for my lessons at whichever local dance school Mom had discovered.

When first grade finished, Dad was dispatched to the West Coast, moving us to Altadena, then to Pasadena, California, where I instantly embraced my surroundings; the towering palm trees were like nothing grown in New Jersey. We lived on Orange Grove Boulevard, which meant the Rose Bowl Parade went right by our house. Every year Dad made money hand over fist by charging parade-goers to park their cars in our backyard.

Because we moved around a lot, we three kids were adept at making friends quickly, and we even managed to keep in touch with people we'd left behind. To an outgoing and energetic seven-year-old like me, moving to a new city and starting a new school was more exciting than scary. In Altadena, Mom enrolled us at Thomas Edison Grammar, where I made friends quickly and settled into our new West Coast environs with ease.

In Pasadena, I became serious about ballet. My teacher was Pamela Andre, a calm, soft-spoken former professional dancer. She had a studio downtown where I took lessons twice a week. This was the big time. Before, Mom had found me whatever local dance school was convenient, and there I bounced around with my classmates pretending to be butterflies, not exactly preparing for the Bolshoi.

Whenever we moved during the school year, my mother had to find public schools that would take us midterm. When we relocated to Pasadena, the only place that had room for me was

St. Andrews, a Catholic school. Before coming out west, we had attended Sunday school at the nearest Protestant church. But once my mother saw how rigorous my education was compared to that of Leah, who was still in public school, she decided that all three of us would attend Catholic school whenever possible.

When the next school year rolled around, my mother put us into a Catholic boarding school in Pomona so that our educations would not be affected by my father's travel schedule. This allowed her to accompany Dad on his longer road trips. The Academy of the Holy Names was a beautiful Mission-style school located next to an orange grove. It was an idyllic setting, apart from the fact that they used to burn smudge pots in the fields to prevent frost from ruining the orange crop over the winter. When we woke up in the morning, we had little black Charlie Chaplin mustaches on our upper lips from breathing in the smoke. Clearly, this was before there was an EPA.

We spent only one year at the Academy of the Holy Names before moving to Monroe, Michigan, where Leah and I were enrolled in St. Mary's Academy, another boarding school. (Don attended the boys' school, Hall of the Divine Child.) I was ten years old when we moved to Michigan, old enough to sense that there was tension between my parents—arguments, sharp words. There was a girl in my class whose parents were divorced, something that was still scandalous back in the 1940s. I had a suspicion that this was where my folks were headed, and I wanted to prevent it. So, one Sunday when my parents were visiting us, I tried out my powers of manipulation on them. "Poor Marlene,"

I said, "her mom and dad are divorced. I'm so glad that's not you two." (I could be a devious, self-preserving little devil sometimes.) I saw my parents exchange a knowing glance. I felt I had guilted them into staying together, at least for the time being. Mission accomplished.

I loved the year I spent at beautiful, pastoral St. Mary's. We ice-skated on a lake and picked apples from an orchard on campus. My teachers, the Sisters of the Immaculate Heart of Mary, were fabulous—strict but devoted to their students. I made a wonderful friend, Bonnie MacKinaw, a tall girl with a terrific laugh, and from my classmates, I learned all sorts of skills, including embroidery and card games. Mom was shocked that I came home from Catholic school a gambler! I was also jacks champion of the fifth grade. Although I wasn't surprised when my parents told me that we were moving again, I was sad to leave this remarkable place and Bonnie.

In 1951, propelled by the fear of the atom bomb (a common preoccupation in the 1950s), Dad moved us to Ashland, Oregon, a small, picturesque mountain town, where we stayed for three years. Ashland seemed remote compared to where we'd lived in New Jersey and California, but that was the point. It was much less of a target for the Russians!

In Ashland, I started junior high and enrolled in the Colleen Hope School of Dance. For the first time, I was moving away from ballet and into other styles, such as tap and tumbling. My mother continued to make the costumes that I performed in at recitals and benefits, painstakingly sewing each outfit by hand, as she had done ever since my snowflake debut. For a routine set to "In a Persian Market," she made me a two-piece fake-leopard-skin number, complete with a matching cap that had huge hoop earrings attached to it, and a floor-length fuchsia chiffon scarf edged in gold trim that trailed off of the cap and attached to my wrists. I had the potent theatrical realization that one's costume was exceedingly important. My outfit made me feel both dramatic and free and inspired me to whirl about the stage clinking my finger cymbals with abandon.

Despite the elaborate costume, I wasn't exactly glamorous. I had no breasts yet, and my waist was still short, so my widest point was my midriff. I might have looked like an egg with legs, but I felt like Isadora Duncan. "In a Persian Market" was in such demand in every Lions Hall and Rotary Club in southern Oregon that I didn't have time to feel bad about my physique.

In addition to giving me dance lessons at a new place called Miss Pat's, Mom took Don and me to the Ashland roller rink several times a week. In the beginning, I skated around the rink, holding Don up until my arm ached. In a matter of months, he was speeding past me like a bullet. Don was as addicted to racing as I was to performing. As devoted as I was to dancing, part of me thought I might become a professional roller skater, if there even was such a thing. I learned to roller-dance with a partner and participated in roller shows in towns all over the Rogue River Valley.

Billie Graham, whose husband owned the rink and had lived in Hawaii, gave hula classes, which, naturally, I had to take. Again, my mother made my costumes—an iridescent hula skirt with colorful tulle and a skirt and lei made out of oilcloth so I could do a hula number in the pool at a swim show. Whenever my mother suggested fun activities, I turned them into performance opportunities.

During those years in Oregon, Dad was gone on more frequent and more lengthy road trips. As a result, Mom was alone a lot, so much that she was virtually a single parent. Since Don, Leah, and I were too young to drive, Mom had to chauffeur us wherever we needed to go, which left her little time to herself. One day I saw her trying to conceal tears while washing dishes, and I offered to stay home from the movies and keep her company.

"You are my darling twelve-year-old, and I love you, but sometimes I really need adult company. Now, you go and have fun."

I didn't want to leave, and I felt bad that there was nothing I could do to make her feel better. I know now that she would have been much happier going back to nursing—something she did several years later.

When my father was home, the discord between my parents became more pronounced. There was a low-grade but palpable tension in the house. As much as I loved Dad, things were easier in the house when he was away.

Except for the strained atmosphere at home, living in Ashland was wonderful—a small-town American idyll complete with a stately old library and a party line on the telephone; I was even a baton twirler on the school drill team. As usual, I made friends easily. Phyllis Knapp and her younger brother, Don, were very tight with me and my younger brother, Don. The boys were absolutely fascinated by cars and anything with an engine—a passion that my little brother would carry into adulthood. Phyllis, who dreamed of being a singer, and I shared intense show business aspirations. Mom accompanied Phyllis on the piano at a talent show in Grants Pass where I also performed the hula. I came in second. Sadly, Phyllis with her sweet soprano voice didn't place. It was a somber ride home through the mountains. But real girlfriends abide and we became even closer after this experience.

Meanwhile, Leah had grown wilder and more independent—and just a little bit boy-crazy. She often sneaked back into our bedroom late at night smelling of alcohol and cigarettes. Long gone were the days of wearing matching outfits and singing around the piano. She had begun hanging out with a fast crowd, and her older friends seemed scary and dangerous to me. When she was only fifteen, Leah ran away to Reno, intending to marry a great-looking blond sailor—an impetuous move that was swiftly shut down by my parents.

While Leah was confident around boys—clearly too confident—I was a complete prude. I was acutely afraid of the romantic side of dealings with the opposite sex. Friends, buddies, pals? Great! Boyfriends? No. It didn't help that my mother had several medical textbooks filled with graphic imagery of venereal diseases. That'll scare you into celibacy if nothing else will. When I heard that a boy in junior high had a crush on me, I avoided him at all costs. I did, however, experience my first kiss during my time in Ashland. It wasn't terribly exciting or romantic. I was helping my neighbor Kenny do some yard chores. His parents had asked us to carry a bucket of slop out to the pigs in their yard. (Ashland was that kind of town.) On our way to the pen, Kenny stopped dead in his tracks with the slop in one hand, turned, and pressed his closed lips against mine. I pulled away, startled, and ran home. It was a decidedly unglamorous kiss, but you always remember your first!

When the lighting company offered Dad a promotion back east, my parents jumped at the chance—they were eager to get Leah away from the kids she'd fallen in with since moving to Ashland. Odd as it might seem, they figured she'd be safer in a city where she'd be less likely to succumb to boredom and run off to Reno to get married, which was what many of her classmates were doing.

Even though it was October, Dad, Leah, and I (maybe my parents believed I'd be a good influence on my sister) got on a plane to New Jersey as soon as we could. Mom stayed behind to close up the house and let Don finish the semester. When we arrived in New Jersey, it was too late to enroll in school, so Leah and I had to wait until January to start the semester. This was terrific. We went on business trips with Dad to New England, and when Dad was working, Leah and I took the train or the bus to Manhattan. We headed straight for the movie theaters in Times Square—some of which were a little scuzzy, though more run-down than disreputable. Still, I felt like quite the adventurer, setting off for the city to catch a double feature before riding the bus back home.

Mom and Don joined us before Christmas, and after the New Year I started P.S. 11 in Jersey City. Before the move to Jersey City, switching schools had never bothered me. I'd come in like gangbusters, make friends, and adjust. But attending P.S. 11 was a huge culture shock for me, so different from Ashland. I was surrounded by all these streetwise, big-city kids with tough-sounding accents. Mistaking my accent for Southern, Gerald (Bubbie) Salerno nicknamed me "Florida." All through grammar school, back when Valerie was still an unusual name, classmates called me "Celery," "Calorie," and the real stretch, "Malaria." Thankfully, some new Jersey City girlfriends came to the rescue: Dottie Norton, a dead ringer for Rosie O'Donnell, Carol Newton, whom we called "Fig," Maureen McGowan, a fabulous volleyball player, Lucille Acovelli, cut-up extraordinaire, and the sweet Carbanaro sisters, Suzanne and Stephanie. These new pals introduced me to pizza, egg creams, the great joy of hanging out at a corner luncheonette, and that famous city pastime, loitering on street corners. My parents threw a graduation party for the whole class at the end of eighth grade. I'd finally begun to take an interest in boys, and I remember them vividly—mostly Italian American, each one more dark and handsome and exciting than the next. We played spin the bottle (yoicks!), and that was about as racy as things ever got for me.

Once we'd settled into an eight-room apartment on Kensington Avenue, I began to focus on dance again. I would move all of the furniture against the walls of the living room so I could practice dance steps until I was exhausted. Mom knew that New

York City was the place for me to study. She found a top-rated school called Ballet Arts, which was in Carnegie Hall. One of the major perks of studying at Carnegie Hall in those days was the chance of spotting Marlon Brando, who lived in the building, which I did once or twice. Studying ballet in the heart of Manhattan in one of the most renowned buildings in town with teachers from famous dance companies filled my teenage heart with hope. Maybe I really could become a dancer.

By the time I was in high school, I was commuting into the city four times a week to dance. I was living two separate lives but equally enjoyable ones. Lincoln High was a great adventure—football, homeroom, cute guys, and a group of great girlfriends: Barbara Zimmerman, Gilda "Cookie" Glaser, Lois Mischel, Ellen Rotkin, and Arlene Kahn, all Jewish girls who would have been Rhoda's high school gang, too.

In the city, I had a circle of friends from ballet: pretty little Barbara Monte; graceful Pat Hayes, who married our teacher, the spectacular Vladimir Dokoudovsky; and exotic Toriana Santiago from the Bronx, who studied Spanish dance as well as ballet.

When I wasn't at Ballet Arts or hanging out with my friends from Lincoln, I was going to the Metropolitan Museum of Art with Kathy Dugan, one of my best friends and an Egyptology buff, roller-skating at the rink in Bayonne, or staging backyard performances for our parents with my neighbor pal, Elaine Gray, who was hilarious. Our big musical number was "Side by Side."

During my second year at Ballet Arts, a new teacher named John Gregory came to teach a class in jazz dance. It was like nothing I'd ever seen taught before—exciting, distinctive, and, well, jazzy. I was still a ballet purist, and I was scared to try something so wild and sexy. Along with a group of curious ballet girls, I watched Gregory's class for two weeks until I worked up the courage to try it. And I loved it. Ballet training enabled me to learn the steps, but the music—with songs like "Night Train"—helped me find the sensual style of jazz. Eventually, I enrolled at the famed Luigi Jazz Center, where I take classes to this day.

Despite my interest in jazz, ballet was still my first and best love. I worked hard to improve my technique, determined to achieve my dream of joining a ballet company one day. When my parents saw the depth of my commitment, they pushed me harder. "If you're going to be taking class four days a week, there's no reason you shouldn't be dancing full-time," they reasoned. When it came to encouragement and support, my parents were world-class. They never wavered in affording us every opportunity to study, work hard, and find success. A lot of little girls wanted to be ballerinas. How many had parents like mine?

Through a classmate at Ballet Arts, I learned about a fully accredited school in Manhattan called Quintano's School for Young Professionals. It was a private school for kids in show business, run by a stylish gentleman named Mr. Quintano out of a dance studio on West Fifty-sixth Street, right behind Carnegie Hall. So I left Lincoln High and enrolled at this new school, where the flexible class schedule allowed me to spend the majority of my time at Ballet Arts while still finishing high school.

Quintano's was a tiny and eclectic school with eclectic students, including Sal Mineo, Carol Lynley, and Tuesday Weld. Our classes—English, German, history, and math—were held at various card tables in different corners of the studio.

My best friend from Ballet Arts, Barbara Monte, enrolled at Quintano's, and we stayed pretty much joined at the hip. Barbara and I were good pals with Mike Mineo, Sal's older brother, and he got us into our first movie premiere—*Crime in the Streets*, starring Sal and John Cassavetes. Like the other girls at the theater, we screamed for Sal even though he was our classmate.

Between being around show business kids and going into the city every day for classes, I felt part of a new, scintillating world. It was probably a good thing that I was out of the house most of the day, as my parents' marriage was disintegrating quickly. Family dinners were particularly tense. There was a lot of drama, a lot of jumping up from the table and storming out, and plenty of sour looks and bitter words.

One particularly strained Thanksgiving dinner was punctuated by Mom slamming pots around in the kitchen while Dad sat at the head of the table, clenching his jaw and kneading his napkin in anger. To break the tension, my very funny but sarcastic sister said in an announcer voice, "And now we bring you *The Emotional Hour*." Don and I burst into laughter. Poor Dad headed for his office. Poor Mom headed for the bedroom. The three of us shrugged and ate more dressing.

My parents tried to stay together for the sake of their children because that was what people did, but we all could see that they might be happier without each other. They were both remarkable people, but they didn't work well together. There was nothing clichéd about my parents' eventual separation—no violence, no cheating, no drinking or gambling, just deep incompatibility.

My father still traveled a lot for work, which relieved the tension in the house. But we sensed that these absences were only a temporary solution. My mother and my brother weren't happy in New Jersey. Don missed his friends and the quieter small-town life in Ashland, and Mom wanted to get out of the marriage and back to working as a nurse. Leah had just graduated from high school and broken up with a long-term boyfriend and needed a change. When Mom told me that she, Don, and Leah were moving back to the house we still owned in Ashland, I wanted to go, too.

But Mom wouldn't hear of me returning to Oregon. "Val, honey, you're really getting to be a good dancer. I don't want you to come back to Ashland with me and ruin your chance for a real career. It's a young person's profession, and you need to take advantage of it while you can. You've already invested so much in it."

Again, Mother knew best. If I moved to Ashland, I would lose two years of first-rate training while I finished high school and consequently might never get into a ballet company. It was painful for me to see them go, but Mom convinced me that staying was the best thing for my future. Close as she and I had always been, it couldn't have been easy for her to come to this decision. But Mom had boundless faith in us and always put her kids' best interests first, no matter the cost to her. She assured me that if it didn't work out for me, I could always join them later. Like she always said about new foods when we were little, "You don't have to eat it, but you must taste it." Mom wanted me to give living on my own a chance.

Since my dad would be traveling for work a considerable amount, Mom had to figure out a way for me to stay on the East Coast and be looked after. She soon discovered the Clara de Hirsch Home for Working Girls in Manhattan (obviously not the *Pretty Woman* type of working girl). The perfect solution— she was confident that I would be safe there, and I could attend Quintano's and Ballet Arts during the week and return to the apartment in Jersey City with Dad on the weekends. My father's office was in the Empire State Building, so if I needed anything, I could contact him or ask his secretary, a marvelous, warmhearted young woman named Angela.

I loved living at the Clara de Hirsch Home. It was a grand mansion on Sixty-third Street between Second and Third avenues. It had a gorgeous foyer and a reception room for entertaining male visitors, who obviously were forbidden to go upstairs. There was a communal kitchen where each resident kept a little basket in the massive refrigerator with her own food in it.

Living in the city on my own was exciting. Even though my father kept close tabs on me, I felt like a big deal. I was on course. I was determined to finish high school in case I decided to go to college, but I was more focused than ever and doing my best to become a working professional dancer.

Despite my independence, I was an inveterate prude. I didn't mind that the boys from the trade school near the Clara de Hirsch Home whistled at me, but I wouldn't dare talk to them. I dressed conservatively in sensible pumps, maybe a black-watch-plaid sheath dress, and *always* crocheted white gloves, even on the grimy subway in the height of summer! It was a 1940s holdover from my mom, who would say, "A lady never goes out without gloves!" A true child of the 1950s, I idolized sweet, demure stars like Natalie Wood, Doris Day, and Debbie Reynolds. The overt sexuality of Marilyn Monroe or Jane Russell embarrassed me. I was convinced that if I had sex, I'd immediately get a venereal disease, get pregnant, or both. I also knew that sex meant losing the respect of the man you'd "given in to." Although, I still think a little savvy self-preservation is an asset for any female.

Since moving to the city, I had much more time and freedom to take performing arts classes outside my comfort zone of ballet. A classmate at Quintano's suggested that I sign up for an acting class at John Cassavetes's studio. I had no idea what I was getting into, but I went for it.

I was nervous—no, terrified—before my first acting class. I dressed in what I thought was appropriate: a pink and aqua tweed skirt, a pink angora sweater with a Peter Pan collar poking out, and high-heeled pumps with seamed stockings. I arrived early to my first class, pencil and steno pad in hand, ready to take down every word Mr. Cassavetes said. Soon the rest of the class began to slink in, shabby, glowering beatnik guys, all of whom were dressed in black and oozing attitude and acute self-importance. I must have looked like a sight gag.

I lasted only a couple of weeks. While I loved hearing Cassavetes, I had no idea what I was supposed to do. Since I was the new girl and something of a refined novelty, a few of the men in the class asked me out. I lied and told them I lived in New Jersey—quite an effective deterrent. I couldn't admit that I lived in the Clara de Hirsch Home for Working Girls. That would have seemed like an open invitation. As my sister once warned me, "With men, if you don't want to do something, don't do it."

"Okay, Leah," I said. "Do you hold back?"

"No! Because I want to do it," she said, and giggled.

Acting class and sexual activity both could wait. Dance was infinitely more important. While attending Quintano's, I auditioned all over town, hoping to get into a ballet company. But I had no such luck. I was so jealous of my pal Pat Hayes, who had gotten into the Metropolitan Opera Ballet Company. In 1956 I finally landed my first paying job as a replacement dancer in the Corps de Ballet at Radio City Music Hall. It was only a six-week run, but I was elated. The Radio City Corps de Ballet might not have had the prestige of Ballet Theatre or Balanchine's company, but to a sixteen-year-old, it was a gigantic deal.

This was in the glory days of Radio City, back when it was a premier movie palace. Following a movie, there was a complete stage show including a full orchestra, a dog act, a magician, an acrobat, singers, the world-famous Radio City Music Hall organ, and us, the thirty-six dancers known as "Ballet Girls" who comprised the Corps de Ballet. The stars of this extravaganza were the much lauded Rockettes. At one show, these poor girls had to do their precision kicking with some perverted fool in the front row watching them through binoculars. Four of these shows were staged per day, which meant a lot of performances. Every time the movie changed, so did the stage show, and we had to learn entirely new numbers.

Backstage was like an actual city. It would have been possible to live there without ever leaving the building. The rehearsal halls were enormous, with a dormitory that had assigned beds where you could sleep between shows, as well as a massive cafeteria and a huge dressing room with many showers. There was a screening room to watch movies between the stage performances. And you could stay there all day, or you could go out and return in time for your performance.

On the first day of rehearsal, I was terribly sick to my stomach, but I was so excited to be working that I made it through the day. I had to work hard to keep up with the strong, seasoned professional dancers who made up the thirty-six members of the Corps de Ballet. The numbers tended to be sweeping, colorful, and dynamic to fill the gigantic stage. In a number set in a gold mine, we rose from beneath the stage on a huge elevator, shimmering gold nuggets in toe shoes. In another number we were spring flowers twirling parasols and waltzing to Gershwin.

It was grueling work, but what could be better? I was a working performer (on my toes!)—dancing, no less, in one of the most legendary theaters in New York City, where my parents had taken me when I was little. There I was, sixteen years old with working papers in hand. (A young person's profession, indeed.) I was now a member of AGVA (American Guild of Variety Artists), the union that covered Radio City Music Hall, nightclubs, and, *I think*, the circus (handy, should I ever decide to reprise my tricycle balancing act). Now that I had my first real taste of the business they call show, I couldn't get enough of it. I was ready for more.

chapter
TWO

When my six-week run in the Corps de Ballet at Radio City ended, life went back to normal. I resumed high school at Quintano's and took a full load of dance classes, both ballet and jazz. I kept my ears open for auditions. I scoured *Backstage* and *Show Business* for possible opportunities and finagled my way into as many nonunion casting calls as I could. As of yet, I was not a member of Actors' Equity.

Barbara Monte and I would hang out at the Colony coffee shop on Fifty-third and Broadway, where a lot of dancers, singers, and actors congregated. Elliott Gould, a very tall, curly-haired dancer, was a regular. He was one of the few straight dancers! We'd share information about what shows and movies were being cast while eating hamburgers and laughing ourselves silly.

During my third year of high school, work was scattershot. I did a few goofy modeling jobs for magazines like *True Romance*, posing on the back of a motorcycle, clinging to a tough-looking guy in a black leather jacket. Eventually, Barbara and I got wind of a movie in Brooklyn called *Rock, Rock, Rock* that was looking for dancers. We took the subway out to Brighton Beach and were cast as extras. Our classmate Tuesday Weld was the star opposite a really great-looking singer named Teddy Randazzo. The film featured performances by Chuck Berry, LaVern Baker, Little Richard, Frankie Lymon and the Teenagers, the Flamingos, and the Moonglows and was presided over by DJ Alan Freed. Barbara and I played teenagers in a prom scene, dancing the Lindy Hop like crazy. It was so great—we had the best time shooting it! The job lasted for three days, we made money (albeit very little), and we got to be rock and rollers in a movie. Best of all, I now had a film credit on my résumé.

During my last year at the Clara de Hirsch Home, I began spending a lot of time with my father's secretary, Angela Posillico. She was a delightful, dyed-in-the-wool Italian-American from East Harlem. My father's office was on the seventieth floor, and I often stopped by to see him or to have lunch with Angela. She even helped me rehearse a scene from Shakespeare for an acting class.

Dad often took us out for dinner, and it was delightful to see him so happy. When I pressed him on getting serious about Angela, he would demur, "No, I'm much too old for her. And she has a boy-friend—Diddy, from the neighborhood." At some point Diddy was dropped, and Dad and Angela started dating. I enlisted Leah and Don to exert pressure from the West Coast, since they also loved Angela. It's the oldest cliché in the book to marry your secretary, but in Dad and Angela's case, it was a perfect fit.

In 1958 they were married at a beautiful, formal ceremony at the Pierre Hotel on Fifth Avenue. Since Mom and Dad had taken so many years to separate and finally divorce, Mom was fine with my father remarrying. She told me she rarely thought about him except when her kids brought him up. To my mother's credit, she never demanded that I dislike Angela. And to Angela's credit, she never said a bad word about my mom. Over time she grew to be one of the most important and influential people in my life.

When I graduated from Quintano's, the ceremony was held at Lüchow's, a glorious landmark German restaurant on Fourteenth Street—a typically unconventional setting for an atypical school. Mom was sorry that she couldn't come in from Oregon, but she had taken me to lunch there before, and the event wasn't exactly going to be "Pomp and Circumstance." There were no caps and gowns or valedictorian speeches, only Mr. Quintano standing at the head of a table, handing out diplomas, while waiters served schnitzel and Sacher torte. Dad was very proud and wanted to buy me champagne, which was silly, because I don't drink and neither does he. So we toasted my achievement with large, ornate glasses of pink lemonade.

After graduation I moved home to New Jersey with Angela and Dad. I still had dreams of being a ballet dancer, but there were more opportunities in show business and theater. I had to face the fact that I might not be ballerina material. I auditioned for dance choruses in summer stock productions, but to my great disappointment, I didn't get cast. I guess I wasn't musical comedy material either! I'd gotten good grades in high school, and throughout the summer I debated whether or not I should go to college. But when fall rolled around, I found myself commuting to New York to audition, and college was forgotten. I also had several "civilian" jobs during the late 1950 and early 1960s. I clerked at the Adam for Eve gift shop in Macy's one Christmas; checked coats (mostly chinchillas) at the exclusive French restaurant Lutèce; did some phone canvassing (yes, I was one of those horribly annoying people!); and had myself hooked up to monitoring devices in a sleep study for a research project about dreams. What can I say, it helped pay the bills.

I used to go to open dance auditions that both union and nonunion dancers could attend—these were indelicately known as "cattle calls." Sometimes hundreds of girls would show up at a rehearsal studio or Broadway theater, hoping to get hired. We signed in at the door and were given a number. We learned the dance steps in a large group and then were summoned in groups of ten to dance for the choreographer. After we danced, we were either eliminated with a curt thank-you or held over for another chance to perform. This process went on until the choreographer had found the number of girls he or she was looking for; sometimes just a single dancer was being cast.

When I was sixteen, I was eliminated in the second round of auditions for Jerome Robbins's *West Side Story*. Every dancer in town wanted to get into that show, and only the cream of the crop made it. When I was eighteen, I went to a casting call for *Li'l Abner,* a Michael Kidd musical that had been running on Broadway for two years. One of the dancers was leaving, and the show needed to find a replacement. My parents had taken me to see *Li'l Abner* for my sixteenth birthday—the first Broadway musical I had ever seen. (Incidentally, the first Broadway play my parents took me to was *The Bad Seed,* about a psychotic, murderous little girl . . . coincidentally named Rhoda. It never would have occurred to me, as I sat there on my birthday watching the amazing, fast-paced choreography, that in two years I would be given the opportunity to audition for *Li'l Abner.*

Almost a hundred girls showed up at the St. James Theatre to land the job. The odds weren't in my favor, but I was peppy and enthusiastic, as usual. I wore all black, with a red bow in my short braid. While we were all being assigned our numbers, one particular girl caught my eye. She was stunning, tall and elegant, with exquisite pale skin and a thick reddish-gold braid down her back. Standing there in her turquoise-and-black–striped T-shirt rolled up into a midriff top, she had such attitude and poise, and a unique beauty that I found captivating. When she registered for her number, I learned her name: Iva March.

I immediately ran over to her. "Iva! My mother's name is Iva. I've never met anybody else by that name." I had momentarily forgotten that the point of the audition was to get the job, not to make a friend.

"So?" Iva said. "My mother's name is Jewel." She wanted to end the chitchat and learn the dance combination.

"Jewel! That's the name of my father's lighting company, Jewel Electric." I couldn't help but celebrate this fantastic coincidence.

Iva politely laughed but told me later on that she'd said to herself, "Well, this one is just going to keep coming at me, so I might as well be her friend."

Michael Kidd wasn't there, so his two dance captains, the glamorous married couple Dee Dee Wood and Marc Breaux, both great dancers with parts in the show, ran the audition. Michael Kidd's production, *Li'l Abner*, was filled with hoedown style, athletic dance routines that involved difficult lifts, and innovative footwork requiring high energy and a lot of strength.

If I'd stuck to traditional ballet training, I never would have made the cut. But my years of jazz with Luigi had given me the strength and athleticism I needed for the choreography. Out of more than a hundred girls, I got the job. Unbelievable! My perkiness, which was right in line with *Li'l Abner*'s hillbilly aesthetic, served me well. I couldn't quite believe that I was joining a Michael Kidd show. After all, it was Michael Kidd's performance in *Interplay* that had inspired me to become a dancer when I was only six years old. I continue to be amazed at the way life unfolds!

Rehearsal meant working with the dance captains during the day to learn the choreography and attending the performances at night. Standing at the back of the house, watching the moves of a dancer whom I was about to replace, was thrilling. Yes, I was nervous and scared, but I was also deliriously happy.

The backstage atmosphere at *Li'l Abner* was welcoming, without a hint of the supposed competitive backstabbing from the other girls in the dressing room. Another myth debunked! Daddy and Angela watched proudly as I got through my first performance without falling off the stage. To my delight, after two months in *Abner,* Iva came into the show to replace another departing dancer. Soon Iva, who was also a Jersey girl living with her parents, and I became fast friends. After work in the city, we would dash to the Port Authority Bus Terminal to catch our respective buses, hers to Short Hills, mine to Jersey City.

Although I was fully enjoying being in a Broadway show, I clung to my childhood dream of getting into a ballet company. Still, here I was, finally getting paid to dance. I was making seventy-six dollars for eight shows a week on *Abner.* As exciting as this was, I found myself thinking that it was simply a diversion until I could return to my original calling. Childhood dreams have a way of sticking with you—although I suppose there'd be a lot more princesses and astronauts out there if everyone stuck by their childhood dreams!

But this showbiz was fun! Each performance I was invigorated by Gene de Paul and Johnny Mercer's terrific score and by hearing the laughter rolling from the audience. I felt that my performance was improving. I began to wonder if this was where I belonged, not in the ballet but in the theater.

After I'd been in the show for six months, *Abner* closed on Broadway; the show was traveling to Las Vegas for an eight-week run. It was an exciting prospect. The only bad part was that Iva couldn't make the trip because she'd gotten into the chorus of *My Fair Lady. Abner* would be the first Broadway musical ever to play Vegas. The producers had to shorten the show so they could run two performances each night. They cut down the acting scenes, which meant that we dancers had much less time to catch our breath between musical numbers. Young and strong as we were, it was still a killer.

The company met in the main concourse of Grand Central Station underneath the constellations painted on the vaulted blue ceiling. We boarded a transcontinental train for Nevada, complete with dining and sleeper cars. I turned nineteen on our journey west. The entire time I couldn't shake the feeling that my life had become the movies. And I loved it.

We opened in Vegas at the beautiful Riviera Hotel. In 1958 Vegas was sparsely populated and the Strip far less dense than it is today. The Sands, the Flamingo, the Sahara, and the Riviera each stood alone, with large swatches of desert between them. After the second performance of the night, the cast of *Abner* lived a vibrant nightlife. If there wasn't a company party, we'd go on a midnight horseback ride or hayride that always ended with a barbecue. My roommate, a tiny redhead named Betty Jenkins, and I would go see Louis Prima and Keely Smith do their lounge show. We even saw Sinatra! Some of the casinos had a policy barring African-American performers from entering through the front door, even if they were coming to do a show. One night at a major hotel-casino, the divine Miss Eartha Kitt ignored the rule and marched in through the front entrance, openly defying all that horrible and ridiculous nonsense. Way to go, Eartha.

Our show ran in Las Vegas for two delightful months: I slept late, spent time by the pool, and then went to the theater—not a bad way to live. I went out with Betty's handsome visiting cousin a few times. Despite the sinful charms of the desert city, it was quite a chaste relationship, as was my style. When I was in my Vegas getup—a Day-Glo bikini and full makeup with fake lashes—who would have believed that I was a virgin?

When I returned to New York, I was asked to join the cast of Michael Kidd's new show *Destry Rides Again,* a musical based on an old Gary Cooper movie of the same name. The show starred Andy Griffith and Dolores Gray. I was excited to be working with Michael again. I had become that rarefied creature: a Michael Kidd dancer!

Despite the rigorous routines in *Abner,* I struggled with my weight. I wasn't one of those dancers who looked as if they might break in a strong gust of wind. Nor was I voluptuous—just average and healthy-looking. But oh, how I loved to eat! I've always been impulsive about food. And I got very good at rationalizing my binges. I used to try to convince myself that whatever cake or cookies I ate, I would burn off in dance class. As if I might be able to burn off a quart of ice cream.

I wanted to shed a few pounds after Las Vegas so I would be slender when *Destry* rehearsals began. I carried around the ideal of the tiny, wispy ballerina in my head—whittled waist and willow limbs. So I began getting diet shots, which worked like magic. They pumped me full of energy, and the weight melted off. Already, at nineteen, I had slipped into the cyclical pattern of gaining and reducing that unfortunately I would repeat way into adulthood.

I was in rehearsals for *Destry* only a week when I began to feel fatigued. But since I was dancing rigorous Michael Kidd choreography all day long, that was to be expected. When the whites of my eyes turned a little yellow, Angela dispatched me to the doctor. I was distraught to learn that I'd contracted hepatitis from the needles used for my diet shots. (These were the days before disposable needles.) Although I didn't feel very sick, I had to drop out of *Destry*. What a heartbreak! It was my first show as an original cast member. When I told Michael through my tears that I had to leave, he kindly assured me that we'd work together again.

I spent a week in the hospital. Then I was released to Angela's care. My recovery entailed two things, eating and rest, which couldn't have delighted Angela more. A nurturing woman, she relished having someone to feed. And I was her willing charge. I lay in bed as she brought me an endless banquet of healthy food, but also pizza and pasta, cannoli and cookies. I gorged. We both loved movies and would watch one after the other while stuffing our faces. I remember the two of us polishing off an entire pound cake watching *The Late Late Show*.

My convalescence helped forge a close bond between Angela and me that would last a lifetime. In addition to preparing wonderful food, she was a great storyteller who loved to laugh. Her childhood sounded like something out of *The Godfather*. I loved listening to her tales of growing up on a Mob-protected block on East 116th Street around guys named Joey Blue Eyes and Bobby the Greek.

After two months in Angela's care and due to my ridiculous indulgence, my weight had gone up to 160 pounds, not exactly ideal for my five-six frame. That was when I got a call to be in the movie of *Li'l Abner*. And so the cycle began again. I was determined to drop weight in time for filming, so I went on a stringent diet and worked out in our living room. I also tried some rather foolish techniques for weight reduction. I remember trying to create my own steam room in our bathtub by wrapping myself in several plastic shower curtains and running the hot water. (I also ate a lot of prunes.)

The *Abner* film was shooting in Hollywood, so I arranged to live with Beth Howland, another dancer in the movie, who went on to play Vera in the television series *Alice*. We spent our first night in Los Angeles in a slightly dingy hotel. The next day we learned that some dancers in the touring company of *West Side Story* were staying at the Elaine Apartments near Hollywood and Vine, a famous address. The Elaine was perfect—a cool Hollywood place with white stucco duplexes, a little patio area dotted with palm trees, and an aquamarine pool. Directly across from the Elaine on Vine Street was the delightfully seedy Hollywood Ranch Market, which was open twenty-four hours. It was heaven.

Since neither of us could drive, Beth and I caught the bus on Melrose Avenue to the fabled Paramount studios. Working on the movie was a totally new experience. While I was accustomed to the backstage camaraderie on Broadway, the soundstages in Los Angeles were incredibly exciting—small bustling cities filled with famous faces. The first time I saw Marlon Brando in L.A.— he was filming *One-Eyed Jacks* on the lot—I started screaming like a crazed groupie. Hope Holiday, an adorable platinum blonde who was a singer on *Abner,* took me by the arm and told me never to embarrass her like that again. "Don't act like a silly fan. You're a professional on a movie," she explained. "Act like one." She's lucky I didn't yell out, "Hey, Marlon, I studied ballet in Carnegie Hall when you lived there."

Although we had early calls on weekdays, we had the weekends off. In our spare time Beth and I would ride the bus down to Grauman's Chinese Theatre, putting our feet in the stars' footprints. We went out to Anaheim to visit a new amusement park that had just opened called Disneyland. And because we were constantly dieting, we'd eat steaks at Diamond Jim's on Hollywood Boulevard. In those days steak was a diet food; at least when served without potatoes and fried onion rings.

When the *Abner* shoot wrapped, I suddenly had time on my hands and didn't know what was going to come next. Work had started to find me, so I developed the ability to live with uncertainty—a great asset to anyone in show business. I knew there would be periods without a paycheck. But in order to survive in the business, I'd have to learn to live with that reality.

When I returned to New York, Iva and I decided to rent an apartment together. From the earliest days of our friendship I've called her "Iva the Oracle" because she always gives the wisest advice no matter the subject: You need something, she knows where to get it, or at the very least will find out how to get it for you. She bought newspapers right away and began circling apartment listings all over the happening Greenwich Village, but we eventually settled on a studio apartment on West Fifty-fifth

Street. We figured it would be good to be in the heart of the city, close to the Broadway theaters where we worked. We often ate at Jim Downey's Steak House, a fantastic show business restaurant and hangout on Forty-fourth Street and Eighth Avenue, where we felt very much a part of the Broadway community. Everybody from chorus members to major theater actors to stars such as Marilyn Monroe and Paul Newman, both of whom Iva and I saw several times, frequented Downey's.

I was moping around wondering what would come next in my life when I received a phone call from Onna White, a choreographer who was working on a new production called *Take Me Along,* a musical based on Eugene O'Neill's play *Ah, Wilderness.* It was being produced by the extremely successful David Merrick, who went on to produce *42nd Street* and *Oliver!,* as well as other huge Broadway hits. Jackie Gleason was going to star.

At Michael Kidd's kind suggestion, Onna was asking me to audition for the show. I was very flattered. She needed strong female dancers for a particularly strenuous Beardsley dream ballet. The first day of rehearsal was a spectacular event. We assembled in a large studio and were introduced to the cast and crew. We listened to the leads read through the script and then divided up—principals, singers, dancers—into different studios to work on our part of the show. When I look back, I realize our studio was a shabby, airless space with less than immaculate floors. The walls were covered in fuzzy pink fiberglass insulation that looked like cotton candy. Looks aside, our studio embodied the hardworking romance of theater, and I was madly in love with all of it.

The show involved all sorts of unusual choreography. In one number with Jackie Gleason, I was a dance hall girl. I wore a black corset with a short flounce, bright orange tights, black patent boots that laced up to midcalf, and a turn-of-the-century wig. (Oh, how we begged the costume designer to get rid of those orange tights, which made our legs look like fluorescent sausages!) The pièce de résistance was a huge pair of dice made out of felt, strategically placed, one over each breast. In my "Dice Girl" costume, I felt like a grotesque Lillian Russell. Along with two other dancers, I jiggled my dice and sang in a squeaky chorine voice, "You can shake 'em if you promise not to break 'em. After all, they're the only pair I've got." It was bawdy and silly and fun to perform.

Jackie Gleason was at the height of his fame when *Take Me Along* opened. His nickname among other comics was "The Great One." It was apt. He was hysterically funny. He had huge hangdog eyes and called everyone "Kid" in a manner that was endearing rather than demeaning.

I'd heard rumors about Jackie's fondness for alcohol. There were certainly nights when he may have had one too many. On those occasions, the pace of the show slowed down a bit, although I'm sure the audience didn't notice. Jackie always seemed to pull it off.

Our opening-night party was held at Sardi's on Forty-fourth Street, opposite Shubert Alley. An area had been roped off for the stars—Jackie, Walter Pidgeon, Una Merkel—as well as the director and producers. The minute Jackie saw the velvet rope dividing the bigwigs from the rest of the company, he got his working-class Irish up. He was outraged and demanded that the rope be taken away. When no one came forward, he moved the rope himself. "There's going to be no steerage class at this party," he said. We were all one company celebrating a successful opening, and he made sure everyone was included equally in the festivities.

There was a terrifying moment during a matinee in the middle of a huge production number. A deranged young man stood up on the railing of his opera box right above the stage, poised to jump. It was John Wilkes Booth time. Jackie signaled the orchestra to stop with one hand, then held the other hand up high like a traffic cop. "Hold it right there, pal." (Yes, he actually said "pal.") He engaged the man long enough for security to pull him back into the box. To a very nervous audience, he announced, "Sorry, folks, everybody wants to get into the act." I love Jackie Gleason for many reasons, and this is one of them.

During *Take Me Along,* I got my first taste of the union organizing that went on behind the scenes in the theater. A few months into our run, Actors' Equity called a strike. They were demanding higher minimum pay and better working conditions for performers—no concrete floors in rehearsal studios, no rooms filled with asbestos.

Although we were locked out, we had to come to the theater every day to prove we were showing up for work. One afternoon while we were waiting in Shubert Alley, our boss, David Merrick, appeared dressed in his "prince of darkness" black suit with his manicured black mustache. As he passed by, he said, "You'll never work for me again."

My friend Gene Varrone, a wonderful tenor singer, called out, "Until you need us, David. Until you need us." As it turned out, Gene was right.

During the strike, most of us attended union rallies at the Edison Hotel ballroom; many stars supported the effort as well. Shelley Winters and Celeste Holm attended one particularly acrimonious meeting. I'd seen many of their films with my mother on "dish night" at Varsity Theatre in Ashland. (Back then, they incentivized people to go to the movies by giving out free dishes to patrons once a week. And I'll never forget Celeste's performance in *All About Eve* and Shelley's turn in *A Place in the Sun*.) Celeste was an elegant blonde, a beautiful, well-spoken woman. I watched as she stood up and said, "Everyone! We must calm down. We are not a union, we are a guild!" She wanted us to think of ourselves as artists, not activists.

Then Shelley Winters stood up and shouted in her brassy voice, "Celeste, sit down! You don't know your ass from your elbow. These kids are dancing for eight hours at a time on concrete and destroying their legs." It was an extraordinary moment. Here I was just starting out, and these legendary stars, women I'd seen only on the screen, were fighting for my professional well-being. It was so moving to actually be part of this engaged show business community.

After the strike, *Take Me Along* settled into a yearlong run, and Jackie won a Tony for his role as Sid Davis. One evening when the show let out, Jim Cresson, one of the principal actors, asked me if I'd ever considered studying to become an actor. He'd heard me fooling around backstage, doing imitations of movie stars, and thought I should consider taking classes. I told him about my experience at Cassavetes's class and how I'd felt like a complete fish out of water. Jim suggested that I go to his acting teacher, Mary Tarcai. Since I had migrated away from classical ballet and into the belly of show business, I figured I might as well explore other paths and signed up.

Mary was an intense, powerful, and extremely direct teacher who always wore black. "I'm in mourning for my career," she explained when anyone questioned her dress code. She'd been caught up in the Communist witch hunt in Hollywood in the 1950s and was blacklisted when she refused to name names.

By coincidence, her classes met in the same studio where my old school Quintano's had been. At least superficially, I felt at home. At first I was terrified to participate in scenes. I wasn't sure of what I was doing. Mary was a rigorous teacher—demanding but supportive and very committed to her students. I often failed miserably in class. "Good," she'd say. "Fail here in the studio, not out there when you're working on a role." Slowly, I began to grasp how to build a character and how to remain true to a playwright's vision. "Acting is not about you self-expressing," Mary said. "It's about you creating other people."

Iva, who was still dancing in the long-running *My Fair Lady,* and I moved from our studio on West Fifty-fifth Street to her aunt Ada's beautiful town house on Embassy Row, on Sixty-seventh between Fifth and Madison. (I can only imagine how thrilled Aunt Ada must have been to have two young dancers under her roof.) Eventually, I moved in with my close friend from *Take Me Along*, Arlene Golonka.

Arlene lived in a seven-room apartment on West 101st Street and Riverside Drive—five girls in all, some of whom were in the business. The atmosphere in the apartment was just this side of riotous. One of our roommates was a very attractive German brunette named Eva, who never missed an opportunity to wander into the living room in her black lace underwear when another girl had a date over, saying, "Ach, I deedn't know zair vas anyvon heah!"

Arlene was an adorable Polish-American blonde from Chicago. She was wildly funny, very talented, and full of energy. She played Belle, the prostitute in *Take Me Along,* and as a principal actor, she had her own dressing room. Lonely and wanting to be with her pals—a lovely redheaded dancer, Nicole Barth, and me—Arlene moved kit and kaboodle into the large chorus dressing room in the basement.

One afternoon while we were previewing the show in Philadelphia, the three of us were having a snack in a coffee shop when Mel Brooks, who was previewing his own show, approached us. "There they are: chocolate, strawberry, and vanilla," he said. Whenever any of us ran into Mel in the years to come, he made the same joke about our hair color.

Iva, Nicole, and I were chorus dancers. There is something truly wonderful about dancing in a chorus, with everyone moving through space as individuals who together make up a whole dance. It's a specific experience that an individual performer can never achieve alone. Arlene was an actor and, like Jim Cresson, she urged me to pursue acting. She would call me from her auditions and beg me to show up. "Val, I'm at the Martin Beck Theatre. I'm auditioning for Abe Burrows. Get down here now," she would whisper from backstage. When I protested that I didn't have an agent, Arlene wouldn't listen. "Just come to the door and tell them you're here to read. If I don't get the part, maybe you will." The extent of Arlene's generosity and enthusiasm for her friends' success was a rarity in the business.

With Arlene's coaching, Mary Tarcai's cold-reading class, and auditions one on top of the other, I felt myself improving, but I hadn't caught a break. Luckily, I had a new source of income— industrial shows, or trade shows. These productions were a big deal back then. These presentations introduced new or featured products to the corporate sales forces before they hit the market with a customized musical stage show. They paid well and became a lifesaver for me. (So was unemployment insurance and, on occasion, Mom and Dad's help when I was between jobs.) For several years I did the Milliken Breakfast Show during fashion week. It was a splashy, beautifully produced musical show put on for the apparel buyers in the posh digs of the Grand Ballroom of the Waldorf Astoria or the Astor Hotel at eight A.M.

The Milliken show, which ran for two weeks, was the ultimate in corporate theater—a first-rate song-and-dance comedy revue that parodied other musicals with special lyrics praising Milliken fabric. Thousands of textile-industry executives and buyers attended these performances, had breakfast, and were in the market buying by nine A.M. Milliken hired only Broadway singers and dancers to model the fashions and always booked marquee stars, like Joel Grey, Nancy Walker, Bert Lahr, Phil Silvers, and later on, David Cassidy.

Although I'd been hoping to move from dancing into acting, I needed a job, so in 1961 I auditioned for the chorus of Michael Kidd's new Broadway show, *Wildcat,* a musical starring Lucille Ball. I'd grown up loving her feature films and her landmark TV show, so seeing Lucy in person was stunning. With her dazzling aquamarine eyes, fiery hair, and luminescent skin, Lucy seemed to radiate light from within. She was wonderful, warm, and friendly to the entire cast.

The first time the cast convened to read through the script, Lucy insisted that everyone introduce him- or herself. I was sitting next to a beautiful, petite brunette named Penny Ann who had worn hip-hugger pants to the audition. When Penny Ann said her name, Lucy looked up from her script and said, "What's a Penny Ann?" Then she looked directly at Penny and said, "Look at those saucer eyes, that's a Penny Ann."

Lucy looked after all of us. The first time she visited us in our chorus dressing room, she was shocked by how grim it was. She came from Hollywood, the land of clean, well-lit dressing rooms, so she was unaccustomed to the lack of glamour backstage in the old Broadway theaters. When she saw the rough, dirty cinder-block walls, she exclaimed, "I don't want you living like this. We've got to paint the room."

A few days later, she returned. "Kids, the union says that we can't paint the dressing room. So how about we all sneak in on the weekend and do it behind their backs." When the management got wind of what Lucy was up to, they immediately saw to it that the dressing room was painted. It was clear that she used her stardom to help us. When I gave Penny Ann a shower for her upcoming wedding to a tall, blue-eyed Israeli named Zvi Almog, Lucy sent a blender. A real state-of-the-art blender was a big deal in those days. I was on Long Island at Penny's wedding when Angela gave birth to Virginia Allyson Harper—Ginger—in New Jersey. That was a full day!

Although the show got lukewarm reviews, people flocked to the theater expecting to see Lucy Ricardo, the wacky housewife from *I Love Lucy*. When the curtain went up, though, they embraced the tough oil prospector Lucy played in *Wildcat*. With her mile-long legs and huge personality, Lucy filled the theater and enthralled the audience.

One night she truly outdid herself. There was a scene that involved Lucy; her sister Janie, played by Paula Stewart; a ritzy countess, played by Edith King; and a little Yorkshire terrier. The dog was unbelievably well trained, and every performance, he dutifully followed behind Edith, Lucy, and Paula as they crossed the stage. One evening as the Yorkie was making his cross, he suddenly stopped center stage, assumed the position, and pooped. The audience went wild. Edith froze. Lucy dashed offstage and urgently asked the stage manager to hand over a broom and upright dustpan. She returned to the stage and swept up the offending little pile and then turned to the audience. "Next time I'll read the fine print in my contract." The audience exploded with laughter and applause. After the show, Lucy later confided to the cast that she was glad it had been a Yorkshire terrier and not a Great Dane.

Wildcat had its share of problems. Lucy suffered bouts of exhaustion and got injured during a performance when part of the oil rig hit her on the head. She was forced to take several leaves of absence during which the show was dark. But when she recovered, she soldiered on immediately. If not for Lucy's immense draw, I think we would have closed earlier than we did.

It was during my run in *Wildcat* that I had my first serious love affair. I had been introduced to a dashing man named Sam by Diana Hunter, a pal, and one of the other Dice Girls from *Take Me Along*. He was a handsome Princeton boy who worked as a producer on a long-running children's television show.

A product of the 1950s and Catholic school, I was saving myself for marriage, so I'd rarely let a guy pay my way on a date; I didn't want to owe anything in return. My catchphrase was "I like you as a friend." Original, huh? I must have uttered this line hundreds of times.

With Sam it was different. A consummate gentleman, he wouldn't dream of letting me pay—and, knowing that I was in love with him, I let him. As my pal Gene Varrone would say, "It was a lovely romance."

Though we were going together, marriage was not a topic of discussion, although I'm sure the question of whether Sam was "the one" was bobbing around in my twenty-two-year-old brain. If it hadn't been before, Angela's aunts, Edith and Carmela, made sure it was when they yelled across the lasagna and roast chicken at a family gathering in New Jersey, "So, Sam, when you gonna marry Valerie?"

I was mortified beyond belief. My sensitive dad maneuvered me into a quiet corner and talked me off the emotional ledge. "Don't be angry at them, Val. They think they're helping you get married and get pregnant. In that order!"

At that point I wasn't sure I was interested in either.

After *Wildcat* ended, I continued studying with Mary Tarcai and auditioning all over town. At one interview I was asked to read a scene with myself. I did it by speaking the lines of one character and then facing the other way and speaking as the other character. Talk about dumb—dumb for the casting person to suggest this asinine direction, and dumb for me to follow through with it.

Luckily, I could rely on being cast in the Milliken show every year. And when Michael Kidd invited me to dance in a Broadway show he was directing called *Subways Are for Sleeping,* I jumped at the chance. The show was produced by David Merrick and starred Carol Lawrence, Sydney Chaplin (Charlie's son!), Phyllis Newman, and Orson Bean.

Subways was about homeless folks surviving in New York City—however, in 1961 homelessness was not as widely understood as it is today, and *Subways* was not a very successful show. The out-of-town reviews were tepid. In order to bring the show to Broadway, David Merrick pulled one of the most question-able publicity stunts of all time. He knew that the critics were going to savage *Subways,* so he found seven New Yorkers with the same names as the seven most well-known theater critics—Howard Taubman, Walter Kerr, John Chapman, John McClain, Richard Watts, Jr., Norman Nadel, and Robert Coleman. He treated them to a free performance and asked permission to use their names and photographs in an advertisement alongside hyperbolic quotes such as "One of the great musical comedies of the last thirty years." He ran the ad underneath the head-line: "7 Out of 7 Are Ecstatically Unanimous About *Subways Are for Sleeping.*" When the newspapers found out they'd been bamboozled, all but one of them pulled the ad. Still, the stunt extended our run.

There was a young dancer in the chorus of *Subways* named Michael Bennett. Michael was eighteen years old, fresh off the bus from Buffalo, with energy to burn. During the show's run, Michael would ask me and Iva to meet him at the Variety Arts Studios on West Forty-sixth Street. The place was a real hub of show business activity. I'd done so many auditions there that the walls knew my name. There was a marvelously dingy coffee shop next door where dancers, singers, choreographers, actors, directors, producers, and musicians ran in and out to get Danish and coffee to take into rehearsals and auditions. The whole place screamed, "I'm in show business."

Michael rented studio space in Variety Arts to practice being a choreographer with Iva and me as his dancers. One night after

Subways let out, Michael asked me, "So Valerie, what do you want to do?"

I wasn't sure what he was asking. After I moment I replied, "I want to act."

"Then go for it," Michael said.

"What about you?" I asked. "What do you want to do?"

"I want to be a choreographer," Michael said. Who knew that this starry-eyed eighteen-year-old would go on to choreograph *A Chorus Line,* one of the most perfect representations of the struggles and the joys of being a Broadway dancer.

After *Subways Are for Sleeping* closed, I was offered a new Michael Kidd show called *Here's Love*. But I didn't want to keep on dancing in the chorus of show after show. If I wanted to act, I decided, I should go for it. Thanks for the great advice, Michael Bennett!

chapter
THREE

I agonized about whether or not to join the *Here's Love* company. I had a strong work ethic, and I knew that turning down a job was not an entirely rational decision. Most of all, I did not want to seem ungrateful to Michael Kidd for his unending support. At the same time, I sensed that now was a moment to take a chance. Under Mary Tarcai's tutelage, I had grown to love acting. So I turned down the show, which was one of the toughest decisions I ever made.

My roommate Arlene was a tireless champion of my acting career. The summer after *Subways* closed, I was cast in a summer stock production of Neil Simon's *Come Blow Your Horn*—as Connie, the same role Arlene had played on Broadway. (Significantly, it was during that Broadway run that Arlene introduced Iva to her future husband, Ron Rifkin, an extraordinary actor to whom Iva is still married.) Generous with her time and energy, Arlene coached me for my summer stock debut.

In addition to her Broadway career, Arlene had become involved with Second City, the famous improv troupe from Chicago directed by the brilliant Paul Sills. Improvisation performed for an audience was a new and exciting evolution in the theater, and Paul and his group were at the forefront. Using Theater Games and acting exercises developed by Sills's mother, Viola Spolin, Second City became the nation's leading improvisational theater company. Viola's pioneering book *Improvisation for the Theater* provided the foundation for Paul's work and the art of improvisation in general. Second City's shows included rehearsed scenes and complete improvisation based on suggestions from the audience, usually laced with political and social satire.

After roaring success in Chicago, Paul Sills brought a core group of Second City players from Chicago to New York and took up residence in Greenwich Village at a cabaret theater called the Square East (where a young folksinger named Bob Dylan took the stage on their night off). Arlene was performing with the troupe at the time and insisted that I come to one of their shows. At first I thought she was trying to get me involved in the group, but I soon discovered that she had an ulterior motive. She wanted to introduce me to someone.

I was still dating Sam. But after two years, we had fallen into a rut. He didn't want to get married, that much was clear, though he also wasn't interested in breaking up. I was content enough with the relationship that I wasn't rocking the boat.

Yes, I had been head over heels in love with him, but I was

even more in love with the whole concept of being in love. I must have been an impulsive, needy, overly dramatic young woman. Poor calm, quiet Sam! Arlene was doing him a favor.

Arlene, good friend that she was to me, worried that Sam and I were wasting time. When she invited me to the Square East, she told me to keep an eye out for her cast mate Dick Schaal during the show. From Arlene's description of him, I knew immediately when Dick came onstage. I was in awe. He was an inspired performer, so free, energetic, and funny. He was a real genius when it came to improv, a master of space work—making an invisible object appear. A lot of people can get out onstage and tell jokes, but Dick could conjure a setting with the way he used his body. He could lean on a lamppost that wasn't there and a park appeared, or sidle up to an invisible bar and there he was in a smokey nightclub. He was a magician, and I was entranced.

In the following weeks, Sam and I decided, in the immortal words of parting, "to take a break." As painful as it was, we both realized that if we weren't getting married, it was time to move on. With Sam out of the picture, Arlene kept pushing Dick on me. "Oh, Dick's joining us for coffee," she said innocently one day. But I should have recognized the twinkle in her eye.

Dick had been a carpenter in Chicago when he discovered Second City. He immediately knew that he needed to switch professions, so he got into Viola Spolin's workshop and left woodworking behind. Dick was quite tall, with a wonderful boyish quality. He had gorgeous thick hair and very dark brown eyes. He was innately humorous both on- and offstage. Best of all, he loved spending time with me. Dick invited me to be a part of his entire world, and immediately our relationship took off.

I started attending the improv workshops Dick taught. He was a sensational teacher. From Mary Tarcai I had learned how to work with what was on the page—how to internalize it and find my own unique way into scripted material. From Dick I learned how to live in the moment onstage, how to allow the moment I was performing to be spontaneous. Using Theater Games, he coached his students to let go of thinking and be open to the next moment. "Get out of your head!" he'd plead.

Dick and I spent a tremendous amount of time together. Although I wasn't officially in Second City, I was very much *of* it. In 1964, two months after Dick and I started dating, the company got an offer to trade theaters with the Committee, a San Francisco-based improv troupe. This trip was exciting for three reasons: I got to travel with Dick, to study in his improv workshop, and to introduce him to my family. Mom had moved to San Francisco where Leah and her husband, Connie, were living with their four-year-old son, Victor, their one-year-old, Anton, and their brand-new daughter, Tanya.

We stayed in San Francisco for three glorious, romantic months. I continued taking Dick's workshop and took sessions with Viola herself, hoping to one day perform with Second City.

At night I would go to the theater to watch Dick and the company. When we had a free evening we'd go to the Purple Onion to see a new young comic named Bill Cosby and hang out after the show at trendy Enrico's coffeehouse with Bill and his beautiful wife, Camille. This trip also allowed me to spend a lot of time with my mother, who, to my delight, greatly approved of Dick. Leah did as well and, for some reason, dubbed him "Little Richie."

Dick and I rented a darling apartment up an extraordinarily steep flight of stone steps high on a hill in the North Beach section of the city. Our landlords had a giant turtle named Giovanni whom we looked after. The weather was warm, the city was beautiful, Dick and I were in love. After only five months together, he started asking if I'd marry him.

"Probably," I said.

"Well, that's better than no," Dick replied.

I quickly changed my mind, though. Yes, I wanted to marry Dick. Badly.

Toward the end of Second City's San Francisco run, a Broadway producer called Dick asking him to play Jesse James in a new show called *Kelly*, about Hop Kelly, who famously jumped off the Brooklyn Bridge and survived. Dick and I hurried to New York and moved into the Wellington Hotel on Seventh Avenue and Fifty-fifth Street so he could begin rehearsals. I called home and breathlessly told Angela and Dad that Dick and I wanted to get married before *Kelly* started out-of-town previews in Philadelphia. My father liked Dick but asked me, "Why an actor? Why not marry a lawyer, doctor, or a merchant?"

"A merchant?" I enquired. "You mean someone with a camel loaded with spices from the Orient?!"

Then we both laughed and he gave me his blessing.

Of course, when Angela heard that Dick and I were thinking of going to the courthouse, she immediately flew into high gear planning my wedding, which she insisted take place at the family home. She put the entire event together in three weeks. We were in such a rush that we didn't have enough time to have invitations printed. So everyone was invited by phone.

I desperately wanted my mother to come from San Francisco, and I kept pushing her to do so even though I heard the reluctance in her voice. My brother, Don, flew in from Palm Desert, California, where he lived with his wife, Diane, repairing and racing cars. Leah was the matron of honor, and Victor was our adorable ring bearer. My sister, Ginger (Angela and my father's daughter), almost three, was the sweetest flower girl ever. My Jersey City friends and my best Broadway pals came—Iva, Arlene, and the now married mothers Penny and Nicole among them, as well as a host of male dancers. Outside of a casting call for *La Cage aux Folles,* there have never been so many gay men in one room! Dick's Second City friends also turned out in force.

Way past the time for me to walk down the staircase into the living room for the ceremony, my mother still hadn't arrived. Don had driven through the snow to the airport to pick her up and hadn't come back. Because he was a professional driver (of logging trucks and race cars), Don could handle driving in inclement weather, so I had insisted that he be the one to go to the airport. Big mistake. Mom's flight had been diverted to Pittsburgh due to heavy snow. I was in the grip of the "bridal crazies" and refused to make my grand entrance without my mother and brother present.

Finally, my father came into the bedroom where I was hiding. "Val, the minister has another wedding. If you don't come down, he's leaving. Now let's get you married."

Don missed the nuptials but got back in time for the party.

Even with my mother missing, I had a wonderful day. We had a buffet of Chinese food, a phenomenal cake (thank you, Angela), and laughed and sang and danced wildly until it was time to return to New York. All the guests said it was one of the best weddings they'd ever attended. We had a one-night honeymoon at the Plaza Hotel, and then we returned to the affordable Wellington, as Dick was in the thick of rehearsals for *Kelly*.

We relocated to Philadelphia with the company and had a sweet, snowy first Christmas in our hotel room. First thing in the New Year, Dick was written out of the show. I guess they didn't need the outlaw Jesse James after all. When Dick's mother found out, she called Dick. "Oh," she said in her midwestern accent, "so you have no job, and now you're married!" But we weren't worried about the future. We were in love. We were going to be actors together, embracing the highs and lows as a team. By the way, *Kelly* ran for a single night on Broadway before closing—one of the biggest disasters in Broadway history.

Dick and I found a quaint apartment with two fireplaces on the corner of Bleecker and Perry in the West Village, for which we paid $190 a month. Dick built bookcases and a small kitchen banquette and Gene Varrone helped us decorate. It was sometimes a struggle to rustle up our rent, but we managed. I performed in industrial and trade shows for companies such as General Electric, Nabisco, and Ford. Dick signed with the William Morris Agency and worked steadily in commercials and voice-overs. He also resumed teaching his workshop.

Dick also did an off-Broadway play by Ronald Ribman called *Harry, Noon and Night* with a young actor named Dustin Hoffman. Onstage, Dustin wore a flowered silk kimono, spoke with a German accent, and walked with a pronouced limp that changed from one leg to the other. If that wasn't bad enough, he had to cut the head off a dead fish every night. I attended every performance, but I never sat up front. The smell! That's the price we actors pay for a chance at being discovered. I must say, young Dustin was absolutely intriguing in every way.

In 1965, after Dick and I had been living in the Village for two years, Wendy, Dick's daughter from his first marriage, came to live with us. Wendy's mother had two younger sons from a second marriage that had broken up. She felt that since she was a struggling single mom, it would be best for Wendy to live with her dad, and my view was, if you have as great a dad as Dick, you should be with him. Nevertheless, I was nervous.

Before Wendy arrived, I had expected a wild child or at least someone who would disrupt the rhythm of our lives. But then in walked this thirteen-year-old angel—sweet, a bit shy, with an innate elegance—who immediately enriched our home. I had to learn how to be an appropriate mother to a teenager, and quickly. Thankfully, Angela had set a sterling example for me as a step-mother. From the start, Wendy seemed to love living in New York with me and her dad. But in order to accommodate her, we needed to find a larger apartment.

Back in the 1960s, it was amazing what an extra twenty dollars a month could get you if you left the Village. For only $210 we upgraded to a penthouse with a long, narrow terrace on Ninety-fourth and Broadway. You gave up chic for space. As usual, Dick put his carpentry skills to use and built us all sorts of louvered cabinets and room dividers. Again my friend Gene— who, in addition to being a terrific singer, was a wonderful interior designer worked his decorating magic.

As much as we would have loved to send Wendy to private school, we simply couldn't afford it. So I found a public school called Joan of Arc, near our apartment. I was terrified when Wendy set off for school. This extremely pretty little California girl walking around the Upper West Side of New York was suddenly my responsibility. I was certain she'd be waylaid by juvenile delinquents on motorcycles. I would follow her to school, ducking into doorways, so she wouldn't see me. Later she told me she thought I was being pretty lame but funny, too.

Although a lot of my time was devoted to helping Wendy

get acclimated, I continued trying to find acting jobs. Dick and I developed a comedy act together, laughing and arguing all the way. We improvised scenes in our living room, which we developed into short sketches that we performed at established downtown clubs such as the Bitter End and the Village Vanguard. We were part of a showcase with other performers, such as Linda Ronstadt and Jerry Jeff Walker, who wrote "Mr. Bojangles." The idea of the show was to draw in casting agents who would put us up for roles, or directors or producers who would say, "These two are dazzling. I must have them." As a result of the showcase, Dick and I were asked to improvise radio commercials and hired for a daily talk show on television called *The New Yorkers* in which we did comedy sketches and interviews. I loved the steadiness of this job, which lasted for months—five days a week, regular salary, not to mention Oscar's, a great seafood restaurant around the corner. Penny's brother, Jeremy Stevens, wrote for the show; later, he went on to write and produce nine seasons of *Everybody Loves Raymond* with its brilliant creator, Phil Rosenthal.

As a result of working so closely with Dick onstage, I was ready to join the Second City Company. My first major performance with the troupe was at the Royal Alexandra Theatre in Toronto. The theater was a gem, and the audiences were eager to laugh. In one sketch I faced one of the biggest onstage challenges ever: I played a little old lady in a talent show who performs a catatonic fit that becomes real. She actually freezes. I had to stay frozen while the scene went on and the audiences laughed wildly. To keep frozen and not burst out laughing was an excruciating task. We got invited on yachts and to country clubs and met many polite and welcoming Canadians. Our show may have sparked the great Canadian Second City tradition.

I continued taking class or attending improvisation workshops and traveled for some industrial shows. I was hired to do a show for the Norge appliance company in Caracas, Venezuela. The salesmen who sold the most refrigerators for the company won the trip to South America. During the evening, I had to do a little nightclub routine, welcoming the men and their wives by singing "Hello, Norge" to the tune of "Hello, Dolly," not a good musical fit. In the mornings, we performed the actual show, which extolled the virtues of Norge appliances within a supposedly comedic musical parody of James Bond. I played Tushy Mucho, an ersatz Pussy Galore. Let's just say it wasn't my finest work. But I did bring home a fantastic leather tote from a Caracas street market.

While Dick landed a respectable number of jobs, including a Broadway comedy by Jules Feiffer called *Little Murders*, starring old chum Elliott Gould, at times our financial situation got pretty dire. I remember one time we were literally down to a quarter. Not kidding. But then work would come, as well as my unemployment check for fifty bucks a week. One great job we did together was as stand-ins for Carl Reiner's Broadway play *Something Different*. Dick stood by for Bob Dishy and Gabe Dell, and I stood by for Linda Lavin and Maureen Arthur. Linda and I became great pals. We used to take an Italian class together before matinees. During periods of waiting to get hired, I never gave up my focus of becoming an actor, but I did involve myself with something quite important to me—the nonviolent fight for civil rights.

I was fortunate enough to have been raised in a fair and open-minded household. My mom never tolerated an inkling of prejudice, no matter how accidental or unaware, from Leah, Don, or me. They raised us to see everyone as equal. Whenever anyone used a prejudicial term to dismiss black people or any other race, my mother would bristle. "Remember," she would say, "women, like minorities, are considered second-class citizens. Treat everyone as you wish to be treated yourself."

It would be several years before I truly understood what she was saying.

After John F. Kennedy was assassinated, a galavanizing event for me, I began to look for more direct ways to get involved in one of the many organizations fighting for social justice in the world. Initially, I thought of joining the Peace Corps—the phenomenal plan put forth by the president's brother-in-law Sargent Shriver. But I had just been cast in *Subways Are for Sleeping,* so it was impossible for me to leave the country. Instead, I decided to take action closer to home.

One of the first protests I attended was a peaceful demonstration in front of a restaurant that served South African lobster tails. I'd read about the event in a free liberal weekly. Although I wasn't sure what effect the action would have on ending apartheid, I felt that I should participate in trying to bring attention to the issue. I showed up at the restaurant and was given a sign to hold. I joined the picket line, circling with a decent-size group of protesters that included James Farmer, the executive director of CORE, the Congress of Racial Equality.

One of my closest friends was a gorgeous African-American singer and actress named Norma Donaldson, who often looked after Wendy when Dick and I were out of town. Norma and I had met at an audition in the early sixties and hit it off right away. Shortly after *Subways* opened, Norma paid me a visit. "Valerie," she said, "I have a friend named Chuck Gordone. He's involved in the Committee for the Employment of Negro Performers [CENP], and they've decided to picket *Subways*."

"Why?" I asked.

"Because of the redcaps," Norma explained. *Subways Are for Sleeping* had a musical number set in Grand Central Station that included three dancers dressed as redcaps—the porters who brought passengers' luggage to and from the trains. "In the entire history of Grand Central," Norma said, "there has never been a single white redcap. And now, on your stage, there are three of them. The producers could have used black dancers and they didn't. It was a conscious choice."

Her logic immediately resonated with me. "I'll join you on the picket line," I said.

Every evening before the show, I'd arrive at the theater half an hour early and sign in to work. Then I'd go outside and walk around the picket line with Norma until it was time for us to go to our respective shows. (Norma was just across the street in

Bravo Giovanni, starring Michele Lee.) While some of my cast mates thought what I was doing was admirable, others thought I was a fool for jeopardizing my job. They also thought I was trying to get them replaced. "I'm not trying to get you fired," I explained to the three guys who played the redcaps. "I'm just trying to make a point for the future."

Norma and I attended meetings of the CENP. Chuck Gordone was an African-American director, writer, and actor who had grown tired of seeing black performers passed over for jobs because of their skin color. I began to understand the difficulty of the struggle. I thought that I had it hard getting cast on Broadway, but for this group of supremely talented performers, even my small sliver of success was an impossibility. The larger issue was lack of diversity onstage. An all-white cast announced to the audience, "These others don't exist."

Around the time I was attending CENP meetings, Arlene introduced me to a man named John Randolph, one of the great progressives who had stood up during the McCarthy witch hunt in Hollywood and was blacklisted. John was a strong unionist and a social justice advocate. He began holding meetings to educate and inspire performers at St. Clement's Church on West Forty-seventh Street.

The primary focus of these meetings was how to aid in the civil rights movement. CORE volunteers Mickey Schwerner, James Chaney, and Andrew Goodman had been murdered in Mississippi in 1964. People were marching on Washington in record numbers. While the theater community was slightly more forward-thinking than the rest of the country, there was a lot of room for improvement. It was not enough to stand at the front of theaters shaking a can to raise money for the Council of Federated Organizations (COFO), uniting voter registration and other civil rights activities in the South, as I had been. Much more involvement was necessary to effect change. We needed to organize.

In the middle of a meeting, during a heated discussion of how best to take action, an elegant woman from Westchester took the floor. She was wearing pearls and a beautiful tailored suit, and she began to talk about women's rights. The reaction to her speech was vehement. "Go back to your suburb," someone cried. Other people, myself included, laughed at her. Women's rights? No one was lynching white women. Why waste our time? It seemed like a silly cause. How unenlightened we all were.

After rudely dismissing women's rights as a social issue unworthy of our attention, the group at St. Clement's decided that we should start a CORE chapter in New York City whose sole focus would be trying to integrate the entertainment industry. We called ourselves Seven Arts CORE, which implied activism across a wide spectrum of the entertainment world, including film, television, theater, and commercials.

Except for one or two all-black shows, Broadway was pretty much lily-white. Seven Arts CORE vowed to change this. *Subways Are for Sleeping* had closed, so all of my free time could be devoted to the endeavor. I discovered that I loved organizing, sharing facts that would compel others to join the effort. I didn't seek to lead but was a dedicated participant, a persistent and energetic soldier for the cause.

When we held sit-ins, I would often volunteer as part of a cadre of protesters who abstained from civil disobedience in order to help bail out those who would inevitably be arrested. I spent a great deal of time at the various courthouses around New York signing protesters out of jail, doing my best to see that they weren't abused, and letting their family members know where they'd been taken.

Eventually, Seven Arts CORE raised enough money to rent a tiny office on Forty-third and Eighth, in the middle of the Times Square melee. During the day, I'd go in and cover the phones and collect donations. From this office we began to organize our actions.

One of our initial goals was to integrate industrial shows. We didn't know if we could tackle commercials right off the bat, so we thought that industrial shows would be a better area to start. We set up a picket line in front of Don Allen Chevrolet in Columbus Circle, demanding that they employ nonwhite performers in their trade shows. The demonstrations took place every weekday and went on for months. Harry Belafonte even joined the picket line. At Easter, we hardboiled white eggs and dipped their bottom halves into black paint as a symbol of integration. Then we sent them to the executives at General Motors as part of our ongoing action. It was either incredibly brave or incredibly foolish of me to take on industrial shows as forcefully as I did. At that time these shows, including the Chevrolet show that I was picketing, were my primary source of income. And at that time it seemed exactly the right thing to do.

Finally, General Motors granted Seven Arts CORE a meeting. They even brought the black-and-white eggs and asked, "What do these mean, and what do you want?"

"The eggs were a little seasonal-integration message," we explained. "And since many nonwhites buy your cars, we'd like you to employ nonwhite performers in your shows." To our surprise, they did. In their next industrial show, Chevrolet hired one black male dancer and one black female singer—Paul Reid Roman and Norma Donaldson! Of course, these two had to perform together (Chevrolet wasn't ready for mixed-race couples), but it was a step in the right direction.

After our success with General Motors, other industrial shows began to employ nonwhite performers. Since I had been hired for these shows for years, the producers knew me. They began to call and ask for my help casting minorities. "We need an Asian American actor," they'd say. "Do you know some teenage African-American dancers?" For a moment I became the go-to girl for minority casting—a small-time volunteer agent.

Every week Seven Arts CORE picketed alongside one of the many other organizations in the city. When a civil rights activist was beaten or killed in the South, we marched in Harlem, in Queens, on Broadway. It was an emotional and turbulent time, although exhilarating as we felt we were making incremental progress. And it simply was not an option for me to sit back and do nothing.

The biggest action that Seven Arts CORE took was organizing an event called Freedom and All That Jazz, a fund-raising concert to bring awareness to the issue of racial equality in the performing arts, held at Central Plaza Ballroom on the Lower East Side, which donated the space for the event.

Civil rights groups from across the city helped us publicize. The auditorium was packed with people drinking and talking. We had a parade of talented singers and dancers on the stage. Then a young unknown comic named Richard Pryor started to perform. He was really skinny and really appealing.

The sound in the auditorium was deafening, and no one could hear his jokes. Instead of giving up, Richard turned to one small section of the audience and focused his attention on them. Soon they were rapt and laughing. People from other sections of the audience wanted to know what was going on. Eventually, everyone was paying attention to his extremely funny act. Richard was really sensational. A great lesson: Do what it takes to get heard.

As the sixties progressed, so did my consciousness. Lack of equality wasn't solely an issue of color; it was also one of gender. The statement I had so carelessly dismissed back at St. Clement's began to make complete sense. It became clear to me that sexism was so widespread, so insidious, so accepted that it was invisible.

I began to recognize sexism and misogyny within the very organizations fighting for equality. In my spare time, I began to read Kate Millet's *Sexual Politics* and Betty Friedan's *The Feminine Mystique*—I was becoming a feminist. I was capable of continuing my commitment to civil rights and of expanding it to include my gender. This shift in my awareness was a fascinating process. I could feel myself opening up, learning facts, wising up. It reminded me of a saying of Mom's: "When are you going to wake up and smell the coffee?" or Dad's entreaty: "Come conscious." I guess I was doing both.

chapter
FOUR

We'd been married a year when, oh boy, Dick landed a feature film! It was the role of a deputy sheriff in *The Russians Are Coming the Russians Are Coming*, an outrageous comedy directed by Norman Jewison. The fantastic cast included stars Carl Reiner, Eva Marie Saint, Jonathan Winters, character actors Phil Ford, Theo Bikel, and newcomer and Dick's compatriot from Second City, Alan Arkin.

The film was shot in Fort Bragg, a small coastal town in Northern California that the director needed to pass off as a New England village. He even filmed a sunset on the Pacific and played it backward so it would look like a sunrise on the East Coast. When the fog rolled in to Fort Bragg, as it did day after day, shooting would be canceled and we'd all trundle off to Carl's motel room and play dictionary or charades. Eva Marie, quietly competitive, invariably won, while Carl's jokes had us in stitches. Here Dick and I were, on location with a big-budget Hollywood movie, but it felt as if we were at sleepaway camp.

Even while Dick was busy working, I had a wonderful time in Fort Bragg. I took knitting lessons from a gentle English woman named Vera House in her modest cottage. Over the course of the shoot, I knitted Dick a beige Irish fisherman pullover that he wore for years.

I took a side trip up north to visit my brother, Don, in Ashland, where he now lived with his sweet wife, Diane, and two beautiful kids, Valerie (my namesake!) and Russell. By now Don was a professional race car driver. He won so many trophies over the years (two hundred!). Diane lined them up in rows in the attic. Val and Russ used to play hide-and-seek amongst them. My Emmys and other awards aren't on display either. I guess Mom had successfully drummed into us, "Don't show off."

After *The Russians Are Coming the Russians Are Coming* wrapped, Carl Reiner enthusiastically proposed that Dick move to Hollywood in order to pursue film and television work. I considered myself a theater person, but over time Dick convinced me that there would be work for both of us in California. Iva and her husband, Ron, were already in L.A., which was a big draw. Arlene had moved to Los Angeles several years earlier and had been working steadily in television. In fact, when she heard we were coming west, she gave us the use of her apartment until we found a place of our own. Iva, the source of all great tips, showed me the bounteous Farmers' Market and introduced me to the best dry cleaners, fabric shops, shoe repair guys, and doctors for every kind of ailment. What a pal! Soon Dick, Wendy, and I moved into one of those typically Californian houses in Laurel Canyon that was perched on what looked like sticks driven into the hillside. I spent a lot of time worrying about what would happen in an earthquake.

I already had my SAG (Screen Actors Guild) card and was able to work. Generous and helpful as always, Arlene got me auditions for small acting jobs and a role on *Mayberry R.F.D.*, on which she played Millie. While I was primarily interested in theater, I was thrilled to be getting any work at all and hoped these little parts would lead to something juicier.

Auditioning is an odd process, because you live in perpetual anticipation of being given a chance. Though auditions were few and far between for me, when one came up, it was a real investment of time, especially since I had to worry about hair, makeup, and what to wear. (Guys have it easy. They shave, throw on a shirt, and go.)

In between auditions, life went on as usual. I was focused on making a home for our family and being a good mother to Wendy. She was the most sweet-natured kid, not an ounce of trouble. However, since she was only fourteen, she needed to be driven to school—and having lived mostly in New York since I turned sixteen, I hadn't had a reason to get my license until we got to Los Angeles. So Dick had to teach me to drive (poor devil!). While I hated it at first and was a bit of a menace on the roads, I came to love how much freedom came with getting behind the wheel of the black Ford station wagon, which I called Blackie, that I bought from our cleaning guy. Why should I spend a lot of money on wheels when I wasn't working? Sweet, tolerant Wendy patiently put up with my tentative driving, never complaining as I banged poor Blackie into the sides of Laurel Canyon, terrified of driving too close to the yellow line and crashing into an oncoming car. "It's okay, Val," she'd say calmly as I bumped into canyon walls over and over again like a pinball.

During those first months in Los Angeles, Wendy and I spent a lot of time together. When Second City was performing at the Lindy Opera House on La Brea and Wilshire, she and I would have a late lunch between shows at Imperial Garden, an enormous, ornate Japanese restaurant on the Sunset Strip. One afternoon while we were sitting at our table, a shaggy-haired guy in weathered jeans came over and asked if we would join him for dinner. I wasn't sure whether he was interested in me or Wendy. Either seemed highly inappropriate, so I politely declined.

Wendy and I continued with our meal until a less hippie-looking fellow came over. "My brother would really like it if you joined us," he said.

"I'm sorry," I said. "We're happy eating by ourselves."

Finally, a pregnant young woman approached us. "It's just a family gathering," she said. "Please come and eat with us."

Wendy and I exchanged glances. We were in a public restaurant. What harm could there be in eating dinner with these three? They seemed perfectly nice, not to mention enthusiastic for us to join them. Wendy and I followed the young lady through shoji screen doors into a small, private dining room.

As we all sat on the floor, eating Japanese style, I couldn't shake the feeling that I had seen the cool-looking, long-haired young guy (the one who'd first approached us) somewhere before.

Then again, in 1968 on Sunset Boulevard, his look was a dime a dozen.

Over tempura, he asked, "What's your favorite song right now?"

"'I Heard It Through the Grapevine' by Marvin Gaye," I said.

"Yeah, wow," he said. "He's very cool."

When we were finished eating, Wendy and I excused ourselves and thanked our very pleasant hosts. On the way out of the restaurant, she grabbed my arm. "Val," Wendy whispered, "that was Jim Morrison."

I may not have been hip enough to recognize the lead singer of the Doors, but at least I'd been cool enough to join him for dinner and give Wendy a unique experience she'd never forget. I regret the missed opportunity to tell him he had the soul of a poet.

As months passed and no work came my way, I started to worry that there was nothing for me to do in California. I missed the theater life I'd left behind on the East Coast. I was nearly thirty years old, which even back then was a little long in the tooth for an actress. Perhaps my ship had sailed.

Fortunately, a call came from Paul Sills, the genius creator of Second City. Every few years, Sills would create a dazzling new theater form. He maintained that theater should deliver powerful, authentic experiences, as well as huge laughs, thrills, and chills. His upcoming endeavor was no exception. He told us that he was developing a production called *Story Theatre,* and he wanted Dick and me to be in the company.

Story Theatre was a direct evolution of Sills's work in Second City. Using his mother Viola Spolin's Theater Games to develop material, he planned to create an evening of comedy, narrative, and movement to tell (or retell) classic folktales and myths. With a company of eight players, he wanted to explore the humor, mystery, and passion at the heart of fairy tales, and examine how the stories we pass down from generation to generation express the human condition. The players would be Dick Schaal, Dick Libertini, Paul Sand, Hamilton Camp, Peter Bonerz, Melinda Dillon, Mary Frann, and Valerie Harper. I was so happy to be invited into this thrilling theatrical process.

Story Theatre was comprised of eight fairy tales or fables such as "Henny Penny," "The Golden Goose," and "The Robber Bridegroom," presented on an empty stage through narration, dialogue, and the use of imaginary objects. Paul planned to have a quartet, The True Brethren led by Hamilton Camp, accompany the performance with songs by Country Joe and the Fish, Bob Dylan, and George Harrison. He decided to develop the show in Los Angeles with an eye to bringing it to Broadway. I was very excited about the prospect of appearing on Broadway once more, this time as an actress instead of a dancer.

Between agreeing to do *Story Theatre* and beginning rehearsal, Dick and I got involved in another production, one with a very interesting man named C. Robert Holloway, who was something of a jack-of-all-trades—a director, set designer, writer, producer, and eventually good friend. He was writing a play with Richard Levine called *The American Nightmare*. The show was a send-up of a staged reading put on by the fictitious and quite dreadful British theatrical company called the Royal Chichester Players.

The play was written in a purposefully over-the-top style riddled with purple prose and sly humor. I played two roles—Hitler's girlfriend Eva Braun at eighteen and Vida Fontanne, a fading stage star who sounded like Tallulah Bankhead. *The American Nightmare* played only a couple of weekends in a tiny black-box theater on Vermont Avenue, but it was a terrifically funny production that I loved being a part of.

Shortly after it closed, I received a call from C. Robert. He told me that Ethel Winant, head of casting from CBS, had seen the play and wanted to talk to me. Since I didn't have an agent, she'd had a tough time tracking me down. Ethel was casting *The Mary Tyler Moore Show* at the time and wanted me to come in and read for Mary's friend Rhoda.

At first I thought C. Robert was joking. I couldn't believe I was being asked to audition with a star like Mary Tyler Moore. When he assured me that he wasn't joking, I asked if he would act as my agent. C. Robert agreed but warned me that he was leaving town and might not be available down the road. I told him that was fine because I didn't think I had a snowball's chance in hell of getting the part.

While I didn't look anything like Mary Tyler Moore, I thought I might not provide enough of a physical contrast to be her side-kick. We were of similar height and both had dark brown hair and small noses. I assumed CBS was looking for a tall, skinny red-head or a short, obese blonde. But as an actor, you audition. You show up, do your best, and hope that if you're wrong for the part, the casting director might remember you for something else.

CBS sent me the script, and I loved Rhoda immediately; I knew I could play the character. When I saw that she was a Jewish New Yorker, I called up my New York pals to hear their accents and refresh my memory. Penny Ann Green and Gene Varrone, who were both from Brooklyn, helped me figure out how Rhoda spoke. It was also Angela's voice that I heard in my head when I began to prepare for the role—the cheery, wise-cracking old-school New Yorker.

Dick began coaching me. We decided that it would be best if I memorized the audition scenes, something you would never do when auditioning for a play. But I wanted to be able to use props and bring a level of physicality that I thought would be impeded by carrying a script. I also wanted to give the impression that I was a quick study, which I'm not.

Dick and I had a little sailboat in Marina del Rey. The weekend before my audition, we holed up on the boat and began to rehearse. I'm sure all of the folks in the neighboring slips thought we were insane as we repeated the same conversation over and over and over.

The material I was given to prepare was the very first scene of *The Mary Tyler Moore Show*, in which Rhoda is outside on the balcony, washing windows in the cold. With Dick's help, I figured out how to pantomime the window and the bucket and communicate the sensation of stepping out of the cold and into Mary's apartment.

The first person I met on *The Mary Tyler Moore Show* was a cute-looking, natural redheaded secretary, Pat Nardo. She had a Bronx accent and a welcoming demeanor that calmed this "bundle-of-nerves" actor. Pat went on to become a very funny writer on both *Mary Tyler Moore* and *Rhoda*. I entered that place of hope, dread, and possibility . . . the audition room.

Jay Sandrich, the show's director, and the creators James L. Brooks (whom everyone called Jim) and Allan Burns were there, as well as writer-producer David Davis, who was always known as Dave. It was one of the best audition atmospheres I've ever walked into—a roomful of smiling, friendly people. It's so nice when you don't have to try to act through your own nerves, plus a veil of negativity from those casting, as is so often the case. Everyone seemed surprised and delighted by the Second City elements I brought to the audition, even laughing aloud when I conjured the cold air with my hands and shut an invisible window. When I was finished, they thanked me for coming in and sent me on my way. Although I felt I'd done well, I had no idea whether I'd be considered for the job.

The next day the network called and said they wanted to see me again, this time to read with Mary. A callback! I couldn't believe it. I was nervous and excited. I'd made it to the next level, and I was going to meet the marvelous Mary Tyler Moore. I harbored zero hope of getting the part. But since I always treated every audition as an opportunity to improve my acting and conquer my nerves, I figured that reading with someone as accomplished as Mary Tyler Moore would be a great learning experience.

Mary had just come from a ballet lesson (like me, she first

trained as a dancer). She wore a pale rose Helanca turtleneck over white trousers. After I gushed about how wonderful she was on *The Dick Van Dyke Show,* I took a step back and looked her over. She was as thin as a reed. "Look at you in white pants without a long jacket to cover your behind," I said. (Hell would have to freeze over before I would go out with my top tucked in and my butt in white.) The guys in the room burst out laughing. I had already become Rhoda the Self-Deprecating.

Mary was sweet and warm and immediately put me at ease. We read another scene from the pilot. It went quickly, and again I had no idea how I did. When we were finished, Mary and I chatted a little so that Allan, Jim, Dave, and Jay could see us interacting, and then I drove home.

When I pulled into the driveway ten minutes later, Dick was standing on the front lawn, waving his arms. "You got it! You got it!" he shouted. He looked a little deranged.

"Get in the house," I replied. "I didn't get anything." Back in New York, I had sweated through six callbacks for radio commercials before being turned down. I had become inured to rejection. "I haven't done a screen test yet," I continued. "This is Hollywood. No one gets cast without a screen test. Plus, I don't even look right for the part." It seemed inconceivable that something so big might work out so easily. This sort of opportunity was the whole reason Dick and I had come to Los Angeles. I couldn't believe it was happening.

"No," Dick said. "You got it. Seriously. They want to know who your agent is."

C. Robert kindly made calls on my behalf but was determined to leave agenting and move to Hawaii. I started out at seven hundred dollars a week to play Rhoda Morgenstern: I was over the moon.

When Dick and I moved to Los Angeles, my only ambition was to work steadily—to get into a play with a decent and successful run, something that didn't close before it opened. Sure, I'd entertained the notion of working in television, but certainly not as a series regular alongside someone as beloved and respected as Mary Tyler Moore! All my ships seemed to be coming in.

After I was cast, Ethel Winant asked me to come into the CBS offices to meet some of the executives. One of the suits was sitting in a chair with his leg slung over the armrest. He looked me over when I came into the room. "Tell me, Valerie," he said, "I understand you're part Spanish."

"Well, I'm supposed to be, on my dad's side. You'd have to do a genealogy search to be sure."

The executive turned to Ethel. "Can we fill our minority quotient with her?"

"I don't think so," Ethel said.

"I once did a Mexican hat dance in grammar school. And I wore black braids and a Mexican costume on Broadway in *Wildcat*," I offered. "But I don't think you can pass me off as Latina."

When I was cast in *The Mary Tyler Moore Show*, *Story Theatre* was getting ready to open at the Mark Taper Forum. I was so invested in Paul Sills's piece that I hoped and prayed I could work out a way to stay in the play while also appearing in the television show. Paul and Gordon Davidson, the director of the Taper, were both delighted that I had landed a series and graciously arranged for another player, the beautiful Mary Frann, to go on for me on Friday nights, the night when *The Mary Tyler Moore Show* filmed. On all the other nights, I would be able to rush from rehearsals at the studio in time for the curtain at the Mark Taper.

I was thrilled beyond belief for my first day of work on *The Mary Tyler Moore Show*. I was also terrified that I would bomb. I had the first-day-of-school jitters driving onto that lot—it felt like something straight out of the movies! I pulled in through the CBS gates and into the parking lot that morning, ready to begin my television career, and there it was: my name on my own parking space. This was huge.

I was one of the first people to arrive on the enormous soundstage. Naturally, I gravitated toward the craft services table loaded with coffee, tea, and mountains of pastries. The first person I met was Gavin MacLeod, who was also perusing the donuts. We introduced ourselves. "Don't these look delicious," Gavin said, holding up a donut. He spoke my language. We were instant friends for life.

Jay Sandrich, who directed most of the seven seasons of *Mary Tyler Moore,* took us on a tour of the set, which reminded me of an airplane hangar. Mary's apartment was in the middle. WJM-TV, the television station, was on the far right; a swing set, which was often turned into Rhoda's apartment, a restaurant, or whichever set was needed for a particular show, was in the area on the left.

Mary was incredibly sweet as she introduced me around. She never drew attention to the fact that I was clearly the greenest person present. In fact, she went out of her way to explain that I was a stage actor. "Valerie's from the theater," she bragged about me as we moved through the soundstage. "She's a Broadway girl, and she's doing a play at the Mark Taper at the moment."

After the tour, we convened around a conference table and began to read through the script. The producers had assembled a unique and talented group of serious actors: Ed Asner was known for playing tough guys. Ted Knight had played Nazis. Gavin MacLeod had played heavies. And Cloris Leachman had been the mom on *Lassie*. During casting weeks, Dave Davis had glanced out of his second-story office window and noticed an actor with the script preparing to audition. Dave thought to himself, *Boy that guy looks like the character Lou Grant.* Turned out it was Ed Asner. Actually, this entire group of actors all had impressive résumés and extensive on-screen experience. I was the newbie. The essential common denominator was that we could all play comedy.

Allan, Jim, Jay, Mary, and her husband, Grant Tinker, who was the head of Mary's production company, set a lighthearted yet professional tone on our first day. I got the impression that we were going to have lots of fun, but we'd lay down some serious comedy, which meant working hard.

Everyone laughed frequently as we read through the pilot. I

thought the script was terrific. A show that focused on a woman's career, not her family or love life, was a new concept. *The Mary Tyler Moore Show* reflected the way more and more real women were living in the 1970s. It was refreshing and invigorating and addressed the changing attitude toward women in the workplace that had been rippling across the country.

The first read-through felt celebratory, like a little party. I was relieved that after they heard me read Rhoda, I wasn't fired— I took it as a sign that they meant to keep me around. When we'd finished the table read, we went into the set and began to rehearse with Jay. I was delighted to find that rehearsing the show wasn't much different from working on a short play. Under Jay's keen eye, we moved through the set, working with props, finding our best positions, playing the scenes, and discovering the jokes.

Some television shows, especially single-camera shows, are shot out of order; the last scene can be shot first, which makes working in that format similar to working in the movies. Since *The Mary Tyler Moore Show* was a multi-camera comedy shot before a live audience, going in sequence was customary on show night. Luckily for me, Jay preferred to rehearse the show so the scenes followed chronologically as well, which was in line with my theater training.

I quickly learned the rehearsal schedule. On Mondays we'd meet in the morning and do a full table read of the script so the writers could hear the whole show and make notes to improve it. After lunch, while the writers—who came to be known as "the guys"—were revising, the actors went down to the stage with Jay and started blocking. When we arrived on Tuesday, the writers would hand us blue pages on which they'd rewritten parts of the script. We'd immediately start reblocking the script with the blue pages. Toward the end of the day, the writers would come down from their offices to see how the rewrites were playing. The script was a work in progress at this stage, so we were still on book. I had to learn how to give as full a performance as possible while holding my pages so that the writers and director could hear how the script flowed.

If there were problems, the guys would hole up in their office overnight on Tuesday and hammer out changes that we would receive on bright yellow pages on Wednesday morning. Sometimes we'd get an entire yellow script, not my favorite development but one I learned to work with. Especially because I knew that every set of changes only made the material stronger.

The biggest challenge for me at first was learning how to hit my mark so I'd be in the right position for the camera. In the theater it's pretty obvious where to stand so that the audience can see you. But I'd rarely worked in front of a camera, let alone three cameras all trained on different angles. Hitting a mark was completely new to me. I had to figure out where to stand so I wouldn't block Mary or another actor and screw up the shot.

On Wednesday afternoons, the guys would come down to watch the official run-though, which initially made me nervous. I felt under-rehearsed and certain that I'd disappoint. When I told Dick about this fear, he said, "Valerie, you've got it wrong.

The writers aren't coming to judge you. They are there to make things better. They are Saint Bernards, coming with brandy to revive you. Help is on the way!" Jim and Allan didn't mind when I started referring to them as my Saint Bernards.

Thursdays, while Jay and the crew figured out the best angles for filming, the cast would drill our lines with Marge Mullen, our script supervisor. On Friday, before set call, the women got their hair and nails done—or, as Mary used to call it, "hairage and nail-age." We'd work through the show scene by scene and then do a final run-through. We'd then break for dinner before the audience arrived, and filming began at about seven P.M.

I loved the pilot script, but you never know how an audience will react. As we were shooting, I heard lots of laughter, so I assumed it went well. Little did I know that it wasn't the audience we were trying to please but the network brass. The other thing I didn't learn until much later was that during the initial filming of the pilot episode a lot had gone wrong. The air-conditioning had failed, the sound went out so the audience couldn't hear, and the network heads were less than thrilled. Jim and Allan knew the show could be much improved and so Grant Tinker arranged for a reshoot several days later. Grant Tinker wasn't fazed and ordered everyone back to the drawing board.

One of the problems the network had with the show was a character they described as "that awful woman yelling at Mary"— Rhoda! They hated her. Thankfully, Jim, Allan, and Jay were kind enough not to share this information with me, while they set about fixing the problem.

It was Marge Mullen who suggested a way to make my character more likable. Rhoda was very funny but with an edge that was essential. The writers needed to find a way to soften her without sacrificing the comedic big-city brashness.

The initial concept for the show was to have Cloris Leachman's character, Phyllis, be Mary's best friend and Rhoda be her foil. Phyllis was supposed to be an elegant, mannered lady looking out for Mary's best interests. But as Cloris began to inhabit the role, she imbued Phyllis with a studied phoniness that made her amusingly insincere. Marge proposed to the writers that they alter the script so that Phyllis's young daughter, Bess, be very fond of Rhoda. The fact that a sweet little girl liked Rhoda and her snooty mother did not would signal to the audience that Ms. Morgenstern was definitely okay. I was so lucky they had the talent, willingness, and belief in the character to write these changes rather than to abandon Rhoda and fire me. And kudos to Marge Mullen!

When we were called in to redo the show, I was unaware that anything had gone wrong with the pilot. For all I knew, reshooting a pilot was routine, so I didn't ask any questions. Luckily, the second go-round was a great success, and CBS ordered the series.

In those days, CBS hosted a big presentation for their upcoming fall lineup of shows. They invited press to the Crystal Ballroom of the Beverly Hills Hotel, where they announced every cast member of each show by name. One by one, we filed onto the stage and took our places on a row of bleachers.

I bought the most hideous dress for the occasion, not on purpose, just an ill-advised selection. It was an unflattering empire-waist number in a homely cabbage-rose print that was more suitable for a set of drapes. What was I thinking? Why did I do this to myself? Was I going for a look? But then you've seen the awards shows: Bad fashion decisions happen to the most glamorous women. Envy the guys in their tuxedos!

My heart was pumping in my chest when they introduced *The Mary Tyler Moore Show* and then called my name. I walked out onstage, praying not to trip, and took my spot on the bleachers. It felt like a high school graduation. I was struck by the enormity of what had happened to me. There I was at the lavish Beverly Hills Hotel, surrounded by real luminaries—Carol Burnett, Sonny and Cher, and Walter Cronkite. I could not believe that I was being presented on the same stage as Walter Cronkite!

From the first day on-set, my confidence began to grow. I worked on the character of Rhoda constantly; I may have driven the writers a little crazy. One day after rehearsal I asked Jim about all the sensational jokes they were writing. "Am I, Valerie the actress, saying these jokes, or is Rhoda the character making them up?"

Jim looked at me for a moment, probably thinking, *Is this a metaphysical quandary, or is this girl just insane?* Then he explained, "Well, you're both funny, so who cares?"

In addition to improving Rhoda's accent and mannerisms and honing her humor, I was determined to define her style. When we first began shooting, I was convinced that Rhoda should look schlubby. No one ever told me that was necessary, but I thought it would be interesting, next to the well-turned-out Mary and the fussy Phyllis, for Rhoda to have a different aesthetic. It's a fact that frumpy can be funny! To help me out, my pal Iva, who has the most exquisite taste, gave me a big bright orange mohair sweater that she was sure would add pounds to Rhoda. It did. When we saw the episode on TV with me wearing the sweater, Iva cried, "Burn it! It makes you look like a dirigible."

I started paying more attention to how my wardrobe could bring Rhoda to life. At first I wore whatever off-the-rack outfits Leslie Hall, our costumer, purchased. I also wore unflattering sweat suits, bulky sweaters, and bright colors and prints—anything to add more weight. Around the third show, I began to notice that Mimi Kirk, Mary's stand-in and personal assistant, always came to work dressed in gorgeous bohemian clothes. She was a very beautiful earth mother from Venice Beach, all batik, macramé, handcrafted jewelry, and the most fabulous head wraps. She wore long skirts she had made out of ornately embroidered old jeans. And since Rhoda, a window dresser, could be eccentric and creative, I thought she might dress a little more eclectically, a little more like Mimi Kirk.

With Jim and Allan's approval, I started copying Mimi's look. Before *The Mary Tyler Moore Show,* I had never in my life worn a head scarf. We started off with a silk scarf tied around my low ponytail, then moved to a handkerchief covering my crown, and finally graduated to one of Mimi's ornate multiple-scarf head wraps. Rhoda's gypsy-woman look became an intrinsic part of her quirky character, while providing a little side benefit—camouflage dressing. Flowing skirts, long vests, and cardigans can minimize a multitude of lumps and bumps. Maybe I'm old-fashioned, but when I see larger women in extremely clingy clothes, I just want to shout, "Tight is not your friend!" But then the feminist in me counters, "Go on, wear whatever the hell you please. Good for you for not caring."

Rhoda's love of eating and her weight problems were a gold mine of comic possibility—and true to life. One of the writers, Charlotte Brown, told me about an upcoming script in which Mary and I are exercising in tights and leotards. Seeing the look of sheer horror on my face, Charlotte patted my arm and said, "You still have time." We both laughed at the all too familiar refrain of having to lose weight to get in camera-ready shape. Luckily, I managed to convince "the guys" that it would be funnier if Mary was in tights and Rhoda was in a baggy sweatsuit. In another episode, as our girls nervously await their dates, Mary offers Rhoda some chips and she replies, "No thanks. I've got to lose ten pounds by eight o' clock."

Women really identified with Rhoda because her problems and fears were theirs. Despite the fact that she was the butt of most of her own jokes, so to speak, running down her looks and her potential, she never acted defeated. Her confident swagger masked her insecurity. Rhoda never gave up.

As the first season progressed, I often found myself getting incredibly nervous on show night. When filming approached, I'd become terrified that I wouldn't be good enough. I was worried that there hadn't been enough rehearsal, that there were too many changes to the script, that I didn't know my part. Mary gave me some calming advice. She told me not to think about the entire show but to concentrate on one scene at a time. On show night, standing just off the set, we'd run our lines for the upcoming scene. When we'd finished filming that scene, we'd dash back to our dressing rooms and change our costumes, reconvene, and run lines for the next scene, thinking of only one scene at a time. It was a very simple but valuable tip.

From the start Mary was professional, supportive, and a delight to work with. She was always on time and always knew her lines. She was a remarkable leader but never acted like "the star." As Mary Richards, Mary was always "straighting" for the rest of us, who played more flamboyant characters. She would suggest to the writers, "Why don't you give that joke to Val? It's more of a Rhoda line." On breaks between scenes, Mary often did needlepoint. A real expert, she turned out beautiful pieces for her home: pillows and chair seats. When she sewed, she wore tiny reading glasses that made her look like a glamorous young granny. The first year of the show, she needlepointed each of the cast members a lovely rectangular pillow with our initials and the signature Mary Richards beret dangling off one of the letters. She must have used up all of her weekends sewing these surprise gifts. Another treasured gift from Mary was a long gold latchkey with the inscription 119 Wetherly, our fictitious address on the show. Ever the generous girl.

While Mary imbued her on-screen alter ego with much of her

own personality, Mary Richards was truly a created character. The real-life Mary was droller, wittier, and much more sophisticated. Mary Tyler Moore's humor was dry. Mary Richards's was sweet and slightly square.

Although Mary smoked, she refused ever to smoke on the show. She was adamant that she not pass along her bad habit to anyone in the audience. "I'm hooked," she'd say. "I don't want to help hook anyone else." She was ahead of her time with a keen awareness and sense of responsibility.

Like Mary, Ed Asner brought much of his own personality and prodigious acting skills to his portrayal of the lovably gruff Lou Grant. In the ill-fated first version of the pilot, Lou was tough and abrasive, which didn't play well. For the reshoot, the writers softened him and smoothed his edges. They wanted him to be hard on Mary Richards but not to eat her alive. Ed played this perfectly. Offscreen, he's strongly committed to a world that works for everyone. It was Ed who invited me to my very first Screen Actors Guild meeting. And no one has done more charity benefits. His rough and rugged exterior masks such extraordinary sweetness that when he lets his softer side show, he is impossible not to love. When he smiles, his entire face shines from within, where the really tender Ed Asner resides.

Ed loved seashells. He often talked about his collection and even offered to bring it in one day to show the cast and crew. I always assumed that if he ever got around to it, he would haul in great big boxes of conch and abalone shells. One morning when I walked onto the set, I saw Mary giggling to herself in the corner.

She beckoned me over. "You have to come look at Ed and his shells," she said. "It's the sweetest thing I've ever seen."

Ed had just returned from a run. He was in his gym clothes and still sweating as he bent over a velvet cloth—the kind jewelers use to display diamonds. He was holding a set of tweezers in his meaty hand, using them to pick up the smallest, most delicate shells imaginable. The sight of this stocky man in a sweatsuit picking up these tiny, fragile shells was both lovely and amusing. Just like Ferdinand the Bull.

As impossible as it was not to love Ed, it was just as difficult not to adore Gavin McLeod, who was charming, hilarious, and my gossip buddy. He was like that kid in homeroom who made you laugh just by looking at you. And Ted, dear Ted Knight, who, when he donned his black-framed glasses, reminded us all of Barry Goldwater. There were times during rehearsal when Ted was so damn funny that he made everyone on the set laugh until we cried and couldn't continue working. The writers created a great comedy role in Ted Baxter, but it was Ted Knight who brought this preposterous newsman to life with his willingness to play an absolute fool. Ted used two local anchormen as inspiration for his character—white-haired Jerry Dunphy for his saner moments and George Putnam for his over-the-top mannerisms.

Ted loved a deli called Art's that was on Ventura Boulevard near the studio. It wasn't long before he had Ed and Gavin addicted to their enormous pastrami sandwiches. To this day, I remember the sight of the marvelous trio sauntering down the street on their way to lunch, laughing and joking all the way.

Every once in a great while, I joined the guys at Art's, but most often I ate lunch with Cloris Leachman. She was a vegetarian and we shared many a terrific salad. I loved Cloris immediately and we became "girlfriends," as she has always referred to us. She was fun, intellectually curious, and thoroughly committed to the art of acting. She also had her hands full with five young children, all adorable—Adam, Brian, George, Morgan, and Dinah—which sometimes caused her to rush into rehearsal at the last minute.

She was unorthodox and outspoken, unable to stop herself from sharing, unsolicited, her tastes and opinions. If she saw someone smoking, Cloris would cajole the cigarette out of his or her hand by the most colorful means. "You don't need that cigarette. I'll give you a delightful shoulder massage or a long, loving hug instead." And she did. The smoker really didn't need the cigarette after that. Cloris was a whirlwind, but a delightful and charming one, overflowing with talent and enthusiasm. She was so dynamic that at times she appeared to be larger than the space she occupied.

I felt incredibly lucky to be a part of such a wonderful television community. At Mimi's cheerful instigation, Sandro, one of the background performers on *Mary Tyler Moore,* helped Dick and me throw a polenta party for the cast and creative staff of the show in our tiny kitchen. We made enough polenta for all of Sicily! Just like in Italy, we served the polenta right on the table without dishes. Sandro brought his mother's polenta pot and special stirring stick, and all of us took a turn at the stove.

Dick covered the table with a large wooden board that served as our shared plate. When it was cooked, Sandro and Mimi spread the polenta onto this plank and covered it with tomato sauce, meatballs, and sausage. It looked like an enormous pizza and it was unlike anything any of us (except Sandro, of course) had ever experienced. There was a lovely communal feeling to this unusual dinner party. And it was delicious.

The social and collegial atmosphere continued on- and off-set. We were all professional, working adults with families at home and children were often around the soundstage having fun, albeit quietly. Mimi's three great kids, Lisa, Jonas, and Mia, helped their mother set out fresh fruit and vegetable platters to transform our junk food-laden craft service table. Incidentally, Mimi first initiated that practice that's now commonplace on television and film production sets.

After Dick and I moved to a larger house, Leah's children—Victor, Tony, and Tanya—began spending lots of time with us in summer and were regular visitors at Auntie Val's workplace. Mary's teenage son, Richie, and I got on very well. I once caught him and Mary's much younger sister, Elizabeth, smoking in my dressing room. I told them I wouldn't rat them out to Mary if they never did it again. After all, Rhoda wouldn't tell on Bess to Phyllis.

The Mary Tyler Moore Show was not a "family show" in the traditional sense; however, the writers did a fantastic job of creating material that was wholesome enough for family viewing but was intelligent comedy. While they never did smarmy stuff, they managed to give the characters, especially Rhoda and Phyllis, a bit of bite. In an episode where Rhoda tells Mary that she's going to stay in a motel, Phyllis quips, "Well, Rhoda, it won't be the first time." This amazing team of writers kept it clean enough for ten-year-olds but allowed adults in on the joke.

They succeeded in creating and maintaining vivid male and female characters who weren't caricatures—Mary Richards and her equally strong cohorts, Rhoda and Phyllis, were wonderful roles to play. Jim and Allan were serious about striking the proper balance between silliness and strength, including when it came to writing the female leads. The characters were sophisticated. They spoke like actual adults and had real adult problems to which they responded humorously.

Jay Sandrich, the show's exceptional director, was politically liberal and brought a terrific sensibility to the set. On breaks, we all sat around and had intriguing conversations about the headlines that day. Jay was extremely well informed and passionate about having a more just society. I had read a lot of Gloria Steinem, Betty Friedan, Andrea Dworkin, and Robin Morgan, and I was a regular customer at the Sisterhood bookstore in Westwood. During my work with *Story Theatre,* Paul Sills urged the female cast members "to get wise to this new wave of feminism." I don't remember ever consciously imposing any of these ideas on the writers, but Jay credits me with bringing a feminist awareness to *The Mary Tyler Moore Show.*

Jim used to say, "I know there's a world of comedy in my wife's purse, but I just can't access it. Allan and I don't do that pantyhose-and-nail-polish stuff well." For an expanded point of view, "the guys" went out of their way to hire female writers—Treva Silverman, Charlotte Brown, Pat Nardo, Gloria Banta, Marilyn Suzanne Miller, Linda Bloodworth-Thomason, and many more. Until *The Mary Tyler Moore Show* came along, comedy writing had been a male-dominated profession. Thanks to Jim and Allan, more women were getting their say in what ended up on television.

While Jim and Allan were adamant that none of their material be sexist, they steadfastly avoided being preachy. In the early days, Treva, who was often the sole woman in the writers' room, had to hold the line on occasion. In one episode, the buffoonish Ted Baxter reveals that he keeps a little black book of women organized according to hair color: Br, Blo, Bla, Rcd. The original script called for Mary simply to stand by while Ted ran his mouth. But Treva stepped in and insisted that Mary give a rejoinder. She explained that Mary could not stand there letting Ted get away with that kind of comment. It was 1971. Our heroine would speak up! Jim and Allan and the boys agreed.

The first season was not a huge ratings success. It finished the year in thirty-third place out of fifty network television shows. But the young TV columnist for *The Hollywood Reporter* trade paper, Sue Cameron, a cute little brunette, pulled me aside after filming. She whispered, "Don't sweat the ratings. This show is gold and will only get shinier." Sue was right. The show was a critical success and snagged a host of Emmy nominations. Naturally, Mary was nominated for Best Actress in her role as Mary Richards. Ed Asner got a Best Supporting Actor nod for Lou Grant. Jim and

Allan were recognized for writing, and Jay Sandrich for directing. And I—Rhoda—was absolutely astounded to learn that my name had been thrown into the ring for Best Supporting Actress!

Remembering all too well the disastrous dress with the cabbage roses, I wasn't taking any chances with the Emmys. I enlisted the help of my friend Gene Varrone to find me the perfect gown. Gene had stunning taste. We found a lovely black silk halter dress at a chic shop in the West Village called Chiaroscuro, where everything was black or white. He thought it would look great with a pair of antique gold earrings that Iva had given me. I told Gene that I was too heavy for such a clingy style. "It's black. The skirt is A-line. Wear it!" he said.

And I did. Dick and I drove our own car to the ceremony. It was terribly exciting being there, and as cliché as it is, I have to say, "It was an honor just to be nominated." When they called my name as the winner in the Best Supporting Actress category, my head began to buzz. I could not believe what was happening. Surely there had been a mistake. My thoughts were to make it to the stage without jamming my high heel through the hem of the gown and to deliver my speech without embarrassing myself or forgetting to thank someone.

Jack Benny and Lucille Ball presented me the award. I can't think of two people more incredible to find myself onstage with at that moment. I was completely stunned. I was so excited that I unthinkingly blurted out: "Lucy, remember me?"

Her face froze in a wide smile. She had no idea that we'd ever met. Why would she? I scrambled to clarify. "From *Wildcat*. On

Broadway." How could I have expected her to remember a chorus dancer from a Broadway show ten years earlier?

"Of course, *Wildcat*," she said. And though she was still at a loss, she gracefully pretended to remember me, playing along for the audience's sake as well as mine.

It was a spectacular night for our little show. Ed, Jay, Jim, and Allan all won in their categories. The big disappointment of the evening was that Mary did not win for Best Actress. She was the linchpin of our show, the force that kept us all together. I had been so sure she would win. When I told Mary how disappointed I was for her, she smiled and said, "It's just show business."

The show's writer-producers clearly felt as I did. The day after the Emmy Awards, they took out a full-page ad in *Variety* that read: "Without Mary Tyler Moore, it would just be *The Show*."

chapter
FIVE

My life changed incrementally during the first season of the show. Slowly, people began to recognize me on the street. This delighted my mother whenever I visited her in San Francisco. She introduced me around her neighborhood of Polk Street as "the famous Rhoda from TV." She didn't care if she was talking to someone straight off the boat from China who had never seen the show. She would point to me and proudly say, "She's Rhoda!" It made me happy to see her showing off her successful daughter. I wasn't a ballerina, but this was close enough.

It was a great feeling not to worry about where my next paycheck was coming from. Although Dick and I now had money, we didn't live extravagantly; we never spent lavishly. I was a successful television actress, but I didn't feel like "star." A star is Joan Crawford, Bette Davis, Lana Turner—someone with glamour and beauty who must live glamorously and beautifully. I was me with a little more capital and freedom.

I clearly remember the first time I bought a piece of clothing without checking the price tag. I was shopping in a sharp little boutique on La Cienega called Bazaar CM and came across some great clothes cut in a 1940s style. I kept picking tops to go with trousers, then a jacket, then another jacket, and one more. When all was said and done, I carted home a bag stuffed with clothes. I had spent over five hundred dollars—the most money I had ever spent at any one time on clothing. Although it felt overly extravagant, it was satisfying to know that I could afford to spend money that I had earned myself.

The Mary Tyler Moore Show was not my only source of income. I was still playing in *Story Theatre* at the Mark Taper Forum, and the producers, directors, and cast members of *Mary Tyler Moore* all came to performances and seemed to love the production. In fact, Dick and many actors in the company, such as Paul Sand, Hamilton Camp, Dick Libertini, Mary Frann, and Peter Bonerz, were all cast in Mary Tyler Moore productions.

When *Story Theatre* went to New York in 1970, the TV show was on hiatus, so I was able to open on Broadway and play there for a number of weeks before filming resumed. It was a dream come true. *Story Theatre* was a huge hit. I felt incredibly fortunate to be in both a hit TV show and a successful Broadway play at the same time. And I felt both productions were so extraordinarily good, I couldn't believe my luck.

When I returned to Los Angeles, pal Linda Lavin stepped into my role in *Story Theatre* until the television season wrapped, and then I immediately went back into the show on Broadway. An actor's life is often either feast or famine, and this was a time of feast. I will be eternally grateful that my employers were willing to work around my schedule so that I could perform in both productions.

As a cast member of *Mary Tyler Moore*, I still thought of myself as part of a small theater troupe. We had a little company of players, and each week we learned a different play, just like in summer stock. Even when I wasn't in a scene, I would watch rehearsal. Whenever the scene involved a bit part—a waitress, delivery boy, stock clerk—I frequently stood in for the actor in rehearsals and run-throughs (performers with smaller roles weren't usually called in until Thursday). I took on all sorts of roles, which was helpful to Jay, because he had a body to work with, and the actors had someone to play off of. It was great fun putting on accents and affecting funny voices. This came to be known on-set as "Valerie's Repertory Theater."

One time after I'd stepped in for a construction worker, I ran across our first assistant director, John Chulay, standing with his back pressed up against the side of the set like a spy from an old movie. He shook his head disparagingly and whispered, "Weak. Very weak." I laughed so hard that I disrupted the rehearsal in progress. Critics—they're everywhere.

The atmosphere on our set was a happy one. Mary's name was a continual source of laughs. Often referred to as Mary Tailor Moore, she said she should go into alterations. While Mary worked in England, the Brits called her by one hyphenated name, Miss Tyler-Moore. But it was Gavin's seven-year-old daughter, Julie, who dubbed Mary "Tiny Miley Moore." We called her Tiny for a long time, which was quite fitting given that svelte figure. To keep it in shape, and for health reasons, Mary was diligent about exercising. She arranged for her ballet teacher to come to the stage to give her lessons during lunch break. Such discipline! On Mondays and Wednesdays, a couple of crew guys would set up a ballet barre and a large freestanding mirror. Knowing my dance background, Mary invited me to join her. No matter how hard I pressed the issue, she never let me contribute a penny toward the cost. "I'm doing it anyway, Val," Mary said. "And I'd love the company."

I think it was Ted who asked, "Hey, Mary, doesn't Grant mind that you're in dance clothes with the crew guys around?"

"Nah. They're all eunuchs." That was the Mary Tyler Moore humor. We laughed so hard, we couldn't start class.

Mary always looked slender and darling in her leotard and pink tights. Obviously, I'd put on weight since my days as a dancer on Broadway. To distract from that, I always dressed head to toe in black. One afternoon when Mary and I were finishing class, Cloris exclaimed, "My God, Valerie, your ass is massive." Not the height of tact but true. Cloris didn't intend to be mean; as a devoted girlfriend, she simply wanted to inspire me to lose weight.

For a while, I had been putting off going on a serious diet because a large part of Rhoda's humor was her struggle with weight. I felt I had to ask permission from Jim and Allan before I started to reduce. Naturally, the guys had no objection. "We won't do fat jokes," they said. "We'll do diet jokes."

It was Mary who gave me the push I needed to get my act together. "Go ahead, lose the weight," she said. "You don't want to be my sidekick all your life, do you?"

"Yes! Yes, I do," I replied. "And so does everyone else in the world." But her support was all I needed to begin watching what I ate. With the green light from everyone, I had no excuse to stay chubby.

Up until that point, there wasn't a fad diet I hadn't tried. Back in New York, perennial dieters Arlene and I went on the Stillman diet, with two other roommates, Michelle Evans and Nancy Cheevers. Michelle went on to become a very successful cookbook author (*Fearless Cooking for Men*, etc.) and Nancy an extraordinary cook, introduced me to that Bible of the 1960s, *The Joy of Cooking*—which was way before Michelle started writing her books! Our apartment was very food focused. The Stillman method was a sort of demented precursor to the low-carb craze. I remember seeing Dr. Stillman, a cranky old guy with wire-rimmed glasses, being interviewed by Dick Cavett and extolling the virtues of eating lamb and beef slathered in butter. He preached that you could consume as much red meat and fat as you liked so long as carbs never touched your lips.

Cavett asked, "What about heart disease?"

"Go to a cardiologist," Dr. Stillman replied. "With me, the weight comes off."

As tasty as his meal plan was, it didn't help me drop a pound. Could have been the mashed potatoes I ate with the steak.

After the Stillman diet, I tried the grapefruit diet—eating half a grapefruit before every meal with the vain hope that the acid in the citrus would burn whatever fat I consumed. There was the watermelon juice fast, the cabbage soup three-times-a-day cleanse, and the hard-boiled egg and prune diet. Any one of these programs might have worked had I possessed the fortitude to stick with them long enough. But I always seem to fall off the wagon. I was never a night-eater, but I do overeat—sneak-eat, car-eat, "perpetu-eat."

Luckily for me, when I decided to get serious about dieting, Gavin MacLeod was beginning the Weight Watchers program. We decided to partner up and keep each other honest. And we knew we would laugh. It was during this time that I discovered that when I was ballet dancing at Radio City Music Hall, he was working there as an usher. Not only that, he married a Rockette!

Weight Watchers was all about selection and portion control—fuel the fire but in moderation. I had a little scale and weighed out my "legal lunches" at home before coming in to work. If I was eating out, I brought my scale to the restaurant. I weighed whatever I ordered, cut off the permitted amount, and fought the urge to eat the rest.

Gavin and I motivated each other. We ate salad with fat-free dressing, celery, carrots, and the permissible portion of chicken. Weighing my food was almost a fetishistic ritual, and it forced me to be conscious about amounts of food eaten and to be wary of overeating. As Rhoda's great line, inspired by my buddy Mary-Frann, expressed so perfectly, "Why am I bothering to eat this piece of chocolate? I should just apply it directly to my hips." On Weight Watchers, eating became a healthy, constructive endeavor instead of a destructive compulsion.

Gav and I were doing very well on the program and were already losing weight. One day at lunch, while I was setting out my little tray of preweighed food, he walked over with a diet soda. When he popped it open, the can began to spout like Old Faithful. Gavin and I stared at the can as it bubbled and fizzed.

I took a closer look, and my jaw dropped. "Gavin," I said, "that's not diet. That's regular soda."

"It's a miracle," Gavin shouted. "A miracle!"

"It is. It's a sign from God: 'You two have been so good. Don't drink this.' We're saved!" We laughed until tears ran down our cheeks. Gavin and I had both attended Catholic school and were well versed in miracles and signs from heaven. Listen, whatever it takes to keep you on the program!

No matter how hard I fought it, the food demon often rose up and grabbed me. During the second season of *Mary Tyler Moore,* Dick and I attended an Oscar party at a friend's house. There was an enormous spread—a tempting buffet of lasagna, pesto pasta salad, garlic bread, and all those deliciously fattening things that Weight Watchers prohibited.

My diet was working for me. I had lost a considerable amount of weight, and I was determined to stick to the program. When everyone hit the buffet, I whipped out my little container of poached chicken and dressing-free salad and ate virtuously.

I was proud to have conquered my demon. After dinner, on my way to the bathroom, I passed through the kitchen and caught sight of a tray of gorgeous brownies all stacked in a tempting pyramid. The food demon began to roar. I ignored it.

When I emerged from the bathroom, I passed those brownies again, but this time I couldn't resist. I shoved a brownie in my mouth. It wasn't as tasty as I'd hoped. This didn't deter me from grabbing another. Before I knew it, I'd eaten three brownies, telling myself, *They were small.* I quickly rearranged the display so it wouldn't appear that any were missing.

A little while later, our hostess brought out the brownies. Before passing them around, she said, "I just want to warn you, there's a little something special in these brownies. If you don't like marijuana, you might want to skip them." I don't even drink, but I had unknowingly eaten three pot brownies! For two days I felt like I was in a sleepwalking daze. That's what I get for sneaking sweets!

Three brownies notwithstanding, I lost a lot of weight on Weight Watchers. However, like many former chubettes, I never felt like a slender person and carried my old self-image in my head. Our writers, especially the gifted Treva Silverman, used this disconnect in people when writing Rhoda. When she loses weight and wins a beauty contest, Rhoda has trouble dealing with it.

Besides being two of the best comedy writers to come down the pike, Jim and Allan, along with the writing team they assembled, created scripts that told the truth about what it means to be human. They always prioritized humor above anything else. Season after season, they brilliantly deepened the relationships between characters on *The Mary Tyler Moore Show;* they never allowed any character to become static but allowed for growth and change.

From time to time the writers introduced new characters, such as Gordy the weatherman, played by the wonderfully deft John Amos. Dear, unique Georgia Engel came in as Georgette, Ted Baxter's girlfriend. Then the phenomenal Betty White joined us. She was warm, charming, and a complete professional. From the day she joined the cast, it was as if she'd been there all along. Betty was utterly marvelous in her portrayal of Sue Ann Nivens, "the Happy Homemaker," whose fussy pinafores camouflaged a man-crazed predator. Betty does have a naughty streak and to this day plays the racy, elderly lady part brilliantly. I can assure you, it's all an act. Betty is as sweet as can be. She just knows what's funny.

The writers did not shy away from hot-button issues of the day—divorce and homosexuality, to name two. But aside from one episode, they never made an issue the central focus of the story line. The exception to that rule was an episode on discrimination in which Mary was invited to play tennis at a country club where Jewish Rhoda wasn't welcome. Mary Frann, my costar in *Story Theatre,* played Mary's beautiful but bigoted friend. After the filming wrapped, Allan said, "This isn't us. This is good for *Maude;* this is good for *All in the Family*. We'll touch on issues only as they occur in the lives of our characters, not as the focus of the plot." The core idea of *The Mary Tyler Moore Show* was to portray people bumping up against people emotionally and intellectually—people coping with others, confronting others, making space for others in a realistic manner. The writers didn't want to make statements. They wanted to reflect life.

Jim and Allan and their entire team maintained the highest level of smart comedy—characters and plot—without resorting to slapstick, vulgarity, or cliché. Rhoda was a perfect example of this fine balance. She was Jewish but the writers refused to have her speak Yiddish or satirize her ethnicity for cheap laughs.

Though Jim and Allan were firmly in charge, they also welcomed our input on how we would deliver certain lines. We were able to offer our emphasis and intention, and if it was funny, the guys welcomed it. After all, we were the ones who had gotten to know each of our characters intimately. This was particularly interesting in the episode when Phyllis tries to set up her brother, Ben, with Mary, only to discover that he's more interested in hanging out with Rhoda. Naturally, this horrifies Phyllis. At the end of the episode, Phyllis tells Rhoda in her own spectacularly condescending way that she's okay with her brother marrying Rhoda, to which Rhoda replies, "Phyllis, I'm not going to marry Ben."

"Why not?" Phyllis says defensively. "My brother is successful. He's handsome. He's intelligent."

"He's gay," Rhoda says.

Before filming, Jim, Allan, and I had a discussion with Jay about how Rhoda should deliver the line. Should she break the news to Phyllis gently? Should she whisper it, to be discreet? I felt Rhoda would be matter-of-fact and not tiptoe around the issue. We all agreed that Rhoda didn't think Ben's being gay was a bad thing. It just made marriage impossible: As in, he's a priest. He's married. He's moving to Tibet.

The audience didn't see it coming. They roared. The laughter went on so long that Cloris and I had to keep on acting silently until she could deliver her rejoinder: "Oh, Rhoda, I'm so relieved." Anything was better to Phyllis than her brother marrying "dumb awful" Rhoda.

While the producers avoided material that was overtly political, there was one instance when politics intruded upon the show. During the third season, a small group of us went to Minneapolis to film some exterior shots. In particular, the producers wanted to show Mary and Rhoda emerging from their iconic Victorian house.

The woman who lived in the house wasn't a fan of the show. In fact, she disliked it intensely, because for the past year people had been constantly ringing her bell and asking if Mary was home. She knew that the producers wanted to film another sequence at her house, and she was ready.

When we showed up, there were enormous sheets hanging over the entire front of her house that read "Impeach Nixon." It must have taken her hours to paint the banners and then hang them. I admired her spirit and effort, not to mention her message. Nevertheless, there was no way we could film the house. We quickly regrouped and shot elsewhere in downtown Minneapolis.

After the first season, *The Mary Tyler Moore Show* really caught on. From time to time we hit the number one spot in the broadcast ratings, and if we weren't number one, we were solidly in the top ten. Emmy nominations for all the actors, writers, and directors kept rolling in. While I was aware of the show's success and Rhoda's popularity, it was still a surprise to win two more Best Supporting Actress awards.

The second time I won an Emmy, Cloris was also nominated for Best Supporting Actress in a comedy. When the presenter announced that there was a tie in our category, I prayed it was between Cloris and me. In the brief second before they announced the winners' names, I imagined the two of us running up to the stage together. Then they called my name and that of . . . Sally Struthers! The camera caught me mouthing her name in surprise. Nothing against Sally, but I was hoping to share the moment with Cloris, my *Mary Tyler Moore* partner in crime. My gifted friend went on to win nine Emmys, more than any other performer, and has earned twenty-three nominations.

My success on *Mary Tyler Moore* led to a lot of other opportunities. Because of my schedule on the show, it was possible to do outside work only on hiatus. Television movies were being produced hand over fist, and I appeared in many of them. I was also cast as Alan Arkin's wife in my first big theatrical film, *Freebie and the Bean*. We shot in that jewel of a city, San Francisco, and I played Alan's Mexican-American wife. The movie posters read: "Guess who's playing Consuelo?!"

Working during hiatus, especially in movies, gave Dick and me more financial freedom than we'd ever expected. Dick was continually doing guest spots and film roles, including Kurt Vonnegut's *Slaughterhouse-Five,* which filmed on location in Czechoslovakia. He took Wendy with him because I was busy working. What an experience for a young American kid to have the opportunity to travel behind the Iron Curtain. Since we were both working consistently, we bought a very pretty house in Westwood on Lindbrook Drive. This house will always have a special place in my heart for being the first house I ever owned.

Dick, expert carpenter that he was, began to build us a loft in our living room. A few days into his project, he landed another film role and had to find a replacement to finish the job. He hired a young carpenter who was a neighbor of Viola Spolin's in the Hollywood Hills. This young guy had a wife and two little kids and needed the money. When he showed up, I was struck by how extremely handsome he was, as well as soft-spoken and serious. While he worked on our loft, I learned that he was an actor, doing carpentry to support his family while he waited for a break. Well, he got one . . . falling from the loft, he broke his arm.

"Look," I told him, "sometimes an accident is a message. You broke your hammering arm. Maybe it's time to stop carpentry and focus on your acting career, Harrison." Yes, his last name was Ford. I'm sure he would have become a star even without my advice. But I like to think that the fall from our loft gave him a push in the right direction!

Gene Varrone, one of the most sought-after tenors in New York and a veteran of more than twenty Broadway shows, had a second career as an interior decorator. In fact, he has decorated every home I've lived in since we met on *Take Me Along* in 1959. He has done apartments for Chita Rivera, Joe Allen, Glenn Close, and many others. Dick and I flew him out and put him up in a hotel so he could decorate our Westwood house. He had exquisite taste, a nose for bargains, and energy to burn. Also, he was like a beloved member of the family.

I loved living in Westwood, which was still a sleepy enclave. Iva and her husband, Ron Rifkin, often joined Dick and me for movies at the lovely old cinemas in the center of town—the Fox and the Bruin. Afterward, we'd get ice cream at Baskin-Robbins. On the weekends, we'd take our sailboat out in Marina del Rey.

The seeming extravagance of buying a house and owning a sailboat aside, Dick and I lived a quiet life. I was aware of the so-called wild Hollywood world of cocaine and other drugs, but that entire scene was utterly foreign to me. Like the rest of the cast of *The Mary Tyler Moore Show*, I lived a normal family life. My costars and I treated our jobs as work—we just happened to work on the artistic side of television. Our jobs weren't some inconvenience that prevented us from dancing the night away in clubs. Being on such a prestigious series was what all of us had worked toward for a long time. And we'd made it. We had phenomenal times together, but not in the mythological Hollywood way you read about in gossip magazines. We appreciated that the winds of good fortune were blowing our way and hoped they'd last.

chapter
SIX

At some point during the first season of *The Mary Tyler Moore Show*, Fred Silverman, the head of CBS, told me, "Valerie, we're going to have to spin you off." After the momentary *I'm fired?* pang of terror, I realized he was saying they actually wanted to give me my own show!

As the second and third seasons progressed, talk about spinning Rhoda off grew increasingly serious. The producers were eager for Rhoda to step into her own spotlight. As season four got under way, I started meeting with Jim and Allan about the new show more regularly. I wasn't entirely sure about the idea, but eventually, the guys and Mary prevailed on me. "You'd have to be nuts not to take CBS up on the offer of your own show," Mary said. Like Mary Richards, she was often the voice of reason. Another sobering voice of reason came from the astute Nancy Walker: "Stop fretting, Val. It's a good job, take it." Yes, I would have had to be nuts to pass up the opportunity.

It was a testament to how much the audience loved and identified with Rhoda that the producers and the network were offering her center stage. She had come a long way from her initial role as Mary's energetic, wisecracking sidekick. She had developed into a fully realized person whom the world seemed to be rooting for. Rhoda, with her insecurities, her eccentricities, and her profound relatability, had become part of the cultural consciousness and left people wanting more. The audience admired her tenacity enough that the network was confident she could carry a show. But could I?

Because *Rhoda* was being developed by the same extraordinary team of writers, I felt incredibly safe. I also felt, as always, a responsibility to live up to their first-rate writing. I didn't want to ruin Rhoda, and I didn't want to ruin a show produced by Mary's company. "What if I bomb?" I asked Mary.

"Then you'll move back to Minneapolis," she said. "You're graduating. You're going off to college. But you can always come home." Talk about working with a net!

Rhoda was moving on—exactly where was unclear. There was some talk around the studio that New York-based comedies were done to death. The network wanted to send Rhoda somewhere rural, like Wisconsin. That didn't sit well with Jim and Allan. Rhoda had already moved from the Bronx to Minneapolis. The writers had mined the fish-out-of-water theme and wanted something new. Rhoda was a New Yorker, they reasoned. She was going home.

Once it was determined that *Rhoda* was going into production, I sat down with Jim and Allan to talk about the direction they were going to take the show. Rhoda was going back to New York, and her family would become a big part of her life. Since her own series had been cancelled, the fantastic Nancy Walker, who played my mother, Ida Morgenstern, on *The Mary Tyler Moore Show,* agreed to come on board, which delighted me to no end. The comedic possibilities of Rhoda and Ida were endless.

The consensus was that Rhoda needed to grow and gain more confidence. Diet jokes, fat jokes, and bad relationship jokes are very funny but not enough to sustain a central character. Everyone agreed that Rhoda needed to find some success and move up in the world.

The guys decided that Rhoda was going to get a job in publishing (from which she was soon fired because they didn't want to do a "workplace comedy" that too closely mirrored *Mary Tyler Moore*). More important, Rhoda was going to get lucky in love. After all the terrible dates she'd endured over the past four years, it was time. Jim, Allan, and Ethel Winant needed to find her a husband.

We started casting while I was still working on *Mary Tyler Moore*. Liberty Williams had played Rhoda's pretty younger sister, Debbie, who gets married on an early episode of *The Mary Tyler Moore Show,* so I assumed that she would reprise the role on *Rhoda*. But Jim and Allan had other ideas. David Davis, a producer on *Mary* who was coming over to *Rhoda,* remembered a young actress named Julie Kavner who had auditioned for the role of Debbie but had lost out to Liberty.

When it came time to cast Brenda, Julie was exactly the

person the producers were looking for—a wonderful comedic actress who seemed like Rhoda but ten years younger. When she came in to read, we were overwhelmed by how singularly funny she was. Her distinctive voice sealed the deal. The guys felt she sounded somewhat like Nancy Walker, our Ida Morgenstern. Even though I was eager to work with Julie, I worried about how they would handle the existence of Rhoda's original sister, Debbie. But this was television. Relatives can disappear bloodlessly.

In a prior episode Ida reprimands Rhoda, "Name anyone who has such problems with their mother as you do, Rhoda!"

"Arnold and Debbie."

"Leave your brother and sister out of this!"

See? Arnold disappears into the cosmos without ever having face time on the show.

Charlotte Brown, one of the terrific writers on *Mary Tyler Moore*, was moving over to *Rhoda* and so was the great actor Harold Gould, who had played Martin Morgenstern, Rhoda's pop. Tall, good-natured Martin and diminutive, strong-willed Ida were a delightfully humorous couple as Rhoda's parents. Luckily I flew to New York and saw Harold in John Guare's *The House of Blue Leaves*. He was sensational and also one of the nicest people I have ever worked with.

The remaining roles to cast were the disembodied voice of Carlton the doorman and, of course, Joe Gerard, Rhoda's new husband. The producers had dozens of actors read for the part of Carlton but hadn't settled on anyone. During our auditions for the part of Joe, Jim and Allan asked Lorenzo Music to read Carlton's lines. Lorenzo had started as Dave Davis's writing partner on *Mary Tyler Moore* and was now coming on board on *Rhoda* as a producer. A former musician, performer, and comic, he also warmed the audience up on show night. He would appear onstage or up in the bleachers and brilliantly improvise amusing patter about what was going on behind the scenes. He was excellent at keeping the audience engaged during the breaks so that they would continue to respond and laugh with the same energy in spite of the stop-and-start rhythm of filming.

No one ever intended to cast Lorenzo as Carlton. But the more the guys heard Lorezno read the doorman's lines, the clearer it became that no one who auditioned was better or funnier. Lorenzo brought such humor into Carlton's voice that the writer-producers decided to go with him over anyone who'd read for the part.

That left Joe Gerard. We auditioned a lot of actors, and I got to kiss a lot of appealing guys in the process. I, of course, thought that my husband, Dick Schaal, would be perfect for the part. While Jim and Allan agreed with me, they had made a pact as writing partners never to work with a husband and wife together, especially in the lead roles. "Valerie," Allan said, "we love Dick. He's wonderful, and he'll be on a lot of shows in guest roles. But it's a rule we just don't break."

One actor they thought would be perfect for Joe was Joe Bologna. But Joe Bologna wanted to bring his wife, Renée Taylor, on board with him to play Rhoda's boss at the publishing house. As anxious as the producers were to cast Joe, they were unwilling to cast Renée in any permanent role and break their rule on married couples. So Joe Bologna turned down the part.

Both Carmine Caridi and Michael DeLano auditioned. While neither of them got the part of Joe, both appeared on Rhoda in different roles in later seasons. William Devane, a fantastic kisser, was offered the role, but he turned it down.

As the production date approached, it came down to two actors for the part of Joe: Alex Rocco, who had played Moe Green in *The Godfather,* and David Groh. Both had the right look for a tough New Yorker who ran a construction company. Both actors auditioned really well. What it came down to was how Joe and Rhoda looked as a couple. And David fit the bill.

David was a really nice guy and very professional—a serious Actors Studio type of performer, not a comedian. That didn't worry the writers, because he gave a great audition and was terrific-looking. But when it came to the marriage, the writers had a tough decision to make. Would Rhoda come on the air in her own show already married to Joe? Or would she meet him in the first episode and give the audience a chance to watch the relationship evolve?

It was decided that interest would build in the show if the audience came along for the ride—if they were there with Rhoda as she met the guy of her dreams. We wanted people to root for Rhoda and Joe, cheer them on as they met, got engaged, and got married.

During hiatus on *Mary Tyler Moore,* Jim, Dave, Julie Kavner, and I and a film crew traveled to New York to film exterior footage for *Rhoda*. Julie had never been to New York, which, given her East Coast sound, was hard to believe. We shot Rhoda walking into her publishing job, getting out of a cab, going into her apartment building. We filmed the sisters in Central Park and the New York Public Library on Forty-second Street. We also filmed shots for the "Wedding Show," even though it wouldn't take place until the eighth episode.

The writers came up with an ingenious plotline in which Phyllis, in town for the wedding, forgets to pick Rhoda up, so Rhoda has to take the subway in her wedding gown. When we went down into the subway to start filming, there was a businessman standing on the platform with blood pouring out of his nose and down the front of his shirt. Someone had hit him in the face and stolen his briefcase. My instinct was to run over to him. I'd taken two steps when the wardrobe lady threw a cross-body block, stopping me in my tracks. "Don't go near him," she shouted. "We only have one wedding dress. You can't get blood on it."

The wedding sequence took all afternoon. They filmed me running all over Manhattan and the Bronx. We did a couple of shots on East Seventy-second Street right in front of the office of my former gynecologist, Dr. Myron Buchman. When I noticed his nameplate was still up, I went in. Needless to say, Dr. Buchman was surprised to see me—especially in a wedding gown and veil. I introduced him to Jim and Dave Davis. "Valerie's a good girl," Dr. Buchman volunteered.

After this hiatus, I returned to film my final episodes of

The Mary Tyler Moore Show. This was a bittersweet time. I was excited to move on to *Rhoda,* but I was sad about leaving behind so many wonderful people whom I'd come to respect and love. I had learned so much from everyone on the show, especially Mary. She had given me a spectacular education in television. I couldn't have asked for a better teacher.

Until filming began on *Rhoda,* I was unaware how much I'd learned about being the lead in a show, as if by osmosis, at Mary's side. I'd watched her be professional, courteous, and respectful in all aspects of the job. When I moved over to my own soundstage, I was prepared.

With Jim and Allan at the helm, the first show masterfully introduced the new characters, brought back the old ones, and showed the transition from Minneapolis to New York City, as well as Rhoda's personal evolution. Rhoda's growth is evident at the end of the episode, when she asks Joe out. "I thank you, *Ms.* magazine, I could never have done it without you," she says. This simple move of having Rhoda take her fate into her own hands and linking it with burgeoning feminism was a brilliant way of signaling that Rhoda had come into her own.

Shortly after the premiere aired, I received perhaps the best fan letter of my entire life from a sweet seventy-two-year-old woman from the Midwest. "Just before the show started I sat down on my couch, so tense, with my hands held tight together and I prayed—Oh Lord, let this girl go over big!" she wrote. I think her prayer was answered.

Very fortunately for me, Mimi Kirk, Mary Tyler Moore's former stand-in and assistant, joined me on *Rhoda* as my assistant. As before, she had an enormous impact on Rhoda's wardrobe. On *Mary,* I might have one or two costume changes per episode, but on *Rhoda,* I could have as many as six or more.

At fittings, our wardrobe supervisor, Shannon, would look at me in an outfit and take a step back to examine her work. "That's not bad," she'd say. Then, with a smile, Mimi would jump in. "Not bad? We're not going for 'not bad'! We're going for sensational." Whenever possible, Mimi added scarves, ethnic jewelry, a hand-crafted purse, anything to give Rhoda an unusual and offbeat touch. Under Mimi's guidance, I began to wear tops made out of doilies or decorative tablecloths, flared pants, and clothes culled from thrift shops. Rhoda's clothes augmented her character. The more confident she became, the more courageously she dressed.

At first I was a little startled by how much more responsibility I had as the star of my own show. People looked to me for answers and opinions. There were more lines to learn, more time in front of the camera, more costumes, more magazine interviews, more publicity appearances, more of everything. But I had many skillful people helping me to get it all done.

When we started out on *Rhoda,* I asked Viola Spolin to come to the set and hold a Theater Games workshop for the cast, staff, and crew. Jim, Allan, and our fabulous director, Robert Moore, even attended a few. These biweekly workshops were fun and quickly created a sense of family within the company. I also set up lunch-break yoga classes, which the group enjoyed.

Rhoda hit the ground running. It felt less like a pilot and more like a seamless outgrowth from *Mary Tyler Moore*. It was well conceived and well executed. There was an immediate feeling of comfort and ease on the set, as if we'd all been working together for a long time. Some of us had been!

From the first episode, the ratings were high. People were familiar with Rhoda and eager to tune in to her adventures in New York. The writers did an incredible job in the opening episodes of investing the audience in Rhoda's job search and her relationship with Joe. They created enough passion and tension that people were rooting for them to get married. From the moment Joe proposed to Rhoda, the media and the television audience began buzzing about the wedding.

The producers did a spectacular rollout for the one-hour wedding special. CBS promoted it wildly. They even linked it to *The Mary Tyler Moore Show*. The episode of *Mary* that aired several days before Rhoda's wedding showed the characters shopping for gifts and preparing to travel to New York. Excitement was building both in TV land and in the real world. It didn't hurt that, shortly before the wedding special, Mary and I appeared on the cover of *TIME* magazine. The title of the article was "Victorious Loser"—a perfect description of Rhoda on the eve of her wedding!

The week before we filmed the episode, gifts began to inundate the studio. Fans sent coffeemakers, engraved plates, and too many toasters to count. Thousands of cards that read "Congratulations, Rhoda and Joe" flooded in. I loved that our audience wanted to be part of the event. All the attention indicated that the show was going to be big.

It was incredibly exciting to film Rhoda's wedding, especially because the show would reunite me with the cast of *The Mary Tyler Moore Show*. It was an hour-long episode and required a longer rehearsal period, which meant more time together. It was going to be like a real party with old friends—like a real wedding.

The writers really did us proud on the "Wedding Show." The script was sensational and gave everyone a chance to shine. The cast laughed all week throughout rehearsal. Lots of colorful actors of all ages were hired to play Joe's and Rhoda's extended families. It was a great wedding! After filming, we broke out champagne in the studio for the whole company.

One of my favorite moments from the wedding episode was when Rhoda is walking down the hall in her wedding regalia, on her way into her parents' apartment, and meets a neighbor taking out the trash played by the laconic Bella Bruck. "Hey, Rhoda," Bella says, "what's new?"

"Not much," Rhoda replies. Little touches gave so much character and texture to—and really Rhoda-ized—the wedding.

On account of all the gifts and the coverage in *TIME,* I had a sense that the show was going to be popular, but I didn't realize that it was going to be record-breaking. More than fifty-two million people—half of the American television-viewing audience—tuned in to watch Rhoda and Joe get married. The numbers were unbelievable. All over America, people hosted their own wedding parties for Rhoda and Joe. They dressed in party clothes, some in black tie, and laid out trays of canapés and toasted the couple. Dinner parties were canceled in deference to or planned in honor of the television event. People who were driving when the show aired pulled off the road and checked in to motels to watch.

On October 28, 1974, the wedding went up against *Monday Night Football* on ABC. During the game, the famed sportscaster Howard Cosell kept a running commentary going about Rhoda's wedding. He indicated that Rhoda was stealing a lot of his viewers. Throughout his broadcast, Howard joked that he hadn't been invited to the wedding, and before a commercial break, he declared, "Let's get over to Rhoda's wedding quick. The chicken liver is getting rancid." It was unheard of for someone on one network to refer to a concurrent show on a rival network. By all accounts, the show was a hit!

After the wedding aired, I was constantly congratulated by well-wishers on the streets. "Congrats, Rhoda, you landed a good one!" It was this hour-long special that permanently united Valerie Harper and Rhoda Morgenstern for life. Before the wedding, I'd often been called Rhoda, but after the special aired, it took on a whole new dimension. The audience felt as if a family member had gotten married.

While the wedding special was a highlight of the first season of *Rhoda,* it was by no means the pinnacle. Rather, it was a fantastic launching pad from which *Rhoda* only grew stronger. The writers had drawn viewers in, committed them to watching Joe and Rhoda's relationship develop, and now that they had the country's attention, they were going to delve into the couple's life together. Because the wedding had been so sensational, there would be no time to rest on laurels. We'd have to work diligently to live up to the hype we'd generated.

Being the central character on a show was much more tiring than I'd expected. While secondary characters rested between their scenes, I was always on. Occasionally, we'd film three shows and then have a week off. Sometimes we'd film for five weeks straight without taking a break. I'm not complaining because it was great to be working, but this shooting schedule tended to wear me down. I often felt that I was playing an eternal game of catch-up. The scripts were fantastic, and I pushed myself hard to be on top of the material.

In order to really be sure of my lines, I began to write them out from memory, along with the lines of everyone else in my scenes. It took me ages to get through a script, but it allowed me to discover what I knew by heart and what I had yet to learn. My hairdresser, Mack Eden, was kind enough to come by my house on Thursday nights to do my hair for filming the next day. He often found me sitting in the living room, eating a pizza, writing out my lines. "Look at you!" Mack would exclaim. "You're a big star, and you're sitting here all alone, eating cold pizza and scribbling away."

I asked Mack, "A big star? What does that even mean?" I was a working actress. And I had a lot of work to do. I wanted to hit pay dirt on show night.

chapter
SEVEN

The first season of *Rhoda* was a smash. I won the Best Actress Emmy, which I accepted in true Rhoda fashion, dressed in a top made from an antique embroidered piano shawl. That night, many members of my *Mary Tyler Moore* family won awards, too—Ed, Betty, Cloris, Jim and Allan, and Ed. Weinberger and Stan Daniels—another terrific writing team. The same year, I won a Golden Globe Award in the same category. While I was delighted with these accolades, the award that was especially pleasing to me was the Golden Globe that the whole cast and all the producers received for Best Comedy of 1975. *Rhoda* was a team effort, and we had a winning team.

Over the course of the first and second seasons, the other main characters in the show really began to emerge—in particular, Carlton the doorman, voiced by our producer Lorenzo Music, who developed an almost cult following. His slurred speech, his loneliness, his comedic interference with Rhoda and Brenda, as well as his loyalty, intrigued viewers. It didn't hurt that the writers found endless ways to tease the audience into thinking they were going to show Carlton. This constant disappointment notwithstanding, the writers were able to sustain an invisible character from season to season by imbuing him with enigma and a fumbling sort of wisdom. Carlton's motto was "Aim low. Avoid disappointment."

Ida Morgenstern grew more demanding, nosy, and clingy, and more beloved by viewers. Her constant nagging and meddling in Brenda and Rhoda's lives—her inability to let anything slide—always hit the mark. No one, not even Mary, was spared her barbs. Nancy Walker ran wild with her role, spewing Ida's vitriol gleefully. It was a delight to watch her and act alongside her.

Then there was Brenda. Brenda was to Rhoda as Rhoda had been to Mary Richards on *Mary Tyler Moore*—an insecure, overweight, unlucky-in-love sidekick. Julie Kavner brought quiet humor and sweet naïveté to Brenda's misfortunes. Julie channeled her own shyness—she absolutely hated being recognized in public—into her portrayal of Brenda. But, oh Lord, she was so good and incredibly funny, always. I've never had more fun or gotten more satisfaction than I did when I was acting with Julie.

The writing team created delightful supporting characters: Charlie, Joe's obnoxious pal (superlative Dick Schaal, my husband); Justin, Joe's business partner (comical Scoey Mitchell); Alice, Joe's eccentric secretary (one-of-a-kind darling Candy Azzara); Myrna, Rhoda's window dressing partner (adorable Barbara Sharma); Susan, Rhoda's friend nicknamed "Easie Susie" in high school, now mother of six, pending seventh (talented Beverly Sanders). During the second season, the writers alternated between shows that focused on Rhoda and Joe and shows that focused on either Brenda or Ida. I always thought it was fun when the shows featured supporting characters, and I thought the writers did, too.

While audiences loved the second season of *Rhoda*, unbeknownst to me, the writers had hit a roadblock. So much of Rhoda's original humor—the self-effacing comedy that had drawn viewers—had been anchored by her hapless love life and her poor self-image. Now Rhoda was happily married and, except for the odd battle with a Sara Lee pound cake, fairly confident in her looks. The writers were struggling to make Rhoda funny.

As the second season progressed, the writers began writing more and more shows for Brenda and Ida and fewer that focused on Joe and Rhoda's marriage. This didn't bother me at all—in fact, I loved sharing the laughs evenly with my talented costars. It seemed fitting that Brenda, single and overweight, should inherit Rhoda's self-deprecating mantle and come into her own, just as I had done on *Mary Tyler Moore*. Soon Brenda's discombobulated love life and countless quips about her body became *Rhoda*'s go-to gags.

Ratings were still high. The audience seemed devoted. As far as I could tell, *Rhoda* was moving along perfectly. So it came as a surprise to me to learn the writers were bored and frustrated with the newer, happier Rhoda they'd created. They'd lost the original hook for their show—the original Rhoda—and calculated that the audience would start to tire of Rhoda's "Sadie, Sadie, Married Lady" routine. Rhoda had lost her vulnerability. She was no longer a "victorious loser," as *TIME* magazine had put it; she wasn't a loser at all.

Eventually, Allan Burns and Charlotte Brown came to me and explained what was going on behind the scenes. "We sit around and try to think up conflicts for Rhoda, but we can't," Charlotte said. "Everything is going too well in her life. So, when in doubt, we go to Brenda."

"That's fine," I told them. I thought the Brenda shows were tremendous.

"Yes," Allan said. "But this show is called *Rhoda*, not *Brenda*."

While I could see their point, I could offer no solutions. Apparently, the writers had tried everything: Rhoda gets pregnant, Joe loses his job, anything to bring the comedy back to Rhoda. Nothing clicked. The show's biggest success—Rhoda's wedding—had become the writers' biggest pitfall. Rhoda, once an independent, wisecracking woman, had settled into the precise relationship she'd always wanted. The only problem was, it wasn't funny.

I was shocked when they told me what they had in store for the third season. Rhoda and Joe were getting separated. This was a nerve-wracking prospect. Rhoda's wedding had been a record-breaking episode, and now we were destroying everything we'd created. However, I could see how a separation might herald the return of old, insecure Rhoda. A failed marriage—what could cause more guilt and self-reproach than that?

Restoring Rhoda's comedic center was not the only motivation the writers and producers had for separating Rhoda and Joe. Here was a young married couple encountering difficulties, arguments, personal struggles that the writing team wanted to show in a funny yet mature way. Unfortunately, the writers were hamstrung by the rules set by Broadcast Standards and Practices. In 1976 the so-called family hour on television demanded conservative material. If the writers of *Rhoda* had been given the freedom to do a show such as *Mad About You,* which aired ten years later and showed a young married couple's struggles warts and all, I think Rhoda and Joe might have stayed together, comedically suffering all the pitfalls of a modern marriage.

Separating Rhoda and Joe was an enormous risk. Nothing like it had ever been done on television. Fifty-two million people had cheered for Rhoda's wedding. Now she was separating. It would be a blow.

Nevertheless, it offered so many new possibilities that it was a risk worth taking. During season two, Joe had become something of a traditional sitcom "wife," taking a backseat to Rhoda. Now he would have something to play with, a new dimension to his character. That would give David Groh some meatier scenes, which appealed to him. The writers knew they could find humor in all the uncomfortable situations that would come with separation—marriage counseling, first dates, awkward run-ins.

Starting work on the third season felt different. The set seemed somewhat empty and less familiar. Ida and Martin Morgenstern had taken off in a camper to tour the country. (In fact, Nancy Walker had gone to a different network to star in her own show.) David Groh appeared briefly in the first episode, in which he tells Rhoda that he's leaving her, then appeared only sporadically. Besides the bombastic Jack Doyle, Rhoda's boss at the costume retail shop played beautifully by Kenneth McMillan, the writers introduced a couple of new characters. Two of these were Sally Gallagher, an airline stewardess, played by the ever funny Anne Meara; Gary Levy, a new neighbor played with inveterate New York charm by Ron Silver; and the wonderfully funny Doris Roberts played Gary Levy's mom years before *Everybody Loves Raymond.* Ray Buktenica brought his marvelously quirky personality to become Brenda's boyfriend, Benny Goodwin. The hope was to bring back the fun Rhoda. Thankfully, hilarious Julie Kavner, that doll, was an absolute mainstay as Rhoda's perennially loveable little sister, Brenda. (Not so trivial trivia: Julie appeared in every single episode—all 105—so Brenda was perpetually at Rhoda's side!)

The fan reaction to Rhoda and Joe's separation was vehement. People wrote angry letters. A psychologist complained to CBS that the network was trivializing marital separation. Viewers felt betrayed, and fans were 100 percent behind Joe. David Groh received nearly a thousand letters telling him he'd been treated unfairly by the show and that he had to get back together with Rhoda. Despite the outcry, the writers stuck to their guns. Good comedy was their priority, and with the couple living apart, they were able to get back to that.

David Groh appeared in only nine of the twenty-four episodes of the third season, each one focusing on some attempt to reconcile the couple. Toward the end of the season, Allan Burns broke the news to me that Rhoda and Joe were getting a divorce. I was floored. I'd thought their relationship was troubled but on the mend. I had no idea that it was about to be taken off life support.

"Listen," Allan said, "we see letters every day from the audience. They're upset. Either we fix the marriage or we divorce you. But this constant back and forth during the separation is killing the viewers. Obviously, the world wants Joe and Rhoda to get back together. But we've done two and a half seasons with Joe. We think we've mined everything there. It's time to move on."

I wished it wasn't so, but when brilliant writers tell you they've hit a wall, you listen. Rhoda was freer and funnier without Joe. She had always been a scuffler and it seemed now was the time to get back to her comedy roots. Rhoda's divorce literally rocked the land of television. There had been divorced characters before, but never had the stars of a show gotten a divorce. It was a gutsy move by the producers, and CBS backed their decision.

Nevertheless, I felt terrible for David, and so did the writers. Charlotte told me later than she and Allan had drawn the "short straw" and had to break the news to David. The whole situation was made worse by the fact that when David came into the meeting, he said, "Hey, guys, I just bought a house in Hancock Park." He'd thought his job was secure. I'm sure he never imagined he wouldn't be with *Rhoda* until the end. I knew that he would be devastated.

Audiences loved David—his looks, his warmth, and the passion he brought to Joe's darker moments. He was great at playing comedic anger. But the show wasn't working. He was a victim of circumstance. David's last day on-set was incredibly painful. He knew that I'd advocated for him and that it wasn't my decision to write him out of the show. Still, it was very difficult to see him go. I prayed that *Rhoda* would open up many doors for him.

With Rhoda newly single, the laughs returned. Suddenly, there was room for a host of zany characters and amusing insecurities. Rhoda was funnier divorced than she had been married, that was undeniable. One of my favorite episodes from the later seasons was "One Is a Number," which guest-starred the respected stage actress Anne Jackson playing a waitress in a diner. In this episode, Rhoda decides to treat herself, a newly single woman, to a night on the town. In 1977 it wasn't entirely common for women to eat out alone. But being able to enjoy herself without a date was an empowering lesson for Rhoda and her fans. Speaking of fans, one of my favorite actors, Eli Wallach, was at the filming cheering on Anne, his wife of twenty-five years at that time—now sixty-four years!

Rhoda wasn't going to be alone for long. Now that she was able to date again, the writers were free to bring in numerous guest stars, such as Judd Hirsch and Michael DeLano, as potential love interests. These characters were more colorful than the reserved Joe Gerard had been, and they put Rhoda right back where the writers wanted her: on shaky ground.

Michael DeLano played Johnny Venture, a monumentally sleazy Vegas lounge singer who woos Rhoda. With his Liberace-style costumes and his comedic velvet-voiced crooning, he brought a lot of the humor back into Rhoda's life. All in all, after the divorce, there seemed to be a little more air in the room, more space to laugh and experiment.

Before the fourth season, Dave Davis (who by this time was deeply involved with Julie Kavner—they are now married) and Jim Brooks announced they were leaving *Rhoda* to develop a new show about New York taxicab drivers that would become the famous *Taxi*. While I was worried that one of the original creators and one of the executive producers were leaving, I was thrilled about their venture. Jim assured me I'd be in good hands—and so I was. After all, Allan Burns was sticking around, as was Charlotte Brown, who had begun as a writer on *The Mary Tyler Moore Show* and had worked her way up in television comedy. She was the first woman writer-producer of a multiple-camera show. Charlotte was fearless in securing wonderful guest stars for the *Rhoda* show. She approached Albert Finney and Alan Bates—her credo was "All they can do is say no." The British icons declined but she did land Vivian Vance as Rhoda's neighbor, and octogenarian Ruth Gordon as Carlton's hugely eccentric mother. Two fabulous ladies! Charlotte had also gotten me involved with an extraordinary, desperately needed organization—the Rape Treatment Center. Gail Abarbanel, the founder, had been a school chum of Charlotte's and deserved support in helping rape victims. As a television star I could assist the organization.

Rhoda got its groove back in the fourth season. Nancy Walker returned to the show to much fanfare, and it felt like the early days. However, I could sense something in the air. The writers were doing excellent work, as were the actors, but the network heads, a constantly changing group, seemed to be shifting priorities. I wasn't sure that CBS wanted us back. So I was surprised when *Rhoda* was picked up early for a fifth season.

During the fifth season, we hit our hundredth episode and celebrated with three large, round cakes that Mimi lined up, each with a digit on top so together they formed the number 100. But there were storm clouds on the horizon. CBS kept moving the show around, airing on different nights at different times. Ratings went down. I wrote to the big brass, explaining that it was incredibly difficult to keep a loyal fan base if the show's time slot kept shifting. The boys in charge ignored my protests and moved us again, six times in total. Charlotte, who had become a very close friend over the years, and her whole writing staff were doing excellent work, as was everyone on the show, but the writing was on the wall.

In December 1978, while on hiatus, we learned that *Rhoda* was being summarily canceled. We'd never be going back into the studio again. The network wasn't even bothering to air the final four episodes that we'd filmed. *Rhoda* was done.

I was saddened by the way the cancellation came about, but I wasn't surprised. After all, that's show business. I was starting to feel that the show had run its course. *The Mary Tyler Moore Show* had already ended. It felt like a groundbreaking era of television was coming to a natural end. My biggest regret was that we hadn't been given an opportunity to write a final episode for *Rhoda*. *The Mary Tyler Moore Show* had wrapped up with a perfect, bittersweet, and amusing finale on which I was thrilled to be able to appear. I wish that *Rhoda* had been given the same opportunity.

The minute I fully grasped that the show was over, I decided to throw a party. And I mean a party—a big, extravagant blast. As usual, Mimi jumped in to set things up. I rented the large party room in Chasen's, a historic and glamorous restaurant in Beverly Hills. Mimi and I put our heads together to put on a fabulous do. I wanted to spare no expense when it came to thanking all the people who had contributed to five wonderful years of *Rhoda*, and I invited everyone who had worked on the show: actors, writers, directors, guest stars, crew, staff, camera operators, prop people, secretaries, everyone.

It was a wonderful party. We had tons of hors d'oeuvres, a fantastic menu, and unlimited champagne. I knew the entire company needed to be together, especially because we were canceled while on hiatus. We needed time to unwind and say goodbye, hug one another, and exchange phone numbers (whether or not we would end up using them).

There was an unquestionable sense of liberation, albeit tinged with sadness, that evening. We all knew that we had contributed to something wonderful, something that would endure. We had done things on television that had never been accomplished. We'd broken records and broken barriers, shifting cultural expectations of what can be shown on TV. It had been a tremendous journey.

I was both nostalgic and relieved that *Rhoda* was over. There are times in this business when you ask yourself in the middle of a dreadful show, "Who do I have to sleep with to get out of this turkey?" There are other times when you wake up in the morning and pray for the show you're in never to end. With *Rhoda,* I was fortunate enough not to experience either of these extremes.

I never grew tired of being Rhoda; I never felt saddled with her. But I wasn't devastated to let her go. When the shock of cancellation subsided, I realized that I was ready to move on. The run had come to a nearly perfect conclusion.

After all, nine years had passed since I'd stepped into the role of Rhoda Morgenstern—four years on *Mary Tyler Moore* and five years on *Rhoda.* It seemed like an impossible stretch of luck. I never imagined that I'd work with such steadiness, that I'd have nine uninterrupted years of continuous employment in a role I loved, a role brilliantly written and conceived by some of the most talented minds in the business.

I knew that it would be impossible to say good-bye to Rhoda entirely. And I didn't want to. Happily, she would live forever in the TV universe—Valerie as Rhoda. To this day, many people are surprised to discover that I'm not Jewish. Fans, usually older women, often came up to me on the street and said while pinching my cheeks, "Sweetheart, darling, I read that you aren't Jewish. Say it isn't so."

I had a stock answer for this. "Listen," I replied, "in my heart, I'm Jewish. And if you go back far enough, we're all Jewish. The Jews are an ancient people. I don't see Babylonians, I don't see Sumerians or Phoenicians, but I see Jews are here. And by the way, Rhoda is Jewish."

This usually got a laugh. "I thought for sure you, Valerie, were Jewish," my fans would reply. "You have the *neshama,*" which is to say the spirit or the soul of the religion. For me, this was always one of the highest compliments I received.

Of course, *Rhoda* wasn't written for a Jewish audience but for anyone who liked to laugh. She was written for anyone who used humor to hide struggle, sadness, and fear. Anyone who wanted someone to commiserate with over body-image issues and boy trouble could turn to Rhoda. Anyone who dreamed big and fell flat had a friend in Rhoda. And then anyone who kept going had her as an ally.

Over the years, whenever I meet fans of *Rhoda,* I'm always treated as a long-lost friend. On the street, in shops, in airports, even on the telephone—everywhere—I'm thanked warmly for the laughs, the encouragement, the comfort when things seemed bleak, and the loving connection that Rhoda provided. Even though we filmed our last episode in 1978, Rhoda lives on in re-runs and in so many people's hearts.

chapter
EIGHT

During the nine years I spent as Rhoda Morgenstern, social and political activism remained a vital part of my life—a passion as important to me as acting. One of the greatest benefits of being a celebrity was that I now had a platform to bring attention to the issues most important to me. The more famous I became, the more responsible I felt.

Often people assume that being a celebrity means that your rights as an ordinary citizen get revoked. I have always thought the opposite—being famous means you can and should do more to bring about the change you believe in. Now that I was in the public eye, I redoubled my efforts to support the ongoing struggle for social justice around the country and the world.

It was well known in Hollywood that I was an activist, and as my so-called celebrity status grew, I was inundated with requests to lend my name to many worthy causes. There are so many fights worth fighting, and I simply could not participate in all of them.

In deciding how best to devote my energy, I took the advice of actor-activist Alan Alda, who said: "Try to lend your name only to those organizations you are directly, actively working with." Since I was someone who wanted to say yes to every request that came my way, the Alan Alda rule helped me prioritize my efforts. (Alan is like a brother to Rhoda. Literally. His father, Broadway star Robert Alda, played Joe's dad on the show!)

By the early 1970s I was beginning to understand that the fight for civil rights, both nationally and globally, was absolutely analogous to the struggle for women's rights. African-Americans, as well as other minorities and women (a majority), are subjugated by a ruling class that unfairly dictates the limits of their freedom. This was, and continues to be, unacceptable to me.

During the late sixties, I began reading a great deal about the burgeoning feminist movement. When I moved to Los Angeles, my interest only grew. In our affluent and free country, women were still being treated as second-class citizens. Too often people mistook comfort and stability for equality. Sure, some women *seemed* happy, stuck at home in the kitchen. But was this prescribed role supposed to be the only one all of us wanted? Come on.

Gloria Steinem's belief that the worst thing done to women is the trivialization of our lives resonated deeply with me. I remembered my mother's frustrations at not being allowed to become a doctor, as well as her forsaking her career as a nurse in order to raise her family—her love for us notwithstanding. Actively fighting for women's rights was something I wanted to do. It was what Rhoda Morgenstern would have done.

Around 1972, I was asked to work on the passage of the Equal Rights Amendment (ERA). Because I was on television in a groundbreaking series featuring women—*The Mary Tyler Moore Show*—I was a natural for appearances to raise both money and awareness about the importance of this change to our Constitution. I already supported the ERA, but in order to serve as a spokesperson, I needed to learn everything about it. Before speaking in public and to the media, I had to learn to communicate the facts clearly and accurately.

My volunteer tutor, a young, pretty lawyer with dark brown eyes, arrived at my door in Westwood in a smart red suit with a big smile. "Hi, I'm Gloria Allred," she said. "I'm here to teach you the legalities of the ERA." This she did, brilliantly. "Gender is not a valid, legal classification of persons," Gloria explained.

The Equal Rights Amendment had been drafted by Alice Paul in 1923 and introduced before every congressional session from 1923 to 1970. Yet it did not reach the floor of the House or the Senate for a vote until 1972, when it was passed out of Congress and turned over to the individual states for ratification. Gloria explained that passing the amendment would prohibit any state from discriminating against any person on account of gender. Its purpose was to write women into the Constitution as full citizens. Sounds basic, right? Well, to this day, the only specific, written guarantee for us is the right to vote. That is simply not enough.

The ERA is a scant twenty-three words: "Equality of rights under the law shall not be denied or abridged by the United

States or by any state on account of sex." As of today, thirty-five states (of the required thirty-eight) have ratified the amendment, and the struggle continues in each session of Congress.

During my yearly hiatus from *Mary Tyler Moore* and *Rhoda*, under the inspired leadership of Sandy Mullins, executive director of the Committee to Ratify ERA, I would travel to various states to work toward passage of the amendment. Sandy had assembled and trained a group of Hollywood actors—myself, Jean Stapleton, Barbara Feldon, Carol Burnett, Anne-Marie Johnson, Ed Asner, Joan Hackett, Cindy Williams, Polly Bergen, Alan Alda, Linda Lavin, Maureen McGovern, and many more— to fight the good fight. We lobbied, rallied, marched, petitioned, picketed, and campaigned intensely to get those final three states to ratify. Once an actress, Timothy Blake, in utter exasperation at our failure to convince certain male legislators to vote our way, said, "Well, Val, we've done everything legally possible. I guess it's time to put on trashy lingerie and head out in cabs." We laughed at the time, but we were so disheartened that we would not succeed after all our work. The struggle for women's rights is the longest nonviolent revolution in the history of the world, and I will be in it until the end.

One of the most memorable events I attended during that period was a giant Mother's Day march in Chicago, where we all wore white with green sashes, the colors of the suffragettes. There were a lot of show business stars at the front of the march, but it was my enormous honor to walk alongside the titans of the women's movement, Bella Abzug, Betty Friedan, and Gloria Steinem.

Gloria was very witty and very beautiful. She communicated effortlessly in a mellifluous, measured voice that underlined her intellect and gave her an air of cultured sophistication. Gloria did me the honor of asking me to pose for the cover of *Ms.* magazine, my favorite publication. The subject of the article was women and money, and the cover featured me, supposedly nude, standing behind a giant dollar bill. (In truth, I was wearing a strapless bodysuit.)

Of these three feminist leaders, I spent the most time with Bella Abzug. She and her husband, Marty, with whom she was completely in love, used to come to the Westwood house for dinner with me and Dick. Although I'd avoided supporting candidates in elections, choosing to work on issues, I gladly stumped for Bella on her home turf in Brooklyn. I was always delighted to lend my support to Battling Bella.

She was truly courageous. A principled member of Congress, she was unafraid to stand up for her constituents, no matter how disparaging her opponents were. Men would say the crudest things about her fight and the rudest things about her person. But nothing deterred Bella. There she'd be, wearing her trademark hat, inspiring us as she got up on the floor of the House and laid it down before Congress.

Bella was a real New York girl—outspoken, tough, and wonderfully funny. She had a deep, hearty laugh that she never held back. (Rhoda could have easily had an Aunt Bella.) Her almond-shaped eyes were mischievous and wise. And her vision was profound, probing beneath the surface to understand the human condition, which she sought to transform. Bella must have been a real beauty when she was younger. By the time I met her, she was an extremely popular, powerful force, a compact tank of a woman with a deep, authoritative voice.

Bella, Gloria, and Betty were not the only remarkable leaders with whom I had the honor of meeting and working in the 1970s. Ever since I stood in front of supermarkets boycotting grapes in the 1960s, I had been a huge admirer of César Chávez and the farmworkers' struggle. While I was on *Rhoda,* Mimi arranged a luncheon in my dressing room so I could meet César, the founder of the United Farm Workers of America, in order to help him work on the passage of Proposition 14 in the next California election. The proposed law provided that a portion of fines collected from supermarket health code violations would help pay the health-care costs for farmworkers harmed doing the brutal job of harvesting. A lot of the cast, crew, and staff on *Rhoda* were eager to meet the famous, respected labor leader, whom I considered the sole survivor of the magnificent triumvirate of social justice heroes of the 1960s, the others being Bobby Kennedy and Martin Luther King, Jr.

Although we ultimately lost Proposition 14, a devoted cadre of celebrities remained committed to supporting César's efforts. Martin Sheen, Ed Begley, Jr., Jane Fonda, Dennis Weaver, myself, and others continued fund-raising, attending conferences, actions, and marches all over Southern California.

César was a brilliant man with a simple, quiet power. He was soft-spoken, kind, and compelling. His studious presence and focused singularity of purpose assured you: "This is a great man!" César and Dolores Huerta, cofounder of the UFW who was honored in 2012 with the Presidential Medal of Freedom, were tireless fighters, determined to improve the poverty-stricken lives of farmworkers and the safety of everyone's food supply. Time spent with them was filled with mariachi music, laughter, and vegan burritos.

Dick and I hosted a number of events and meetings on César's behalf, including one lovely dinner party that Diana Ross attended in order to meet César. César came with a number of security guards, handsome, somber young Mexican-American men with terrific mustaches and beautifully embroidered white shirts. Several searched the house, while one stood guard at the door, one in the back, and one on the roof as we dined.

The primary purpose of this dinner was to introduce César to a man who had recently become an influential figure in my life—Werner Erhard, the founder of est. Werner had immersed himself in the study of hunger and César was pleased to meet to discuss issues of food and poverty. In 1975, at the suggestion of my friend, the actor Anthony Zerbe, Dick and I had signed up for the two-weekend session of Erhard Seminars Training (est). The training was at the forefront of the Human Potential Movement that swept across the country in the 1970s. Est married spirituality to psychology and self-empowerment to deep and often painful personal examination. Facing yourself is tough love at its best.

The purpose of est was to help people shift their contextual state of mind from attempting to feel satisfaction in their lives to actually being able to experience that satisfaction. Werner's seminars strove to free people from their pasts and allow them to live fully in the present from moment to moment (just like excellent actors try to do in their work).

Est was a wonderfully empowering experience for me. It took a lot of the struggle and conflict out of my day-to-day decision-making and helped me to imbue my life with more focus and intention. I learned that there was a difference between committing to try to live a certain way and actually living the way you intend. Werner spoke of how unsuccessfully a lot of us live our lives. "Imagine if your life is a car. What would happen if you got in, started the motor, and then took off, steering the car with your hands on the rearview mirror? You'd wind up in a ditch or worse." Werner explained that the training helped you to get your hands off the rearview mirror and onto the steering wheel of your life. Sounds simple, right? It worked for me.

The two weekends of est training were tough and at times emotionally eviscerating. But I noticed a marked change in myself. I was happier, more alive, and everything seemed lighter. Most of all, I stopped feeling desperate and uptight about things in my life that I couldn't control.

Based on the premise that the world could really use some transformation, the training was geared to transforming individuals who will then transform the planet. In 1977, Werner, John Denver, and Professor Bob Fuller of Oberlin College founded a separate organization called the Hunger Project, which put forth a powerful and effective approach to ending world hunger. Much of the thinking behind the Hunger Project was from the work of Buckminster Fuller. (Bucky himself participated in many of the huge Hunger Project events across the country.) I was asked to be on the advisory board and eagerly agreed.

Werner invited us to envision ourselves as part of the end of worldwide hunger. Given the enormity of the problem, other organizations were doing Herculean work that focused on alleviating hunger. The Hunger Project's goal was not the *alleviation* of hunger but the *end* of the persistence of hunger on the planet. A mighty endeavor!

The first step was to shift people's mind-set about hunger. We invited people to visualize a world without hunger and to ask themselves if they'd be willing for world hunger to end forever. "But it can't!" they'd say. And that's the same kind of resignation we would later encounter in the developing world, where the hungry people themselves thought they were powerless.

And then we would ask people, "But would you personally be willing for it to end?"

Those who answered yes started on a process, however subtle, of becoming part of the solution instead of part of the problem. The notion that hunger could only be alleviated, not eradicated, was so firmly entrenched in the cultural consciousness that changing people's way of thinking was like swimming upstream against a strong current. Despite the opposition, we opened up a global conversation that hunger exists, it doesn't need to, and each of us can make the difference.

Werner held four-hour symposiums in cities around the

country to provide people with the facts about hunger-related deaths. As a celebrity, I was in a position to assist in disseminating this vital information. I traveled to East Africa on a Hunger Project fact-finding mission, visiting various countries that included Kenya, Uganda, and Somalia. When I was in Nairobi, I stepped out of the hotel elevator and a Kenyan couple stopped, stared, and the woman shouted gleefully in her African accent, "Rhoda!" Hard to believe the reach of American television! I expected the trip to be daunting, filled with refugee camps and untold thousands of displaced, suffering, hungry people. But when I arrived, I was overwhelmed by the beauty, resourcefulness, and courage I encountered. The hunger camps were lined with small domed huts, formed from thorny branches that stretched across the barren landscape as far as the eye could see. They looked like a mass of desert igloos.

Our delegation was greeted by crowds of gorgeous Somali women in vibrantly colored dresses and spectacular head wraps. Even the slings holding their babies were intricately patterned. I'd expected to see people in rags, ill and tragic, but here were these women of all ages, working with what little they had to make a functioning community. The only men I encountered were elderly. It was a stunning, accurate view of what hunger looked like in that region of Africa and of the brave people confronting it.

Upon returning from Somalia, our delegation, along with Liv Ullman, John Denver, and John Amos (who played Gordy the weatherman on *Mary Tyler Moore*), appeared before a United

My father, Howard Harper, a professional hockey player in the 1930s . . . hot stuff on ice.

My mother, Iva Mildred McConnell, a bright-eyed nursing student, class of 1933, Calgary, Alberta, Canada.

Mom and Dad in Chinatown, Los Angeles, in the 1940s . . . obviously, just look at her hair!

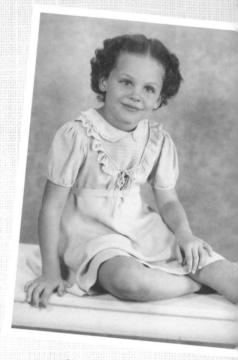

Me, age three, with my sister, Leah, age five, struggling to hold our baby brother up for the photo—Don was not amused.

At age six, I already knew how to pose for the camera.

Our mother used to dress Leah and me in matching outfits—I loved wearing the same dresses; Leah did not.

My brother, Don (seven), sitting on a log, and me (nine), doing an impression of a pin-up girl at a beach in Vancouver Island, British Columbia.

Me and some great girlfriends, 1953–'62.

Me at age fifteen leaping on West Fifty-seventh Street in front of Carnegie Hall as part of a demonstration to save it from demolition. We succeeded!

Rhoda and Joe's wedding! October 28, 1974.

My then-husband Richard Schaal on an episode of *Rhoda*.

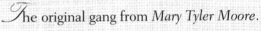

The original gang from *Mary Tyler Moore*.

Ed Asner and me with our second-season Emmys for *The Mary Tyler Moore Show*, 1972.

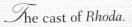

The cast of *Rhoda*.

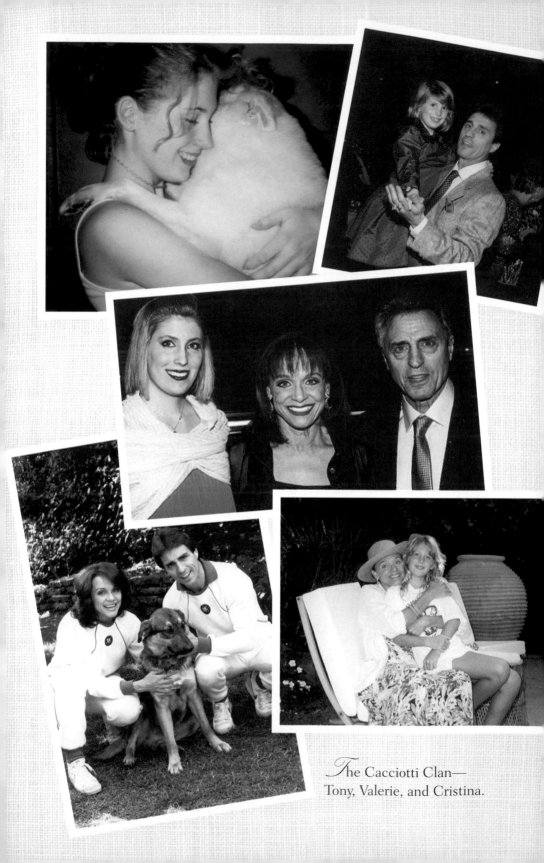

The Cacciotti Clan—
Tony, Valerie, and Cristina.

Susan Blakely, me, Sandy Mullins (executive director of the Committee to Ratify the ERA), and Carol Burnett at an Equal Rights Amendment celebrity workshop, 1974.

Chatting with César Chávez at a "Yes on 14" fund-raiser with friends Arnette and Anthony Zerbe (also César fans).

On a Hunger Project visit to Somalia, East Africa, 1980.

So proud of Tony's public servant son, Michael!

Me and my pal
Mary Tyler Moore.

Cheering "girlfriend" Cloris's
induction into the TV Academy
Hall of Fame.

Me as the outrageous Tallulah
Bankhead in *Looped*, my Tony-
nominated role on Broadway, 2010.

Nations-assembled panel and the Congressional Committee on East Africa to report about our mission. One fact we were determined to communicate was that only about 10 percent of hunger-related deaths are a direct result of famine. The other 90 percent are due to chronic undernutrition that, over time, leaves people vulnerable to diseases and other conditions that result in death. The underlying cause is, of course, hunger.

There were many organizations fighting world hunger with relief, aid, and food distribution. Getting food to hungry people is something that must be done. But it is only a temporary solution and cannot transform the underlying conditions that cause hunger to persist.

Under the miraculous leadership of our extraordinary founding president Joan Holmes, one of the most wonderful people I have ever known, for over twenty-five years the Hunger Project has continually adjusted its course of action to achieve its purpose. It has pioneered ways to empower communities with the opportunities they need to end their own hunger.

Since its inception, the Hunger Project was a brave endeavor that would take many, many years to be fully realized. It has been my observation that the media does not generally look for good news—"if it bleeds, it leads." It is also an impatient beast, demanding an event to report rather than a process. Back in 1978, *Mother Jones* magazine in particular took exception to the Hunger Project, accusing the organization of indulging in "happy talk" and a whole lot of New Age nonsense. They published an insulting cover with a cartoon of John Denver, one of the project's founders, and me wearing my Rhoda scarf, dancing in front of a pile of starved African babies. The accompanying article dismissed our mission, claiming that we were fools for thinking hunger could end. It was incredibly painful, as I was a big fan of the publication. In retrospect, the article was a reflection of the prevailing mind-set, that what was needed to end hunger was to provide goods and services to the poor, rather than provide an enabling, empowering environment in which people can end their own hunger. To their credit, after they saw the success of our organization, *Mother Jones* printed a retraction and an apology several years later.

Ending hunger is not only a moral imperative but a practical necessity. It is central to resolving an entire nexus of issues—population growth, civil unrest, war, environmental destruction—that threaten the quality of life for everyone. These days it is almost universally recognized that the severe subjugation of women is a social condition that holds hunger in place. The vast majority of the world's poor are women. They eat last and least, and their health often goes ignored. The deeply entrenched subjugation of women is reinforced by violence and the threat of violence. Inspiring women's leadership at all levels of society is critical to ending hunger. The Hunger Project has made the empowerment of women one of the pillars of our programs. After thirty-five years, our mission continues to be the sustainable end of hunger worldwide. A tall order, but we are on our way.

The est training and my subsequent involvement with the Hunger Project ushered in a period of intense personal change.

Dick and I attended several est seminars together, including a six-day training in Northern California. We began to be happier with each other and less judgmental. We also began to examine the truth about our relationship. What did we want out of our marriage? Were we holding each other back from total fulfillment?

I'm not sure when exactly our marriage stopped working. My career kept me so busy that there was never any time to sit back and examine what had become of Dick and me. I was always dashing from event to event, and Dick, naturally, was at my side. "Hey, Dick, grab your tuxedo!" I'd call. And we were out the door. I went, so he came; we were married, after all.

Sure, we had our share of minor arguments, but nothing traumatic. We had just slowly grown apart. One day we were sitting on the bed chatting, and I said, "Hey, we're roommates."

"Yes, but is that enough?" Dick replied.

To his credit, Dick never resented my success. He'd worked continually in film, on TV and stage, including numerous guest spots on both *Mary Tyler Moore* and *Rhoda*. He'd even costarred on Cloris Leachman's spin-off, *Phyllis*. If he was unhappy about the disparity between our careers, I never saw or felt it. In fact, Dick used to joke, "How can I be jealous? We're never up for the same parts."

In many ways, Dick and I were fundamentally different. I have always been a complete teetotaler and a nonsmoker. Dick, on the other hand, enjoyed both these things. At night, in front of the TV, he'd drink beer while I polished off a complete box of Van de Kamps chocolate chip cookies and milk without help.

So I'd be throwing stones from a glass house if I called him an addict.

Before taking any drastic measures regarding our marriage, we decided to go see Dr. Bob Lazalere, a relationship expert who was part of the est staff in San Francisco. We both knew and respected Bob very much and thought he would be a great resource for us. Our first consultation was over the phone. "Before you come to see me," he said, "I want each of you to ask yourself one question. Don't answer this question yet, just hold on to it in your mind for the few days before we meet. Think about it without answering. *Are you willing for your relationship to work regardless of the form?* When you come up here, we will discuss how to answer this."

I thought about Dr. Lazalere's question all week. When we got to his office, he asked us some very basic things about our marriage. "Valerie, what's something Dick does that has always annoyed you?"

"He never washes the cat food fork," I blurted out. I didn't even have to think about it. Dick would dish out the cat's food, then leave the fork in the sink to get all crusty. It was such a simple thing, but I had never mentioned it. It made both of us laugh.

"Listen," Dr. Lazalere said, "you two obviously love each other. But how invested are you in your relationship? Are you willing to make it work regardless of whether or not you stay together in a traditional sense?"

"What do you mean, exactly?" I asked.

"There are a host of options. You could stay married as you are now. You could be married but live separately. You could legally separate. You could divorce but live together. You could figure out a situation in which you see each other every other week. The possibilities are endless. Those are all forms that two people can agree upon. But the most important thing to do is ask yourselves, are you committed to having a relationship that works even if your marital status changes?"

This was brilliant! I didn't have to be furious with Dick or he with me. Divorce didn't have to mean anger, hostility, recrimination, or bitter rancor—none of which I felt in any part of my heart for Dick. Nor did I want to.

After our counseling session, I finally admitted to myself that I was lonely inside my own marriage. Dick and I were both going through the motions, which got in the way of each of us living to our fullest. We needed to acknowledge a simple truth—we were better off as friends and should keep it at that. And we didn't have to end our friendship because we were getting divorced. Hurray!

Thankfully, Dick felt just as I did. No one was hurt, humiliated, or deserted. We both wanted out of the marriage, and we both took responsibility for that decision. There was no blame, no finger pointing. It was a mutual decision, and once we made it, we both felt unburdened. I've often told pals, "Our divorce was better than many marriages."

Even though we had come to this landmark decision, neither of us wanted to move out of the house at that moment. I was busy filming *Rhoda,* and I had a couple of TV movies coming up. Since the tabloids had been viciously and erroneously predicting the end of my marriage since my first year on *The Mary Tyler Moore Show*, I was not going to give them the satisfaction of a big juicy story during production.

Now, who would be the person to file for divorce? It was a mutual decision; why should one of us be to blame? But gentlemanly Dick insisted I be the plaintiff, which didn't feel truthful to me. Then Gene piped up, "Val, you want to look like a *puttana*?!" (That's Italian for "naughty lady.") I really didn't, so I agreed.

Once our divorce proceedings got under way, my lawyer called and said, "Listen, Valerie, I know you and Dick are friends and all, but one of you has to move out of the house. It looks weird to the judge if you're still living together." Obviously, there was no room for a pleasant divorce in court.

It was an easy decision that I should move out. Dick's parents, both in their late seventies, were living with us at the Westwood house, and no way was I going to disrupt their lives. Besides, I was looking forward to getting my own place.

After we came to that decision, we had a quiet dinner party to break the news to the Schaals, Dick's daughter, Wendy, and her new husband, Stephen. Our caterer Maurice prepared and served a really lovely dinner. When dessert and coffee came, we made the announcement as gently as we could.

Dick's mother, Margaret, was flabbergasted. "But you've been getting along so well," she exclaimed.

"I know, Mom," Dick said. "But one of the reasons we're getting along so well is that we know we're getting out!"

I burst into laughter when he said this. It was true. We were both so relieved that the marriage was over that we'd really begun to enjoy ourselves. There was no tension, no drama.

After we told our immediate family, I began to let my closest friends realize that I was moving out. Some of them took the opportunity to commiserate, calling me up to let me know they were on my side and had never liked Dick to begin with. "No, no. Don't say it," I said. "You're talking about a friend of mine." It remains so to this day. I didn't want to hear anyone speak badly of him on my account. Cloris had a great expression for divorced people to use: "Never call him or her your ex, but rather your once-upon-a-time husband or wife." Sweetly accurate, huh?

Dick helped me hunt for a new place to live. I was eager for a major change, and I thought living near the water in Malibu was just the thing. Dick drove me out to Old Malibu Road, above the Malibu Colony, to look at a perfect little house at the water's edge. I fell in love with it immediately. Unfortunately—or, as it turned out, fortunately—the week after I spied this house, a giant storm swept it out to sea. Luckily, I found a great apartment in a picturesque building farther up Old Malibu Road.

Dick helped me move, and when I pulled out of our driveway in Westwood for the last time, he came out to wave good-bye. "Drive safe," he said.

"Of course. You taught me to drive," I replied. We both smiled, with tears in our eyes. The moment was bittersweet, poignant, and celebratory—another familiar movie scene, except in this case the parting couple was happy to say good-bye.

I loved my seaside apartment. It faced the ocean and had

a fifty-foot balcony, much like a widow's walk, from which I could watch the ocean. When my friends stopped by, they were tempted to pity me. "Oh, look at you, poor Val. You're a lonely woman by the sea!"

"No," I said. "I'm anything but lonely. In fact, I'm thrilled to be alone." And in beautiful, luxurious Malibu!

It was true. I had shared a room all my life, with either my sister, a roommate, or Dick. I had never lived by myself. I was excited. I had worked hard for nine years, and now I was truly independent. *Rhoda* had finished. My marriage had come to a graceful end. The 1970s were wrapping up. I was ready for whatever came next. Now all I had to do was get used to the incessant pounding of the Pacific Ocean.

chapter

NINE

As excited as I was to be living alone out in gorgeous Malibu, I kept waiting for a plague of loneliness to strike. It never did. As I had hoped, I found it liberating to be on my own.

During the last years of my marriage to Dick, our house had become quite busy and full of activity. Leah's children spent a lot of time at our house, sometimes their entire summer vacations. Penny and her husband, Zvi, visited with their four wonderful kids, Daphna, Michael, Danit, and Sharon, who to this day call me Aunt Val. Since we had the means and the space, they were always welcome. I loved taking them around Los Angeles—I went to Disneyland more times than Minnie Mouse. While my nephews, nieces, and friends were only temporary visitors, Dick's parents had moved in on a permanent basis. Although my absolutely perfect housekeeper, Audrey Harris, was always on hand, it seemed I was constantly rushing between home and set, worrying about whether there was enough food in the fridge, trying to remember who needed to be shuttled where or who was expecting to spend the evening with me.

In Malibu, for the first time in ages, I was free to do with my time exactly as I wished. Weird. With *Rhoda* over, I could finally relax. I loved sleeping as late as I pleased, buying only the food I wanted, staring out at the ocean from my balcony with no lines to learn. I'd worked hard from a very young age to find success, and now I actually had the time to relax and enjoy myself.

In addition to my new bachelorette pad, I thought it was time for a new car. I no longer needed my large white Cadillac Seville, which I called Blanca—a family car that could accommodate Dick, his parents, and Leah's children when they were in town. So supportive pals Norma Donaldson and Charlotte Brown, accompanied me to Beverly Hills Mercedes and encouraged me to buy a cream SL convertible with a brown soft top—a sporty little car for my new single lifestyle. I named her Crème Caramel. Delicious!

Charlotte, Norma, Arlene, and other friends often came out to Malibu. I hosted small but raucous dance parties to the tunes of Rod Stewart and Donna Summer and celebrated this new phase in my life. Soon I discovered that Helena Kallianiotes, a raven-haired Greek-American actress who had been in the classic Jack Nicholson film *Five Easy Pieces*, had organized a Monday-night private event for actors and their pals at the Reseda roller rink, calling it "Skataway." Disco roller-skating with flashing lights and mirrored prom-ball was the epitome of cool at the time, so Charlotte and I bought skates and had great fun at the immensely popular event. Helena went so far as to have white customized roller club jackets made for people who regularly came to the rink. My Skataway name was "Valve Job."

The place was always filled with famous and familiar faces. I remember one evening when Jon Voight turned up. It was shortly after the Academy Award ceremony when Sir Laurence Olivier had been presented with a lifetime achievement award. Olivier had made a tremendous speech about what it meant to be an actor. His words were erudite, inspiring, and very beautiful. As he was wrapping up, the cameras cut to Jon, who was looking on with an expression of rapture, awe, and appreciation, as if Olivier had given voice to something essential to Jon's soul. I think he had.

I didn't know Jon personally, so I decided to write him a note: "Olivier's speech was exceeded only by your reaction to it." I handed it to him and told him to read it at his leisure. As I skated around, he waved, smiled, and gave a courtly little bow. Soon we became friends and fellow advocates for a wide range of issues from poverty and homelessness to the Hunger Project.

Some people, I guess, might be unnerved by so much change—being newly single and, in a sense, out of work. But I embraced it. I visited my family back east before Ginger enrolled at MIT. As she moved into her dorm room, several classmates inquired, "Are you Valerie Harper's sister?" Ginger's "Yes, I am" was followed by excited girlish chatter. Then a boy in the corner calmly asked, with his Southern drawl, "Yo' name Brenda?" Life becomes art. That Christmas I got Ginger a T-shirt bearing the phrase.

During each season of *Rhoda,* I had done some theater during hiatus, and I thought now that the show was over, I would return to the stage. Instead of theater, however, the early eighties presented a slew of movie roles, both theatrical and television.

My first feature film after *Rhoda* was *The Last Married Couple in America* by John Herman Shaner, which starred George Segal and Natalie Wood. Arlene was also in the picture, playing their neighbor. George and Natalie were a married couple, and I was a divorced friend of Natalie's chasing after George. Some friend, huh? The legendary eight-time Academy Award winner, Edith Head, was costume designer for the film, and Mimi and I were thrilled to work with this extraordinary woman. Mimi assisted her and even got screen credit. During a fitting, I remarked about Edith's lovely gold chain necklace with eight miniature Oscars hanging from it. "Yes, Valerie," she said, "I find it helpful to wear this to job interviews."

The Last Married Couple in America was one of Natalie's last movies before her death. She was a dream to work with, relaxed and calm, which is often the case with a star of her magnitude. She was a gorgeous little thing but never fussed about her looks and never seemed insecure over her appearance. During a touch football scene, Natalie noticed that the elastic on Arlene's tracksuit pants had snapped and insisted that her own personal wardrobe assistant do a quick alteration so that Arlene didn't have to deal with safety pins. So thoughtful! When I told her I had been an extra on her 1973 film *Love with the Proper Stranger,* she laughed and said, "I loved that film. Lots of nominations and Steve McQueen." (Trivia: Arlene Golonka was also in this movie!)

We had several scenes together, one of which was at a restaurant where my character Barbara shocked Natalie's character Mari by admitting that, besides my face-lift, I'd had my vagina tightened. Natalie decided she wanted to do a spit take with her water. We had to repeat it several times so our director, the prolific and terrific Gil Cates, could get the shot. "This is so much fun," Natalie said as she spit out her water again and again. "This is what the vaudevillians have been getting to do for years."

During that scene, a question about the dialogue came up. My character was supposed to use the word *screwing* in one of her lines. This sounded a little harsh to both of us. Someone suggested *laying,* which seemed dated. Suddenly, Natalie had an idea. "You know, what about *bangin'*? Some of R.J.'s card-playing buddies use that expression." (Everyone called Natalie's husband Robert Wagner "R.J.") *Bangin'* was perfect. Natalie had nailed it.

After *The Last Married Couple in America* wrapped, I was offered a role in a great Neil Simon comedy called *Chapter Two.* I had played Alan Arkin's wife on Neil's hilarious TV special, *The Trouble with People,* and I was looking forward to working with this superb writer again. *Chapter Two* was directed by marvelous Robert Moore, who had directed the majority of the early *Rhoda* episodes, and it starred Marsha Mason, James Caan, and Joe Bologna. It was fun being reunited with James after *Freebie and the Bean,* as well as finally getting the opportunity to work with Joe, who had been up for the part of Joe Gerard on *Rhoda.*

In *Chapter Two,* I played a soap opera actress who tries to have an affair with Joe Bologna's character. As Rhoda Morgenstern, I had been unlucky in love for so long that this was a nice change. I could swap my eccentric clothes for something more sophisticated and sexy (in one scene all I "wore" was a bed sheet). As excited as I was to do the film, there was a catch—a bathing suit scene. Much worse than a sheet. With my butt? It would be *Cellulite on Parade* in movie theaters nationwide. I had to get into shape.

Several of my pals from the Reseda roller rink, including Kathy Smith, who later became a nationwide workout aficionado, knew a personal trainer who specialized in working with movie stars. Personal training was new, and I liked the idea of hiring someone to whip me into shape for the role. Tony Cacciotti, the recommended trainer, had worked with John Ritter, Richard Gere, and John Travolta, three of the hottest actors in the business at the time.

When I called Tony to ask if he trained women as well, he told me he did but that he was unfamiliar with *The Mary Tyler Moore Show* or *Rhoda* and was therefore unaware of my size and shape. It turned out that the following day we would be in Beverly Hills at the same time. I was getting my hair colored at Jon Peters Salon, and Tony had a lunch appointment nearby, so he agreed to drop by the beauty shop. Well, he'd get to see the real me—my hair a mess, wearing a homely salon smock.

When Tony walked in to Jon Peters, I was struck by how attractive he was. He was a great-looking Italian-American guy with thick dark hair and beautiful, soulful hazel eyes. He was wearing a yellow-and-blue-striped rugby shirt with a white collar, which couldn't hide his impressive physique.

I did my best to ignore his looks and focused on the problem at hand. I got down to business. "Okay, I have this movie coming up, and I need to get my body into shape for a bathing suit scene." Then I lowered my voice. "Especially my thighs and butt," I added.

I started to stand up from the hairdresser's chair so Tony could see the problem for himself. He waved me back down. "Sit. I can see from here." *That bad, huh?* I thought. He certainly had his work cut out for him.

I had no idea what to expect from working with a trainer. "Let's try one session," Tony suggested. "If you like it, we'll continue."

A few days later, he came out to my beach house. He brought weights with him and set up a little workout bench, and we got going. Tony was impressed by how strong I was.

"I used to be a dancer," I explained.

"Well," Tony said, "those muscles are still under there somewhere."

To find them, we were going to have do some deep excavating through layers of fat. Rhoda would have hated it! Just imagine the wisecracks she'd make as she kvetched her way through the whole session. But from the very first day, I loved working out with Tony. He was so knowledgeable and encouraging. Every day we did a basic workout of weights, stretching, and a run on the beach, and then each session we would do a different activity.

We'd work on parallel bars and rings at Muscle Beach in Venice. We did gymnastics, calisthenics, or yoga. Tony was a dedicated devotee of yoga. We worked out six days a week, and on Sundays I took a long walk on the beach to recover.

Tony was a big advocate of health food, and rather than dieting, he got me eating properly and drinking a lot of juice made from fresh tomatoes or carrots. I drank so much carrot juice that I acquired an orange glow, which unfortunately didn't look so hot on camera. But this new strict regimen of healthy food and exercise definitely produced results: The visible changes in my body were impressive. Within three weeks I began to see serious changes in my muscle tone and waistline. I was so excited about my body and the effectiveness of my wonderful coach that I completely overlooked just how physically beautiful he was.

Even though he was my trainer, I felt that Tony and I were colleagues. He had been an actor, director, and stuntman, always maintaining a lifelong interest in physical fitness. He'd started out like me, in New York theater, both on Broadway and off. He'd appeared in several movies, including *The Longest Yard* with Burt Reynolds and *A Hero at Large* with John Ritter, whom he'd gotten in shape for his part. He'd also appeared in numerous TV shows, including more than a hundred episodes of Chuck Barris's *The Gong Show*, doing stunts and sometimes wearing the most ridiculous getups. Tony was familiar with the industry, and it was easy to talk to him about my work.

Shortly before *Chapter Two* started filming, I threw a little party at my house and invited Tony. When Arlene and Norma got a look at my new trainer, they dragged me off into a corner. "That trainer is incredible!" Norma exclaimed.

"I know," I replied. "Look at me." I showed off my new physique.

My friends weren't interested in how *I* looked. "He's so gorgeous," said Arlene. "Are you guys going out?"

"No. He's my trainer. We're working out together."

"You fool!" they said in unison.

Dating Tony didn't occur to me. He was always dashing from our sessions to one date or another, while I was going home to soak in a hot tub to prepare for the next day of sweat and pain. But I was so thrilled with the results from my sessions with Tony that I asked if he could come to New York, where *Chapter Two* was filming. I wanted to keep up my fitness regimen, and I needed my fitness guru! Tony put his other clients on hold and accompanied me to Manhattan. It was strictly a business deal, with me paying for all of his expenses in addition to his salary.

The studio had booked a large suite for me in which Tony was able to set up a small gym. When we weren't working out indoors, we ran in Central Park or on other trails Tony mapped out. He found all the best health food restaurants in the city and made sure that I ate properly. When I wasn't working out or filming, I often visited my younger sister, Ginger, Dad, Angela, and her wildly funny mother, Vee, in New Jersey. In his spare time, Tony was very socially active—his dance card was always full.

Two weeks into the shoot, Tony asked if I wanted to accompany him to the Museum of Modern Art on my day off. I hadn't been there in years, so I agreed. As we strolled through the galleries, I discovered that Tony had been an artist, a sculptor, in fact. "Now you're sculpting real human beings," I said, which made him laugh. We were both incredibly taken by a very famous Andrew Wyeth painting. The haunting *Christina's World* is a melancholy rendering of a woman lying in a tawny field looking toward a farmhouse. We stood shoulder to shoulder, admiring it for quite some time in the hushed gallery.

After the museum, engrossed in conversation, we walked all over the city and down into the Village. It was a lovely Manhattan summer night. Eventually, we stopped to get something to eat. While we were waiting for our veggie wraps, Tony looked at me and said, "Valerie, would you like to get close?"

I was startled. It was the most gentle and gentlemanly come-on I had ever heard.

"I don't know," I said.

Tony didn't seem disappointed. "Just think about it," he said.

On the way back to the Plaza, he kissed me. I kissed him back. I guess I didn't have to think about it very long. He spent the night in my suite. The next morning he said, "There is no way you are paying for my hotel room or expenses anymore." He even insisted on reimbursing me for the return flight to California.

"Well," I said, "do you want to move in to my suite?" And he did for the remainder of the shoot.

The minute I opened myself up to Tony romantically, I fell hard. I was deeply, profoundly in love with him. I guess I had been all along without realizing it. We've been together ever since.

After we returned to Los Angeles, Tony stayed at my place in Malibu, where the crashing surf often startled him out of a deep sleep. He'd bolt out of bed, making me scream. Then we'd both howl with laughter at our mutual foolishness. Within a month, he'd gotten rid of his apartment in Venice, and we set up our life together.

Loving Tony was easy. He was so full of life. He was committed to health—spiritual, physical, and mental. Although he no longer acted, he was knowledgeable about the business and fully supportive of my career. He wanted me to be the best version of myself that I could be and was always available to help make that happen. Like me, he neither drank nor smoked. As his longtime friend Vidal Sassoon observed, "Tony is one of the most honorable men I've ever known."

With Tony, I was unbelievably happy. I was completely in love, and I felt (and looked) terrific. It was as if everything fell into wonderful alignment. Ours was a dazzling relationship right from the start—romantic, sensual, exciting, and supportive.

I'm not entirely sure I believe in fate or karma, but over time, Tony and I began to discover that we were meant to be together. In fact, we had met two times before but didn't know it. We figured out that back in 1958 Tony had lived around the corner from the apartment I shared with Iva on West Fifty-fifth Street in Manhattan. Tony didn't remember me, but he remembered Iva and her long mane of red-gold hair. He'd even tried to pick her up once or twice. Back then Tony was going by his stage name, Tony Bogart. Years into our relationship, when he told me this, I screamed, "Tony Bogart! I remember a Tony Bogart."

In 1958, when Iva and I were in *Li'l Abner*, we used to go out to support our team in the Broadway Show League baseball games in Central Park. The casts and crews of each show would form a team and play in the league. Very few women played. Most of us were just cheerleaders. (I didn't think to let this bother me back then.) We'd wear outfits inspired by our shows: The *Li'l Abner* gals would shout from the sidelines, dressed in shorts with patches and midriff tops with our hair in hillbilly braids.

One afternoon Iva and I were walking across the field to watch the guys from *Li'l Abner* play, and we saw a beautiful man in the outfield make an amazing catch. With the ball in his glove, he looked over his shoulder and flashed us an enormous smile. I said, "Oh my God. What a hunk! He's gorgeous! Who is he?"

"Val, he's completely your type," Iva said. Back then she was partial to blonds.

When we got to the dugout, we asked some of the players about the fantastic outfielder. "Oh, yeah. That's Tony Bogart," someone said. "He's a part-time actor but a great baseball player; worked out with the Dodgers during spring training. He's our ringer. We pull him in when we need to win."

I remember thinking, *What a name!* Tony Bogart. It takes guts to name yourself after Humphrey.

Many years after Tony and I had first gotten together, I was cleaning out an old appointment book and came across a business card I didn't immediately recognize. "'Tony Gardner,'" I read aloud. "Who is Tony Gardner?"

Tony overheard me. "I used to go by that name while I was teaching yoga in Laurel Canyon."

Suddenly, I remembered how I got the card. Shortly after Dick and I had moved to Los Angeles, a good-looking yoga instructor had tried to pick me up in a supermarket by giving me his card. I'd brushed him off but hung on to the card. "You hit on me when I was married!" I said, putting the pieces together.

"I had good taste," Tony replied.

I had really hit the jackpot with Tony. Love and romance, all that really good earth-shaking stuff that you dream about, were only part of the package. He was completely committed to me on every level as I was to him. We became a team in every possible sense—our lives were fully entwined—and we knew we would be together for the long haul. He named our first production company TAL Productions, which stood for Together at Last. Tony brought his four beautiful sons into my life. Michael, Ron, John, and another, younger Michael all accepted me wholeheartedly. His eldest, Michael, a committed social justice advocate, went on to become mayor of South Pasadena.

Not long after Tony and I started living together, I was cast in a really interesting movie directed by Paul Newman called *The Shadow Box*. The film was an adaptation of a Tony Award-winning Broadway play by Michael Cristofer. It followed three families dealing with hospice care of a loved one. The terrific and talented cast was comprised of Christopher Plummer, Joanne

Woodward (Mrs. Paul Newman), Melinda Dillon, Sylvia Sydney, Ben Masterson, and James Broderick, father of Matthew. James played my husband, Joe (yes, another Joe!). Paul arranged for the shoot to take place at a summer camp in Malibu Canyon, a short drive from our apartment.

To see Paul up close was an experience. Those famous eyes were everything they'd been purported to be—glacial, sparkly blue, but so warm. Warm ice? Who'd ever heard of such a thing? But it was true. Of course, Paul had a beautiful face to match his eyes. I had to concentrate very hard on what he was saying so as not to get distracted.

Paul was an absolutely marvelous director and approached the film as if we were staging a play. He was passionate about this project, and the budget permitted him to do it the way he wanted. He provided us with at least two weeks of rehearsal time before filming commenced, a rare and thrilling luxury. I have never in my life had the experience of rehearsing at such length for something that was going to be filmed, not presented onstage. It was tremendously gratifying.

There was a big gymnasium in the camp where we filmed. Paul had the floor taped off in sections as is customary when rehearsing a play. We began to run through our scenes, slowly growing confident with the material until we were able to go off book. As time went on, we were doing actual run-throughs, performing the entire movie from beginning to end without stopping. When filming approached, I said to him, "Paul, this is amazing. I feel that we've all become our characters. It's as if we've been running in Philadelphia for months and are now ready for Broadway."

As a director, Paul was both generous and thoughtful. He set an amazing tone on-set. His attention to detail and his respect for the cast and crew were unparalleled. He'd spent so much time on the other side of the camera that he knew precisely how everyone wanted to be treated. Every day at four in the afternoon, he would have popcorn made for everyone on set to lift our flagging energy for the remainder of the day's work.

I loved hearing him talk about Joanne in her role. "She always plays these brainy women—teachers or spinsters. But she's a gorgeous dish. I wanted her to show that off in this part," he said.

He and Joanne came to dinner at our apartment in Malibu. Paul was suffering from a chronically bad back. Tony instructed him to lie down on the floor and began to go through a series of relaxation exercises based on Kundalini yoga. When Tony was done, Paul exclaimed, "I feel sensational. I'm pain-free. My body was so relaxed, I felt like I was part of the floor." Then he stood up and grabbed me by my lapels. "Harper," he said, "do you know how lucky you are to live with this terrific trainer? I wish I lived with a great trainer." Paul Newman was complimenting my new boyfriend! I knew I had a keeper.

chapter
TEN

Tony and I stayed in the Malibu apartment only a year. The winter season was horrible. There were endless rainstorms and landslides that often made it impossible for us to get back to our home. The roads were blocked and closed for days at a time. Eventually, we had to take a suite in the Beverly Wilshire Hotel in order to be certain we had somewhere to sleep at night.

As much as I loved living at the beach, getting back and forth was a real problem—a long commute through horrendous traffic. I'd bought a house in the celebrated Malibu Colony as an investment property. It was an older house that needed a great deal of work. But we knew that we needed a more reasonable place to call home. I sold the house in the Colony and moved from the Malibu apartment to Brentwood, where Tony had found us a rustic little house once owned by the Goldwyn family.

Kenter Canyon in Brentwood reminded me of Laurel Canyon without the beads-and-moccasins vibe. Our house was on

Rochedale Lane, up on high ground, tucked into the hillside. It had lofty high-beamed ceilings, brick floors, and an expansive living room with a wall of sliding glass doors. Naturally, Gene flew out to help us decorate.

One major change in store for me in Brentwood was that Tony insisted we get a dog—the "best security system there is," he assured me. Ever since I'd bitten the delicious-looking tail of that yellow Lab who'd promptly bitten me back, I'd been scared of big dogs. Jesse, the shepherd-Lab mix Tony brought back from the ASPCA, was no exception. I insisted he stay in the kitchen.

Slowly, Jesse started making inroads deeper into the house. First the living room, then the bedroom, and soon he was sleeping in our bed. Before I knew it, I was mad about this big, floppy-eared sweetie.

Jesse was quite a character and had a serious case of wanderlust. The canyon was full of unruly vegetation, and many houses didn't have fences or gates. One night Tony and I were summoned to the yard of the neighboring house, where we found Jesse entwined with Benjamina, a black chow chow. Her owners, tired of her howling, had foolishly tethered her outside when she went into heat. She was easy pickings for all the neighborhood dogs. But it was Jesse who got caught in flagrante delicto.

To our horror, we discovered that the dogs had become stuck. While Benjamina's owner tried to separate them by hosing them down, I called the vet. He told me to immediately stop the hosing, lower our voices, and calm down. Our hysteria was making the dogs panic. He instructed me to position Benjamina so the dogs would be the same height. Once she was up on a low stone step—magic! Jesse and Benjamina simply walked away from each other.

But the deed had been done. About two months later, Benjamina gave birth to an eclectic litter of puppies. Some looked like terriers, some like chows, some like shepherds. We didn't want another dog, but our neighbors were trying to find homes for this motley crew.

"Tony," I said, "not only did Jesse mate with Benjamina, he got caught in the act. As the grandparents, we have to take at least one of the puppies." So Billy came into our lives. He was a pale sienna-colored darling little guy who fit into the palm of my hand.

After Jesse's dalliance with Benjamina, we knew we had to get him fixed. We didn't want him roving the canyon looking for available females. And we certainly didn't want to keep adding puppies to our canine family.

Even after Jesse had his operation, he kept wandering the neighborhood. Instead of mating, he started bringing home a slew of female dogs that were really long in the tooth. These "old-timers," as Tony dubbed them, would hang around our house, sometimes for weeks on end, until we could locate their owners. Eventually, Jesse brought home a chunky male named Paco—he wore a red bandanna around his neck and was constantly mounting Jesse. He was the quintessential "Latin lover" cliché and gave poor Jesse a taste of his own medicine.

After we moved to the Goldwyn house in Brentwood, I continued to work in movies, often traveling to shoot on location. When possible, Tony came with me. One evening as we were packing to leave for Monaco to film a TV special and attend a celebrity benefit tennis tournament, a call came from a shocked and tearful Angela. Dad had died of a heart attack while playing tennis on his court. I nearly fell over with disbelief.

We flew directly to Glen Rock, New Jersey, and were part of a traditional Italian-American three-day wake for my beloved father. It was comforting to be with family to acclimate to the shock of loss, and allow the memories to flow. The funeral parlor was overflowing with mourners and with gorgeous flower arrangements. My favorite one was made of white carnations in the shape of a four-foot-long tennis racket. I could almost hear my darling dad saying, "Go to Monaco and enjoy the tennis."

Not long after Monaco, Tony and I traveled to Brazil, where I filmed *Blame It on Rio,* starring Michael Caine, Joe Bologna, Michelle Johnson, and a newcomer named Demi Moore, who played my daughter. Fate seemed intent on reuniting me with Joe Bologna, with whom I'd costarred in *Chapter Two*. Yet again, we were playing extramarital lovers. This time I would be stepping out on my husband, played by Michael Caine.

Blame It on Rio was a remake of a somewhat risqué French comedy about two fathers (played by Joe and Michael) who take their daughters on a beach vacation. During the shoot, Tony and I lived in a wonderful hotel right on the Copacabana. It was lively and colorful during the day but a little seedy—not to mention dangerous—at night, when the streets were crawling with knife-wielding transvestite pickpockets.

I had been to Brazil once before, on a celebrity cruise with Dick and other Second City performers. During the trip, Ruth Buzzi, who is more fun than you can imagine, from NBC's *Laugh-In* and I became exercise and sightseeing pals. We had gone up to visit Corcovado—the magnificent gleaming white statue of Christ that overlooks Rio. The hilltop was shrouded in soft clouds. As Ruth and I approached, we saw just one other tourist enjoying the beauty. It was a big star we had both worked with—Rock Hudson. We all laughed so hard at the incongruity. Then Rock, in his best Old Testament-prophet voice, intoned, "And the swirling mist parted, and there appeared . . . Valerie Harper and Ruth Buzzi."

This time around, I saw much more of the country. Filming on location is always a wonderful experience. Since you are working, you get to know the city or country in a more intimate way than if you're a tourist, and you get to interact with all sorts of local people on the production. Our cheerful young driver, Nacimento, tried unsuccessfully to recommend restaurants to Tony and me. All of the menus were laden with red meat. I don't think he grasped the concept of vegetarian, let alone vegan.

Between filming and sightseeing, Tony helped me stick to my workout regimen. Every morning we went out for a run. Up and down the Copacabana beachfront we passed unremitting soccer and volleyball games that went on day and night. Rio de Janeiro is situated way, way back from the shoreline, so everyone in the city can enjoy this glorious, enormous beach. Running is an excellent way to get to know a new place fast. We often saw Demi on the beach with her bicycle. Her commitment to fitness, as well as health food, pleased Tony, and he admired her for keeping it up.

Demi was a very sweet kid. She was talented and had that special quality that was to one day become famous. I think she was going through a breakup while we filmed; she seemed a little fragile. Since we played mother and daughter in the film, it was natural for me to take on a parental role with her. When our director, Stanley Donen, grew understandably impatient with electrical power failures or construction noise, Demi assumed, incorrectly, that it was because of her performance. So I found a quiet corner where we could rehearse our scenes, run our lines, and gingerly inch ourselves off the actor's precipice of self-doubt.

Tony and I spent many wonderful evenings with Michael Caine. A favorite place of ours to have dinner was a French restaurant called Café Verde, which served the most delicious hearts of palm salad I have ever tasted. Michael was incredibly warm, terribly intelligent, and full of interesting stories about the places he'd traveled and the movies he'd made. In the film *Zulu*, in which he, a Cockney, was cast as a snobbish upper-class English officer, Michael said he mirrored Prince Philip's walk and demeanor to appear sufficiently aristocratic. (The prince, always accompanied by guards, walked with his hands clasped behind his back, having no need to use his fists to defend himself.) Actors do many things to bring authenticity to a part. I thought this one was particularly creative.

Even after decades in front of the camera, Michael's passion for acting hadn't waned. He came to the set every day full of enthusiasm and ideas. He was always looking for ways to improve his performance and get even more out of a scene. Michael was a pleasure to work with, a wonderful actor, and a delightful man.

The original movie on which *Blame It on Rio* was based was a sexy romp of a film that only the French could get away with. In some scenes, our version seemed like a borderline skin flick. It didn't help that the plot revolved around Michael Caine's character having an affair with his best friend's teenage daughter, played by Michelle Johnson.

It wasn't Michelle's fault that she was extraordinarily buxom, but Stanley Donen seemed never to miss an opportunity to have her bouncing about topless. There was a scene early in the film where Joe and Michael stumble upon their daughters, Michelle and Demi, at a topless beach and are duly embarrassed. Perhaps Stanley figured, "Well, we've seen her chest once, so let's see it again. And again." If not for Michael Caine's innate grace and elegant charm, which greatly minimized any offensive tone, the picture would not have worked at all, despite a truly funny Larry Gelbart script.

Several months after *Blame It on Rio* came out, I got a letter from a nun at St. Mary's Academy in Monroe, Michigan, where I'd gone in fifth grade. "I know you're a St. Mary's girl," she wrote, "so how could you appear in such a movie as *Blame It on Rio*?"

I wrote back and explained that I wasn't in any of the more explicit scenes, and I'd had no idea the director would have the young actress take off her blouse so many times. Sorry, Sister . . . and come to think of it, just how is it that you saw the movie?

While I loved doing films, Tony and I thought that it would be a sound career choice to develop a new TV show of our own. We had already done a two-hour dramatic pilot called *Farrell for the People,* which hadn't been picked up but proved to be a very good experience. I played Liz Farrell, an assistant DA in New York City based on Linda Fairstein, the pioneering head of sex crimes prosecution for twenty-six years. Linda, now the famed crime novelist, fourteen books so far, helped us enormously with the film. The two detectives with whom she worked closely were Charlie Bardong, played by Gregory Sierra, and Jay Lynam, played by Ed O'Neill.

It was shortly after *Farrell* that Mary remarried. Robert Levine, a Jewish doctor, was precisely what Ida would have wanted for Rhoda. Tony and I attended their elegant wedding at the Pierre Hotel in New York. Another reunion occurred on *The Love Boat* Nile River cruise with my old *Mary Tyler Moore* buddy Gavin MacLeod ("The Captain"). He tried to insist we take his state room, which was larger. Same sweetie. Tony and I both had parts in the show and the trip was beyond fascinating—seeing the ancient Egyptian sites, riding a camel, visiting exotic marketplaces. I saw a pretty, young shopper in her black traditional dress kneeling by a basket selecting fruit with one hand. In the other arm she held an infant and over her shoulder she balanced a sleeping two-year-old girl. This extraordinary mom gripped the sleeping child's dress firmly in her teeth to prevent a fall while getting the food shopping done. Touching. And on Mother's Day, too!

For years Tony had immersed himself in the business side of show business, an area I have little knowledge of and no interest in learning. As the head of our production company, TAL Productions, Tony arranged a meeting with Lee Rich, the president of a company called Lorimar. They were responsible for some of the most successful television series of the era, *Dallas, Knots Landing,* and *Falcon Crest.*

Lee suggested we team up with another production duo— Tom Miller and Bob Boyett, who had a deal with Lorimar to develop a show. Miller and Boyett had come off some major successes, *Happy Days* and *Laverne & Shirley,* and were interested in launching a new series. Lee thought that together we might come up with a vehicle in which I could star.

Tony set up shop for TAL Productions on the MGM lot right next door to Bob and Tom's office. They were eager to develop a show for me, and it was decided that Tony would come on board as co-executive producer. Bob and Tom generously shared their considerable experience and know-how with him.

Of the many ideas we tossed around, we decided on one we liked for a series. The beauty of the concept was its simplicity—a mom at home alone, coping with three boys. With such a basic canvas, there would be lots of room to explore different story lines. Nobody wanted the mother to be a widow, which seemed too sad; or divorced, which would lead to a lot of dating drama; this show was to be centered around family, around a mother's relationship with her sons. We decided to make the husband an airline pilot, a job that would excuse his frequent absences.

So the concept for *Valerie* was born.

Now we had to sell it to a network. This proved more difficult than we'd anticipated. CBS was interested in the show but was willing only to commission a pilot, with no guarantee that they'd pick up the series. NBC, however, offered to order a pilot and seven episodes. NBC it was, then. We knew we had to prove ourselves quickly to encourage the network to order additional shows. We got down to work, deciding stories, crafting the pilot. I was excited to be getting back into a series, especially one in which Tony and I would have creative input and control. I expected everything to go swimmingly, especially because I loved my young costars. They were wonderful kids and so much fun. Jason Bateman, an excellent actor even back then, played my eldest son, David. Danny Ponce and Jeremy Licht—both so talented—played my younger set of fraternal twins, Willy and Mark.

I had been involved in only two series before, both run by Jim Brooks, Allan Burns, and later, Charlotte Brown. I trusted entirely these three, their writing staffs, and their style of working. During the nine years they wrote for me as Rhoda Morgenstern, we never butted heads. Above all else, these writers set and maintained an atmosphere of creative give-and-take in which suggestions were welcome.

When we got down to rehearsing *Valerie,* I was in for a shock.

I was used to an open discussion among the writers, directors, and the actors. After we finished a run-through, the writers would whisper among themselves, then gather with the producers and staff, away from the actors, to talk about improvements. Then off they'd go to their offices to rewrite. It felt cold and corporate. I sorely missed the collaborative energy on the sets of *Mary Tyler Moore* and *Rhoda,* and I'm afraid I was guilty of pushing my way of preparing the show onto my colleagues.

One thing I don't regret was my requirement that we rehearse until a scene was really working and that everyone use their props. As Mary often warned, "You don't want any unpleasant surprises on show night." One time we were doing a winter scene, and I suggested the boys work with their mittens and scarves during the final run-though. The director thought it was unnecessary and nitpicky. I ceded the point. But that night in front of the audience, when the kids made their entrance, they were all tangled in their scarves and dropping their mittens. Mary's "unpleasant surprise." We had to stop the scene and reshoot. It's not simply a question of wasting time and money; rather, it's better for the live audience and the show if things go smoothly.

In addition to having a more rigorous rehearsal period, I also wanted *Valerie* to be funnier. After taping one middling episode, I went up to one of the staff members and said, "Hey, we filmed that whole scene and there wasn't a single laugh from the audience."

"Don't worry," he said, "there will be in post."

I couldn't believe it. Rather than make the material better

so the audience would react on show night, it seemed fine with him to add canned laughter in post-production. Coming from *Mary Tyler Moore* and *Rhoda,* where the audience's laughter was paramount, I found that attitude appalling.

Some of the episodes were terrific. I'm extremely proud of one very realistic, hilarious episode for which we won an award. It was an artfully written script about David (Jason Bateman) surreptitiously buying condoms. Serious subject matter like smoking, drugs, sex, and the pitfalls of modern adolescence can be communicated through comedy. Having raised Wendy and having spent a lot of time with Leah's kids, I understood how important these issues are to adolescents and their parents. I'd seen it all—moodiness, crushes, sibling rivalry.

In 1987, during a hiatus from the second season of filming, Tony and I took a trip to Italy. We were sitting in a café on Via Veneto, watching the high-class hookers stroll by, when Tony said, "Valerie, you should be a mother."

I'm not sure if it was the Chianti, the warm Roman air, or the fact that I wasn't a Mom but played one on TV that brought about the announcement, but I thanked him nonetheless.

"I think we should adopt," Tony concluded.

At forty-six, I'd pretty much accepted the fact that pregnancy wasn't in the cards for me. I had thought about adoption and was so happy that Tony was considering it, too. Since we had the wherewithal to give a child a wonderful home and upbringing, when we returned to Los Angeles, we began looking into adoption.

Through Tony's screenwriter friend Robert Klane, we discovered an amazing attorney named Durand Cook, a local lawyer who specialized in adoption. Durand was committed to bringing together children and parents to create a perfectly matched, mutually loving, newly organic family. We were thrilled to be beneficiaries of his knowledge, skill, and love. Durand assured us that it would be no problem matching us to a child. He handled domestic and international adoptions, both open and closed. Since I was famous, we decided to go with a closed adoption. Durand looked for a situation in which the birth mother wanted anonymity as well.

One day Tony called to tell me that Durand had found a little girl for us. That afternoon Tony came home with a photo album filled with pictures of the most adorable blond four-year-old child. Her story was an unusual one. Her birth parents' marriage ended in divorce and her mother, then in the Marine Corps, put the eighteen-month-old baby into private child care with a woman known as Nanny. Other children were in Nanny's care only during the day, but this little girl lived with her full-time.

When the birth mother left the service, she and her boyfriend traveled constantly for work and paid Nanny to take care of her child. When the little girl was approaching her fourth birthday, the boyfriend, who himself had been adopted, encouraged the mother to put her daughter up for adoption. They both agreed that it would be the best thing for the little girl.

Durand explained that the child would be flying from North Carolina to California that evening, and we could see how things went over the weekend. "Remember," he said, "unlike an infant, a four-year-old is a fully formed little person. Let's make sure this is a perfect fit." He told us that there were five other adoptive couples waiting in the wings, so we shouldn't feel any pressure if things didn't seem right.

Many couples only want to adopt an infant. But for us, her age was perfect. Over the years, I had grown accustomed to children of all ages coming to live with me. Wendy, Dick's daughter, moved in with us when she was thirteen and quickly accepted my role as her stepmother. My sister's children, Victor, Anton, and Tanya, had been staying with me off and on from the time they were babies. I was very comfortable taking on mothering duties at any stage in a child's life. With a four-year-old, we could avoid diapers, all-night screaming, and when she turned eighteen, we'd only be sixty instead of sixty-four.

We later learned the poignant fact that the birth mother had the painful duty of picking up the little one in North Carolina to bring her to California. When she and her boyfriend arrived at Nanny's house, the little girl asked, "Are you my mommy?"

"No, but I'm taking you to meet your mommy," she answered. It must have broken the mother's heart. She sat apart from her boyfriend and child. What an unbearable plane ride that must have been.

Although we had agreed to a closed adoption, Tony's curiosity got the better of him. He wanted to get a glimpse of the birth mother. Due to nerves, we made an illogical choice. Instead of Tony's SUV, we took my two-seater—a white Mercedes convertible I called Blanche. I was swathed in black—a black scarf, a black sweater, and black glasses. It was a warm March evening, but I didn't want to risk being recognized. Truth be told, I probably stuck out like a sore thumb. Since then a celebrity wearing a baseball hat and dark glasses at night has become de rigueur and is a veritable attention magnet! We pulled up to the curb outside Piedmont Airlines—in those days you could—and I slunk down in my seat.

Tony sneaked up to the gate—in those days you could—and lurked behind a pillar, not wanting to blow his cover. One of the first passengers off the plane was a tall, pretty redhead who ran over to sit with Durand. She seemed nervous and unsettled during their brief conversation. He gave her some papers, which she hurriedly signed, and then she ran off. Tony kept watch as every passenger deplaned. Finally a man with a goatee appeared holding a little girl in his arms.

When I saw Durand emerge from the terminal, I got out of the car, my heart thumping. He was carrying a beautiful blond child in a pink coat, holding a stuffed alligator (I still have that coat and that alligator).

When Durand reached me, he whispered, "Boom-Boom [her nickname], this is your new mommy."

She turned toward me and jumped into my arms. "Mommy, you picked me up!" she exclaimed. Every day at the day care where she lived, she had watched as parents came to get the other children. She had always been left behind, and now she, too, was being picked up. It brought tears to my eyes.

Just then Tony reached the car. "And this is your daddy," Durand said, pointing out Tony. "Daddy," she said, jumping into his arms.

Her openness was shocking and delightful. It was not at all as we had imagined. I had worried that she would be scared and shy. But she was remarkably agreeable and excited—so full of life, from the second she came off the plane. She adopted us on the spot. She sat on my lap and chatted the whole way home.

When Durand had told us that he'd found a child for us, Tony and I were in the process of moving from our house in Brentwood to a larger place in Beverly Hills to accommodate what we hoped would be our growing family. Our new house wasn't ready, and our old house was entirely in boxes.

We had rented a place in the Malibu Colony for the summer while the renovations were finished on the Beverly Hills house. We hadn't yet moved. On our first night as a family, Tony and I and our new daughter literally camped out among our moving boxes and wardrobe carriers in Brentwood.

Our little girl had been called by her nickname Boom-Boom because of her unceasing energy. Perfect for us! Her name was the classic Celtic name Siobhan, which the hospital had misspelled as "Sibeon." That's too close to "simian" and the inevitable schoolyard taunts. Obviously, she couldn't go by Boom-Boom Cacciotti, which sounded like either a stripper or a Sicilian boxer. And Siobhan Cacciotti wasn't too great, either. We felt that we should change her name, but she certainly needed to be a part of such a decision.

"Boom-Boom is a cute nickname," I said, "but would you like to have a real name?"

She immediately agreed.

"Well, let's pick one together," I said. "Something that sounds good with our last name."

"Yes," she concurred quite seriously.

"Would you like Carla, Mia, Christina?" Tony asked.

"I like Chris," she said, smiling. "You know, from *Cagney & Lacey*. She's blond, like me." She meant Sharon Gless's character, Christine Cagney.

So Boom-Boom became Cristina Harper Cacciotti. Initially, I chose the American spelling, Christina, but Tony's mother, Filomena, who was originally from Italy, sent a card that read, *Buonvenuto, Cara Cristina*. And her spelling stuck.

My sister, Ginger, Angela's daughter, a darling, lively twenty-five-year-old, happened to be in Los Angeles when Cristina arrived. Angela, who was back in New Jersey, gave Ginger marching orders to welcome Cristina. "Ginger, take my credit card and shop. I mean *shop*! I don't care if you max it out. I want you to go into every store and buy more than you can carry—dresses, toys, games, anything a four-year-old might want. I want you to walk into Valerie's house like Auntie Mame." Angela went about shopping for Cristina the same way she went about serving food: "You don't ask, you just put." (Translation: "You don't ask people if they'd like something to eat. You just put it out—and lots of it!") Ginger followed her mother's orders and swooped down on us with an avalanche of gifts.

Two days after Cristina arrived, we moved out to the pretty home right on the beach in the Malibu Colony and made an amazing discovery. There on the wall of the bedroom for Cristina hung a giant rosy pink neon-glass signature that read "CiCi." This was literally a sign! Durand had told us that we didn't need to be married to adopt, but we knew it would facilitate the process if we were; plus, we'd always intended to get married. And since the "baby" had already arrived, we arranged a quick shotgun wedding.

I took Cristina with me to pick out rings. It was going to be a three-ring ceremony, celebrating that we were now a trio. Cristina picked out a little gold ring with a tiny ruby. For Tony and me, I bought traditional gold bands. At the jewelry counter, I held Cristina in my arms so she could see into the display cases.

"Hey, Val! Who is this beautiful little person?" a voice near me asked.

I looked up and saw Shirley MacLaine. "Oh, Shirley, meet my daughter," I said. "A very recent addition."

Shirley fussed over Cristina for a while, then she and I got involved in our own conversation. Eventually, Cristina grew bored with all the adult talk and started tugging on my hair. "Mommy, Mommy, can we go outside?"

"I can't believe she's completely accepted me as Mommy so soon," I said to Shirley. "Can this be possible?"

"Val," Shirley said, "it's a miracle. Accept it. You are her mother, and she is your daughter. You two have found each other in the universe."

"Of all the people to have run into at this emotional, thrilling, and scary time in my life, who better than you, O spiritual one, Shirley MacLaine?" With a shake of the red hair, a flash of the famous smile, and a kiss for each of us, Shirley blessed this adoption.

The next day Tony and I were married by a female judge right on the beach in Malibu. My mother's presence was wonderful, as she was both welcoming Cristina into our family and witnessing my marriage to Tony. After all, she had missed my first wedding. Tony's eldest son, Michael, and my treasured friend Gene also joined us for the tiny, impromptu yet tender ceremony. At a beautiful beachside Malibu restaurant, we had our wedding dinner where Cristina was the belle of the ball.

When Tony and I decided to adopt, I prepared myself for a difficult transition, especially because the child coming into our home was four years old. The media tends to amplify horror stories of maladjusted kids rebelling against their new families. But with Cristina, it was effortless. She was so completely at ease with us in her new home. She was very comfortable talking about where she came from, her old life back in North Carolina, and Nanny's dog, Scooby-Doo. One of her favorite television shows was Jim Henson's *Muppet Babies*. Whenever the little Muppet Babies and their caregiver, Nanny, were all in a scene together, Cristina would point at the screen and say, "That used to be me."

That first summer on the beach was a magical time. I loved watching Cristina play in the sand in her little bathing suit. The sun made her beautiful blond hair even more golden. Whenever she got out of the water, her wet hair turned dark, and she'd rush over to me, holding strands of her wet hair in her hands. "Look," she'd say. "Now my hair is just like yours and Daddy's."

One night not long after Cristina came to us, I woke up in the middle of the night to her shouts. "Mommy! Daddy!" she cried. Tony and I rushed across the hall to her bedroom. Cristina was sitting up in bed. She didn't look the least bit terrified, sad, or troubled in any way.

"What is it?" we said, dashing to her bedside.

"Nothing," Cristina said. "I was just making sure you'd come if I called."

I admired her logic. She wanted to know where she stood with us. She was only four years old and couldn't possibly know how much she meant to us from the moment she leaped into our arms at the airport.

chapter
ELEVEN

Cristina made Tony's and my world complete. It was as if we had always been a family. If only our work lives could have been as perfect as things at home. Not long after the joyful arrival of Cristina, things on *Valerie* began to unravel. In 1987, before the third season, Tony and I entered into a serious contract dispute with Lorimar. Suffice to say, we had some extremely tough negotiations, but at the eleventh hour, we came to a suitable agreement, and I prepared to go back to work for season three.

As was customary, we filmed the show on a Friday evening, and I looked forward to the season ahead. On Monday morning, Gina Trikonis, the costumer for *Valerie,* was at my house energetically putting together outfits for the upcoming show. Incidentally, Gina, a spectacular dancer, was in the original Broadway company of *West Side Story* in 1956 (that I failed to be hired for!). Also, hearing her talk about her daughter Christina inspired me to consider the name for my new child. Kindred spirits, we were looking through shoes—and having fun doing it—when a call came from Lorimar. For reasons of their own, Lorimar wanted out of the deal they had made with Tony and me the previous week; they wanted to go back to before we had renegotiated and reached an agreement. They told me I should "walk away."

Gina and I were in complete shock. I had just been fired.

When I called Tony in a panic, he wisely advised me to calm down and do nothing until he reached our lawyer, Bill Hayes, a top name in entertainment law. Coincidentally, Bill was the attorney who had handled the creation of Lorimar years earlier. Bill told Lorimar, "You wrongfully fired Valerie. See you in court."

Being fired from our own show—an eponymous one, no less—was painful and humiliating. That night Tony and I sat on the floor of the unfinished bedroom of our house in Beverly Hills, with him holding me as tears ran down my cheeks. The floor was strewn with moving boxes and packing material. We sat in silence, mourning *Valerie*'s demise. I had to put it in perspective. That very week Joan Rivers's husband, Edgar, had killed himself, and a large passenger plane had gone down on its way to Los Angeles. These were the real tragedies. All we were confronting was people in our business behaving inappropriately.

During this period, I tried my best to hide my distress from Cristina. When she asked why I was crying, Tony said, "Mommy's feeling a little sad."

"Don't worry, Mommy," she said, putting her hand on mine, "I will hold you." This was the same thing she said whenever we saw something gruesome—like a nest of tarantulas—on television. I was so touched by the fact that Cristina took on the job of comforting me.

The following week, my good friend Carol Kane took me to lunch at a cozy spot called Trumps. A mutual acquaintance stopped by our table and asked me what had happened on *Valerie.* "Well," I said slowly, "I was fired."

After he left, Carol said, "You don't have to tell people you were fired. You could just say you left." Sure, that would have been less painful, but it wasn't true. And I didn't want to lie about what had happened.

My friends and coworkers supported me thoroughly, which was reassuring. Shortly after Lorimar made their decision, I called each of my three television sons. I didn't want them to hear it through the grapevine that their TV mom had been fired. Jason offered to make calls to have me reinstated, as did Jeremy and Danny. Danny's mother, Diane Ponce, went so far as to have a meeting at Lorimar on my behalf. As much as I wanted to be back on the show, I didn't want the kids mixed up in this.

Within days the rumor mill was in full swing. There were reports that I'd been unable to perform on show night—that I'd taken my anger out on my TV family, endangering the boys and throwing furniture. Since I was a woman, the ever popular accusation that I was unbalanced, hormonal, and menopausal was flying around.

These allegations were particularly upsetting because Tony and I were well into the adoption process, and we desperately wanted to avoid a public smear campaign by the rag sheets and a prolonged court battle. We certainly didn't want anything getting in the way of finalizing Cristina's adoption. Tony and I were afraid that one of the social workers who made random, unannounced visits to our house, checking up on Cristina, would be influenced by a slur in the gossip "press."

At the suggestion of my publicist, Michael Levine, I called a press conference. I sent out seventy-five handwritten letters inviting the press to attend. Michael told me that we needed to determine our SOCO (pronounced *socko*) "single overriding communication objective," one crystal-clear message to get across to the press. This was simple: to clear up the lies. I was going to demonstrate to them that, contrary to any rumors or allegations, I was perfectly stable, had done my job, and had been wrongfully fired.

There was a huge media turnout. They all listened as I read my statement with Barry Langberg, a lawyer from Bill Hayes's firm, by my side. Many members of the press knew me personally from having interviewed me for over eighteen years. I told them that Tony and I were not about to "walk away" from *Valerie*, as Lorimar suggested, and we were not going to let my reputation be ruined. Lorimar and NBC could expect a fight. We were going to court.

The first battle I had to face was over the name of the show, which NBC wanted to keep even after I was fired. My name! Needless to say, this wasn't acceptable. Get rid of me, but hang on to my name to maintain viewer loyalty? That wasn't going to happen without a lot of resistance.

We had a hearing to work out the issue. My lawyer Barry Langberg, a terrific litigator, came before the judge and said, "They fired her wrongfully, as we will prove at a later date, but they want to hold on to her name. If she goes, her name goes with her."

Opposing counsel stood up. "Valerie Harper is a second-rate actress. Nobody knows who she is. Her name means nothing."

The judge, a charming curmudgeon with a sharp wit, banged his gavel, silencing the opposing counsel. "Do not be pejorative in my courtroom," he said. "My wife loves Valerie. And she knows the show. When I hear *Valerie,* I think Valerie Harper. What other Valerie is there?"

"Valerie Bertinelli," Lorimar's lawyer said.

"Who's she?" the judge asked. "I'm inclined to have Ms. Harper take her name with her."

During recess, I told Barry I didn't want them to use my name. But he explained that my case could take years to come to trial. There was a huge backlog in the California court system at the time. He thought it was in the best interest of my career if we got to trial as quickly as possible. Both Lynn Redgrave and Raquel Welch had been involved in court cases that dragged on for years. Barry wanted me to be able to get back to work immediately. So he made an agreement with the Lorimar and NBC lawyers: They would be able to keep my name on the show if they would agree to share the costs of hiring a judge to hear the case. This was a perfect way to get the court case under way without a long delay.

Rent-a-judge (the colloquial name for this program) was a unique system in California designed to beat the backlog in the courts. It allowed the plaintiff and the defendant to split the cost for a retired judge who would preside over a case. We contracted Los Angeles Superior Court Judge William P. Hogoboom, and our court date was set to take place in about three months.

Between the hearing over the *Valerie* name and the court date for our trial, NBC offered me the starring role in *The People Across the Lake,* a television movie with Gerald MacRaney. The film, a murder mystery, was set to shoot in Vancouver, British Columbia, and I was reluctant to leave Cristina. Barry convinced me otherwise.

He explained that NBC's offer to hire me signals to the entire industry, the media, and the country that I am completely employable—not unprofessional or unstable, as was claimed. The very network I am suing wants to star me in their film.

So I went to Vancouver. And Tony took great care of Cristina. Working with Gerald MacRaney, "Mac," was a total pleasure and a great comfort to me at this harrowing time. A wonderful actor and such a good guy, Mac helped me through my anxiety about the impending court case. Over the course of the shoot, we had many engrossing conversations as we commuted back and forth from Los Angeles to Canada on weekends. During one of these flights, Mac described a gorgeous aquamarine and pearl choker that he was going to give to his fiancée, Delta Burke. He said, "She's got those gin-clear blue eyes that a man knows perfectly well, once he's lost in them he'll never find his way out." Tony and I were at their splendid wedding and Delta looked dazzling in the choker. It's been happily ever after for them ever since.

As a result of doing the film, I dropped my suit against NBC, which was exactly what they wanted. Since they'd hired me for a movie, I could no longer accuse them of blacklisting me and ruining my reputation. Now that they were out, the case would be between Lorimar and us.

In the suit, I claimed that Lorimar had wrongfully terminated me and ruined my reputation. Lorimar countered that my erratic and unprofessional behavior led to my firing. They alleged that during the final show I taped, I put the child actors at risk, and most important, I had been unable to perform.

Barry suggested that I ask some of my costars to make declarations on my behalf. When I called Judy Kahan, who played my neighbor on *Valerie,* to see if she would be willing to make a statement about my behavior on-set during that final show, she immediately replied, "How many languages do you want it in?" What a gal!

At Barry's request, Carol Burnett had generously agreed to help with testimony and to watch footage of the final taping of *Valerie.* Barry had won a case for Carol Burnett against *The National Enquirer,* which claimed that she had fallen down drunk out on the street. Carol, who has had a family member struggle with alcohol, couldn't stand the false allegations and went after the tabloid. With Barry's help, she achieved an amazing victory over the *Enquirer,* something no one had done before.

The depositions and the trial, which lasted over two months, were grueling. I was deposed at length—tedious and often painful questions about my time on-set and my strained relations with the writer-producers. My mother, who was sick with lung cancer, had moved in with us and was particularly ill during the trial. Every day I couldn't be with her because I had to be in court was a struggle for me; my lovely friend Norma Donaldson would come sit with my mother so she wouldn't have to be alone. When Norma was unavailable, Vera, our crackerjack Yugoslavian nanny, took care of both my mother and Cristina—my older and my younger blondes, as I used to refer to them. Vera, with her sparkling demeanor, was a sensational cook and had worked in several top-notch Roman trattorias. She kept everyone in our house well fed, well cared for, and smiling, especially during this difficult period.

Despite the help I received from both Norma and Vera, there were times when I didn't feel I should leave my mother's side. One day when my mom was really suffering, I called the opposing counsel and explained that I had to stay home. They were very gracious and canceled that day's deposition.

The lynchpin of the case was a tape of the final show I filmed—the show that Lorimar claimed directly led to my firing. Lorimar contended that my behavior that night was unstable and threatening. As often happens, cameras roll between takes on show night, so a complete document of the evening had been recorded. Before the trial, Barry called Carol Burnett as an expert witness to assess the evidence.

The scene that concerned Lorimar most was one in which I, as the mom, was supposed to scold Jason's character, David. They maintained that my acting was overly aggressive and that

I was out of control with my young costar. The director had asked me to do the scene three times, each time with a different intention.

Carol Burnett, an undeniable expert on television comedy acting, had already watched the tape of the entire evening. When she got to the three takes of the scene in question, her evaluation was: "This is great. She did the same scene three ways, so the producers had three choices when they edited it. She was soft with her son. Then she was tough on him. Then she was in between. One scene, three distinct ways. Not only is this a good performance, it's great."

Carol also had something complimentary to say about the raw footage of the evening—the filmed record of what happened between takes. "Look," she said, "Valerie doesn't seem angry or upset between takes. In fact, you can see her laughing with the boys and joking with the audience. She's going beyond her duties as an actress. This is not unprofessional behavior in the least."

The show's director, Howard Storm, also came to my defense and in court told the judge that he had instructed me to bring anger to the scene during one take. "That last take was a little soft, Val," he remembered saying. "This take, really let David have it." I had, appropriately, been taking his directions.

After Carol's powerful testimony, Lorimar had to take off the table their allegation that I was "unable to perform." It was clear I hadn't endangered the boys and that I'd comported myself professionally all evening. Soon all they were left with was the charge that I was unhappy in my job. People are unhappy in their jobs all the time, but they don't get fired for it. Truth be told, I wasn't unhappy. I wanted our contract upheld.

An executive from Lorimar accidentally tilted the verdict in my favor when she got on the stand and admitted that Lorimar had never bothered to draw up a long-form contract with me. We had signed a short-form contract, which is an interim agreement. But the parties involved were required to sign the official long-form document if the series was to proceed. An old friend from *The Mary Tyler Moore Show* days, Sue Cameron, was very helpful when she took the stand to verify specific contract terms.

Barry had complete command of the courtroom. He was a tremendous counselor with amazing attention to detail. He saw us through to victory. The court ruled that I'd been wrongfully fired and that Lorimar was to be held accountable.

The next day there was an enormous picture of me on the cover of the *Los Angeles Times* business section, under the heading: "SHE WON!"

I felt vindicated. I had beaten Lorimar and reclaimed my reputation. All the false claims that had been bandied about before and during the trial could be put to rest. The industry and the public no longer suspected I was an unstable actress on the verge of a breakdown. It was proven that I had been wrongfully terminated. As Bill Hayes, the dean of entertainment law, said, "Val, not since Bette Davis took on MGM has a female actor taken on a huge Hollywood corporation." I'd stood up for myself and Tony had stood right up with me. Thanks to Barry Langberg and our excellent legal team, we won.

I'm sure there were people out there without the facts who viewed me as a greedy actress suing for more money, but money was not the primary issue. Fair treatment was. I had been wrongfully fired, and now the public knew. Even today, entertainment lawyers refer to the Valerie Harper case as being beneficial to actors because it's now harder for studios to back out of short-form contracts.

The judge awarded me a substantial settlement for loss of income for season three of *Valerie*. He also ruled that I was to be a profit participant on future syndication. Although mine was by no means an earth-shattering case, winning was a huge deal for me. Since Barry had ensured that the trial would take place as soon as possible, my career could get back on track, and business could resume as usual. No one was happier about this than Mom. She laughed out loud and shook her weak little fist: "You kids did it! You won!" This was pure joy—joy that we were able to experience together.

Now that the case was settled, I was free to stay at home with my daughter as well as with my mother, who was entering the last months of her life. I didn't want to miss out on precious time with her because of some legal entanglement. My mother was furious about her lung cancer. She had never smoked, and as a nurse, she had devoted her life to taking care of others. It just didn't seem fair. This was her second go-round with cancer, too. She'd been diagnosed with encapsulated lung cancer five years earlier and had invasive surgery to remove the tumor.

My mother was still working as a nurse in San Francisco when her cancer returned. Way back before PETA, I'd given her a full-length, white mink coat that gave her such pleasure. In her dramatic fur, she came to be known as the Queen of Polk Street, as she was an extremely popular "gal."

Living in San Francisco and working in the nursing profession, my mom had lots of devoted friends, many of them gay men. She called them her "lavender boys" because it seemed more respectful to her. When her illness progressed to a point where it seemed best for her to come live with me, I threw her a going-away party in her San Francisco apartment building. The party room was wall-to-wall gay guys, all of whom were excited to see Rhoda Morgenstern in the flesh, but even more interested in seeing off their beloved Iva. I dressed my mother in her favorite dress and did her makeup. All of Polk Street turned out for the party—waiters, bartenders, pals, nursing colleagues. It was a terrific send-off.

Tony and I moved my mother into the ground floor of our house in Beverly Hills. I converted an office into a comfortable bedroom and decorated it with favorite items from her San Francisco apartment. Our dogs, Jesse and Billy, often sat with her, keeping her company and standing guard.

Her condition worsened by the day. As she grew sicker, she began to imagine that she was at sea. "Valerie," she said, "that air! It's just wonderful. Don't you love the smell of the salty ocean air, Tony?" Then she'd comment on how adorable Cristina was. She had a fascinating way of weaving this imaginary shipboard experience right in with reality.

If Jesse and Billy wandered into the room, she'd say, "It's so wonderful that the captain allows dogs on board this ship, don't you think? You know, this is such a stable vessel, I barely feel it moving."

One afternoon my mother asked me, "What does 'three bells' mean?"

"Oh, Mom, are we back on the ship?"

"What ship?" she said. "We're in your house. I just want to know what 'three bells' means."

I was trying to enter her fantasy, but she just wanted a straight answer about naval timekeeping. I felt the fool! But, oh, it was funny.

One day Mom was in extraordinary pain. She asked me to give her enough morphine, enough to end her life. Her doctor had told me how to handle the situation.

"Mom," I said. "Why don't you take the regular dose now, wait a couple of hours then see if it's still what you want to do."

In two hours, I came back into her room, praying that she had changed her mind about the morphine, and asked how she was feeling. "What time is *Perry Mason* on?" she asked.

"In about an hour," I said.

"Okay, let's watch *Perry Mason* instead." It seemed like a better option than assisted suicide.

Another day Mom took my hand and said, "Val, I'm so sorry you have to preside over this death watch."

"Listen, you," I said, "when you're dead, it will be a death watch. But you're alive, so it's a life watch."

She had taken care of terminal patients throughout her career, and she knew firsthand how draining it could be. One morning when I came into her room, she said brightly, "This is the best day of my life." Then she told me about a dream she'd had. "It was wonderful, Valerie. I saw Mom and Dad and Aunt Kate and all my uncles. We were at a picnic on a hill, eating delicious food. Everyone was wearing white dresses and suits and we were all laughing. I'm not afraid of dying anymore, because I know where I'm going." My whole life, she had been such a positive fun-loving person. She always tried to see the good in everyone and everything. Two days after her dream, she died.

Tony and Cristina were out on the lawn when Mom passed. I signaled to Tony that it had happened, and they returned to the house. Cristina ran up to me. "Mommy, Mommy," she said. Then she looked at Tony. "What's my line?"

"I'm sorry Grandma died," Tony said.

"I'm sorry Grandma died," Cristina repeated to me earnestly.

It was so wonderful that I couldn't help but smile. *What's my line?* Clearly, she's the daughter of a theater couple.

I was deeply saddened by my mother's passing. Even though I was prepared, it was still a wrenching final good-bye. During the last weeks of her life, she had become so fragile and wasted away from her illness. Carl Reiner told me, "When a parent dies of something slow and painful, for a while you will remember how she was when she died. But then that image fades, and you'll remember her as she was before."

Carl was right. When I think of her now, she's wearing her

pretty red dress, pounding out a ragtime tune on the piano, or she's sashaying in that white mink coat. Then there is her boisterous, heartfelt laugh, the costumes she sewed me, the air baths, "The Blue Danube" on her record player, her patient smile during the hours and hours of ballet lessons she watched. Rhoda and all my other successes gave her such pleasure. It is impossible for me to even reflect on my career or on my life without thinking about my mother's part in it.

chapter
TWELVE

In 1990, a few years after we won the court case, I was offered a deal at CBS to develop my own show. Both Tony and I really admired Paul Haggis, one of the talented writers and directors of the hit show *thirtysomething*. (Today, of course, he is an Academy Award winner.) We were delighted to discover that he was eager to partner with us.

Paul came up with a fantastic idea for a show called *Desperate Women* that involved four women from one family living together under one roof. My character was a political wife originally from Brooklyn whose politician husband has left her and their teenage daughter. The other women were my recently widowed mother, my aunt, a nun who has lost her faith, and a Southern-belle divorcée friend. I absolutely loved the script and was excited to be part of a show featuring such strong female characters.

CBS was on board at first, but then their enthusiasm waned

and they wanted to bring in a new team of writers to develop another half-hour comedy. Tony, as producer, stood firm. He and I both felt that it was wrong for the network to lose such a fine writer just because they'd gone sour on the project. "We love Paul and his writing," Tony said, "and we've been working with him all year. How about you give him another chance to come up with different material?"

Paul, an extremely prolific writer, had another idea that he turned into a show called *City*. It was an unusually funny script with a touch of zany. I played the city manager of an unnamed metropolis dealing with budget cuts, corruption, and bureaucracy. LuAnne Ponce, the sister of Danny Ponce, who played my son on *Valerie*, was cast as my daughter on *City*. We both dyed our hair auburn so we would look even more alike.

One of my favorite episodes guest-starred adorable Estelle Getty (Sofia on *The Golden Girls*) as a very confused former city manager. In between rehearsals for *City*, we shared funny theater stories, as Estelle had, like me, started out on the New York stage. She loved telling one story about a handsome young man with a ton of sex appeal and no talent who was cast as a Roman centurion in some gladiator period musical. He was to knock on the city gate and say his one line. A ball of nervous tension, he pounded so hard on the gate that the entire set, fake stone walls and all, crashed down onto the stage. When the laughter from the audience and cast subsided, this foolish kid belts out his line: "Open up, in the name of Rome!" All week every chance she got, Estelle repeated the ill-fated line to me, even slipping a note under my dressing room door. She was such a doll—a kind, wonderful, completely genuine person.

A wild collection of exuberant, unpredictable, and some certifiable characters populated my office at city hall, and the on-screen relationships were witty and eccentric. All of the actors were really super in their roles, and we were lucky enough to have Allan Burns come on board as a consultant.

Paul was incredibly quick and funny, capable of producing brilliant material consistently. *City* was smart and dealt with a number of issues, from socioeconomic discrepancy to political ethics. Since the network wanted the show on the air quickly, we had to produce it in about half the usual time. Paul spent all weekend in the editing room, getting the show ready for that Monday's evening airtime. *City* burst into the Nielsen top ten, where it stayed for a few weeks. But slowly, ratings began to decline. Although we had reasonable numbers for the duration of our thirteen-episode first season, CBS didn't renew us for the fall.

It was a big disappointment. *City* was a strong show and well received, and I felt that if we had been given the chance, we would have picked up speed in the second season. CBS thought otherwise. When we were canceled, Paul threw a wonderfully raucous party at the Reseda roller rink with pizza and a huge cake. I think I ate six pieces, using the show cancellation as an excuse. I was sad to see this fabulous group break up. I had so hoped that we would make a go of it together. The cast and crew said our good-byes, and we all moved on to new projects.

Throughout the 1980s I starred in numerous television movies and often Tony and I took Cristina on location, many times to New York City. She loved hotel life (room service, tiny shampoo bottles, mini-bar goodies) and one time my new motherhood was sorely tested. Flipping around the TV channels my precious little daughter landed on a late-night porn channel where the scene was a group orgy! Horrified, I quickly changed the channel saying, "Oh, that's boring." Then I thought, *I'd better "parent up,"* and I casually asked, "What was that?" and Cristina said, "I think they were trying to be models." Whew! Close call!

After *City,* I also did many guest spots, including a *Perry Mason* movie special that Mom would have loved! My *madrina* (Italian for stepmom) Angela was celebrating Ginger's wedding to a handsome Irish-American, Jim Gilmartin, in what used to be known as a "mixed wedding." All three Cacciottis were part of the wedding party. The reception was a fabulous "do" in the Grand Ballroom of the Plaza Hotel with two hundred guests, including the *Mary Tyler Moore* cast mates who could make it, Gavin and Georgia, plus my second family, the Almogs. Penny and I teared up about her wedding having been on the same day Ginger was born.

I did one outrageous part on a show called *Promised Land,* which starred my good pal Gerald (Mac) MacRaney. *Promised Land* was written and produced by the *Touched by an Angel* super-talented team, Martha Williamson and Jon Andersen. The show was a family drama that filmed in the environs of Salt Lake City, Utah. I was cast as an eccentric children's book writer, an eclectic dresser who wears crazy flowing robes and lives a wildly unorthodox life and turns out to be a cocaine addict. Go figure. In the script, Mac's young son is fascinated by me and comes over to my mysterious mansion. The first time, he encounters me sitting on my porch flanked by two enormous snarling black dogs. The next time, I'm sitting in the backyard with a lion. I'd gotten over my fear of dogs and in fact had recently added a third canine to our family—a ball of white fluff named Archie. But a lion? It was going to be an interesting shoot.

I got to Utah a couple of days early. The director told me that I should drive out into the desert to a ranch and meet Simbi, my feline costar. When I heard the name, I breathed a sigh of relief. Simbi was clearly a miniature Simba. I was expecting to meet a diminutive, playful cub.

Out at the ranch I was greeted by a tanned, blond, long-haired husband and wife named John and Bev Pinder who had rescued Simbi when he was little. They told me all sorts of charming stories about their lion—how bonded he was to their dog, a crazy black mutt called Edsel, and how much he enjoyed frolicking with their cattle. They gave me some fragrant branches of herb that Simbi enjoyed, so he would like me and feel safe with me. I went around to the back of their house, ready to meet this gentle creature.

Simbi was no cub. He was an enormous four-hundred-pound lion, a veritable king of the jungle. He was massive and pretty terrifying. The couple instructed me to approach him holding out the branches. When I got within reach, Simbi lowered his head and put his mouth around my ankle. Not a bite, just a hold.

"Do not move," John said.

I didn't. Did the guy think I was nuts?

"Simbi, let go." Slowly, the lion released his jaws. Later that evening, bruises welled up under my skin.

The couple had a very strange method for getting Simbi to obey. Bev would wield a pink and teal plastic lawn chair while saying, "Bad lawn chair. Bad lawn chair." That giant beast was petrified of a cheap, spindly chair. To him, it was worse than a whip. While she waved the lawn chair, John held a vacuum hose. He had only to show Simbi the vacuum cleaner to make the lion cower.

When it came time for me to film the scene with the lion, the Pinders were ready with their strange tools. They stood nearby, lawn chair and vacuum at the ready. The stage manager took all necessary precautions. The craft services trailer was shut down. There could be no cooking smells or sounds of clattering dishes. The crew was instructed to wear gloves to minimize noise. They even went so far as to banish menstruating women.

Luckily, Simbi performed without a hitch. He didn't snarl or growl; nor did he open his jaws. The lawn chair and the vacuum did not come into play. But Simbi was definitely my scariest costar. And I've had some doozies.

In one telephone scene, an actor I was working with was told by the director to "let the anger out" and pulled the prop phone out of the wall, taking a chunk of the wall with it. It took an hour to repair the set and reattach the phone. Another well-known actor I worked with on a television show was a sweetheart all morning, helping me with my role. After lunch, he became a snarling, furious lunatic. Major Jekyll and Hyde demonstration! I think he'd hit the Scotch at noon.

After my harrowing guest spot on *Promised Land,* I did a couple of pilots that didn't get picked up. It was becoming harder and harder to get a show onto network TV. I also appeared on a short-lived, but excellent, comedy called *The Office* (different *Office*), written by Susan Beavers, who now writes *Two and a Half Men.* It was a very clever sitcom about a secretarial pool and interoffice politics. It was great fun to be directed by Jay Sandrich again and to work with a terrific actress, Debra Jo Rupp, who later played the mom on *That 70's Show.* When *The Office* was canceled after six episodes, I began to entertain the notion of getting back into theater. I missed the stage and thought that perhaps the fates were telling me it was time to return.

As so often happens, out of the blue, I got a call from a man named Julian Schlossberg who was a producer on an off-Broadway show called *Death Defying Acts,* a collection of three one-act plays written by David Mamet, Elaine May, and Woody Allen. The show had been running for six months, and they were looking to bring in an entirely new cast. Julian, a truly lovely guy, wanted me to replace Linda Lavin in the May and Allen plays. Here were Linda and I changing places once again, and not for the last time. Although Linda and I look nothing alike, fans often mistake us, asking me how Mel from *Alice* is doing and asking Linda, "How's Bren?"

It was a perfect reentry into theater. *Death Defying Acts* featured an ensemble cast portraying delightful nutcases on the verge of nervous collapse while facing their own mortality. It was witty and mischievous, written by three gifted playwrights at the top of their game. The show was running at the Variety Theatre, a historic off-Broadway theater on Third Avenue, which once showcased vaudeville, burlesque, and later porno movies. Ah, the ever changing face of Manhattan.

Our family moved to New York. We rented an apartment in the Tower Records building on Fourth and Broadway in the Village. It was a real show business building. Diane Keaton, Cher, and Tempestt Bledsoe (of *The Cosby Show* fame) had all been tenants at one time. Our duplex was owned by Thomas Keneally, the gifted Australian author of *Schindler's List*. His previous tenant had been Jude Law.

Cristina, now twelve, was excited by the move. She loved our apartment because she had her own little bedroom and bathroom, accessed by an open stairway. The day we moved in, she discovered a clear shower curtain in her bathroom with a funky black design. "Mommy, can we keep this?" she asked, unfurling the curtain. Stretched wide, the pattern revealed itself: SEX printed in giant black letters across the clear plastic.

"Sure, honey," I said. "But we have to wash it first."

"Okay, Mom. But don't worry. I'm sure Jude Law is a very clean person."

Cristina didn't just love the apartment; she loved New York. On weekends, she often visited Angela and Ginger in New Jersey. We enrolled her in the seventh grade at the exquisite Grace Church School, built by the same architect who designed the famous St. Patrick's Cathedral. The school was walking distance from our house, a few blocks north on Tenth and Broadway.

I was able to walk to the theater on Third Avenue between Thirteenth and Fourteenth streets, where *Death Defying Acts* played, so my entire world was centered in the Village. In my fifties, I suddenly had the bohemian downtown life that Iva and I had dreamed of when we were eighteen-year-old dancers. My treasured longtime friend Gene lived around the corner on Lafayette in what had been Enrico Caruso's building. Whenever possible I spent time with him and his partner, Lad, who was an artist. Although we never saw Caruso, Gene and I once shared a glimpse of a pale blue figure whom we presumed to be the ghost of Lady Astor. She, too, had lived in Gene's building. Dressed in a long gown and bonnet, she would walk into his closet as she put on her gloves. Later on, Gene, who saw her often, found out that his closet had originally been the door to the hallway she would have taken to go out.

The minute after relocating to New York, I started rehearsing with my new cast mates, Kelly Bishop, John Rothman, Brian Reddy, Aasif Mandvi, Paul O'Brien, Tari Signor, Cynthia Barlow, and Dan Desmond. There was barely enough time to prepare before opening night. Woody Allen's act was about an Upper West Side woman whose husband leaves her for a much younger girl. It was, as you can imagine, classic Woody—ripped from his own headlines.

In Elaine May's play, I was a depressed hooker on hold with a suicide hotline. Elaine's writing was hilarious and so insightful about the difficulty of getting through bureaucracies like the phone company. The only trouble was, Elaine's piece featured numerous page-length telephone monologues that I had very little time to learn. With phone calls, you have to learn the lines and intentions of the person on the other end of the call. Yes, double memorizing.

At night, after rehearsal, I'd head over to Washington Square Park and walk around the perimeter with Archie, our snow-white American Eskimo (sort of a spitz), on his leash, running my lines aloud until past midnight. This was before everyone had cell phones, when a person talking to herself on the street still looked crazy. Although, in the Village I think I came off as commonplace. Sometimes Tony watched me from a distance, making sure I didn't get mugged and Archie didn't disturb the peace with the shrillest barking ever heard on earth. Occasionally, he had to come out to the park and drag me back to the apartment when it got too late.

Learning the monologues was difficult and frustrating. I had no choice but to pinch my buns together and get down to it, memorizing pages and pages of text so that the words flowed from idea to idea. Some actors strategically place crib sheets around the set, on tables, on the backs of chairs, wherever, to prompt them. I have never felt that would work for me, especially since I'm nearsighted. I was also afraid that this theater was small enough that the audience would be able to see if there were notes anywhere. I devised a strategy with the stage manager. He would stand just offstage and if I got lost, I'd simply walk in character to the wings, continue speaking into the phone and say, "I don't know what you're saying," while staying in character. God bless him, the stage manager would always throw me a whispered line, and we'd be back on track. Before long, I no longer needed the "walk to wing" survival system.

Death Defying Acts was directed by the extremely talented Michael Blakemore, a witty and wise Australian. He had directed the first cast and was rushing to prepare the replacements in time. He knew that we were pushing our luck. On opening night he said, "Ladies and gentlemen, we haven't had enough time. Godspeed."

After the first few performances, the whole cast started to get our sea legs. Whenever Cristina came to the show, which was frequently, she would be the first to jump up and give me a standing ovation on my bow. I suggested she let the audience stand if they wished to. "But Mom, sometimes they're shy. If I stand, they'll all follow." My own little ovation shill!

Once I'd mastered my roles, *Death Defying Acts* was great fun to play. However, there was one dreadful occurrence during the run. It was the only time in my entire career when I missed a cue. I was backstage chatting with crew members when Kelly Bishop came into the hall, yelling my character's name: "Carol! Carol!" I rushed onstage. John Rothman started shouting, "Carol, where have you been?"

I could see how angry he was—and with good reason. "In the

bathroom," I yelled back, joining John in trying to play it off for the audience.

It was the most horrible, humiliating feeling to have left my fellow players stranded out onstage, adrift. With my carelessness, I had endangered the play. I had never missed a cue before and haven't since.

When my off-Broadway run ended, Tony and I decided to remain in New York. We sold our house in Beverly Hills and rented my sweet friend Carol Kane's apartment on Central Park West and Sixty-fourth. Several luminaries lived in the same building, including Madonna. Cristina enrolled in high school at the Convent of the Sacred Heart at East Ninety-first Street and Fifth Avenue, and our lives resumed uptown.

During the run of *Death Defying Acts,* Tony started looking around for material that he could develop into a theater piece for me. As with *Valerie,* he thought it wise to have ownership in a project and not just be a gun for hire, so to speak.

Inspiration comes from the most unexpected places. Every year we received a Christmas card from Carol and Dom DeLuise on behalf of Pearl S. Buck International, a humanitarian organization devoted to fighting prejudice and cultural intolerance, as well as facilitating international adoption. "You know, Val," Tony said, looking at the pretty white-haired woman surrounded by beautiful mixed race children on our yearly card, "she seems like a fascinating person. I bet you could play Pearl."

I was interested because Pearl Buck had been my mother's favorite author. She seemed like a great subject to dramatize and someone worth investigating. Tony drove out to Bucks County, Pennsylvania, and met with Janice, Pearl's living daughter. He got her blessing to begin to develop a play about her mother.

The more I learned about Pearl's life, the more passionate about the project I became. A daughter of missionaries, Pearl was taken to China as a baby and raised bilingual. After coming home to attend Randolph-Macon Woman's College in Lynchburg, Virginia, Pearl returned to China to care for her ill mother. There she met John Lossing Buck, an agricultural specialist. They married and moved to a small town in rural China. Her experiences with peasant life there became the inspiration for her Pulitzer Prize-winning novel, *The Good Earth*. Later, she became the first American woman to win the Nobel Prize for literature.

In 1934 Pearl and her family returned to the United States to escape the fallout from the struggle between the Nationalists and the Communists, which had created an unstable environment for Westerners. While Pearl continued to write prolifically, she became a champion of many humanitarian causes, especially cross-cultural understanding and racial harmony as a means of achieving world peace. She was an outspoken supporter of the civil rights movement in the United States.

Since she had such an unusual background, referring to herself as "culturally bifocal," and had accomplished so much, I was drawn to Pearl's story. Tony and I thought it would be interesting to develop a one-woman show that incorporated many of the fascinating characters from Pearl's life—her Southern mother; her elderly nanny, Wang Amah; and Tzu-Hsi, the Dragon Lady empress of China. He got in touch with Marty Martin, who had written the one-woman show *Gertrude Stein Gertrude Stein Gertrude Stein* for the wonderful Pat Carroll. Marty got to work writing the play, which he called *The Dragon and the Pearl*.

After Marty completed a draft, we started to workshop it. Developing a one-person show is a slow process that involves a lot of researching your subject and reworking the script. The first director we hired, Kathy Berlin, who ably started us out on this process, suggested that I try working with an earpiece so I could be fed lines if needed during performances. But the sound in my ear only confused me. I wanted to think the thought, feel the feeling of the character, and have the lines right there without struggle or tension.

Also, I knew that if I momentarily lost my way, I'd paraphrase to get me through the moment. I knew the story, after all. And I was the only one onstage. I could improvise without fear of confusing other actors. I was thankful for all those years of Second City improvisational training under the tutelage of Viola Spolin and Paul Sills. They gave me the tools to perform the show when my lines weren't as absolutely solid as they should be.

The first thing Tony had to do was find us a venue. He picked up a directory of American regional theaters and began cold-calling them. He explained the nature of the play and that I was the star. Since *The Dragon and the Pearl* was in the development stage, we wanted to start in a small theater, work out the kinks and see what we had before we brought the show to a bigger city. I had no idea that Pearl would take us on a journey of several years.

Tony booked our first tryout at a summer theater in New Hampshire that had a roof made of corrugated iron. When a New England downpour hit during a performance, I could not make myself heard over the pounding on the metal roof. The audience was very goodnatured and would wait out the deluge while I walked around the stage in character, occupying myself with props (books, files, tea!) until the rain abated.

We stayed in New Hampshire for five weeks in a large, comfortable cottage next to the woods. Cristina spent hours checking Archie for ticks while I diligently checked her. After Marty completed more rewrites, we brought *The Dragon and the Pearl* to Chicago with yet another excellent director, Susan Booth. What a hardy breed Midwestern theatergoers are—wrapped up in parkas and mufflers like mummies. Through the blizzards they came! One gave me an invaluable tip about walking on ice-covered sidewalks. Having watched me fall twice in one block, this kind fellow called out, "Hey, don't pick up your feet!" It worked. I shuffled along and reached the theater without falling a third time. Once during our run there was a complete blackout in the theater and the Chicagoans all stayed in their seats as I finished the show "radio style" in the pitch black.

Despite the supportive audiences, the show still wasn't working. So it was back to the drawing board once again. Back at home in New York, through Joanne Woodward, we met a gifted young director named Rob Ruggiero who was interested in working on the play. Under his direction, we brought the show to Cambridge to the Hasty Pudding Theater in Harvard Square. Rob had a terrible time hearing me in rehearsal as the Krokodiloes, the Hasty Pudding's a cappella group, were singing at the top of their lungs next door.

When we returned to New York to rework the material we mutually decided to part company with Marty. Tony and I were still committed to finding a way to tell the great story of Pearl S. Buck. My husband was determined to see our project through to a New York City theater and when he decides to do something, rest assured, it gets done.

Through Rob we found a talented playwright named Dyke Garrison with whom I could collaborate. I had read most of the over one hundred books Pearl had written and I had done an extensive amount of research on her. For two months, Dyke, Rob, and I gathered around my kitchen table on Central Park West and created the show from the multifaceted elements of Pearl's life. Rob, a terrific dramaturge, kept pushing us to "find a strong dramatic event" and "a more powerful first act break."

We decided to open the play with Pearl as an old woman at her home in Bucks County, waiting for her visa to arrive so she could visit China. Pearl had written so openly against the Communist Party that she had become persona non grata, barred from the country she had loved for many years and where her parents were buried. Suddenly, we had a through line. As she waited for the visa, memories would return to her—eighteen different voices. A knock from her secretary on the door would trigger a memory of when Pearl and her family hid from the Chinese Kuomintang as they searched villages, looking to execute foreigners. A host of characters parade through Pearl's life. We called this new version *All Under Heaven,* taken from a Confucian saying that states that everyone on earth is all one family regardless of race, religion, or gender. It was also the title of Pearl's final book.

Tony came up with the brilliant idea of asking Pearl's alma mater, Randolph-Macon Woman's College, to host the first production. Pearl is a beloved figure on campus, so the school was more than willing. The students built sets and did a lot of the tech work, and we opened to much regional fanfare. The run was such a success that we extended it.

When we knew we were ready to bring the play to New York, Tony asked the college to back us. He offered them a deal they couldn't refuse. It was advantageous for them in terms of publicity for their prestigious but small college, as their name would be tied in to the production. The very set built in Lynchburg, Virginia, by their young female students would appear on the New York stage. We opened in an off-Broadway theater on Fifteenth Street called the Century Center for the Performing Arts. It was a beautiful space that had a Victorian atmosphere with wall sconces designed to resemble gas lamps. It was perfect for Pearl.

The theater was a little jewel and, like many old New York buildings, had a small behind-the-scenes mouse infestation. I could hear the little guys scurrying around as I performed. The problem got so bad that the stage manager had to set out glue traps. As I made my entrance for my very first New York preview performance, I stepped in one of those damn traps and came clattering onto the stage with the thing stuck to my shoe. I floundered for a second, then played it as if Pearl were angry with her renovation contractors for leaving traps around her house. Rob rushed backstage at intermission, appalled but pleased about the energy it lent to our opening scene! Apparently, Pearl's agitation played well with the audience. However, I had to go through the evening in stocking feet.

The esteemed television journalist-host Charles Gibson, whose wife was an alumna of Randolph-Macon Woman's College, hosted an elegant opening-night party. Mary and Robert, Iva and Ron, Nicole, and other pals were there. We got lots of great press coverage, including a segment on *Entertainment Tonight* and a terrific review in *The New York Times* that allowed us to open the play in many other venues after the New York City run.

In the 1990s while I was doing television movies and guest slots, Tony was hard at work building and opening a charming Italian restaurant on La Cienega Boulevard that he named Regina Coelia, after an infamous Roman prison. As I was packing to fly to Chicago for a three-episode guest appearance on the TV series *Missing Persons* starring Daniel Travanti, the 6.7 Northridge earthquake hit. After the initial jolts, Tony rushed with a ten-year-old Cristina to check on the restaurant, which was minutes away from our Beverly Hills home. No structural damage, but olive oil as far as the eye could see, mixed with wine, broken dishes, smashed glasses. Cristina, an accomplished ice skater, said, "Daddy, it's like the rink!"

After four years with New York as our base, we had decided to return to the West Coast, where Tony produced *All Under Heaven* in Los Angeles.

We leased a house on our old street in Beverly Hills. Cristina was happy to enroll in Beverly Hills High so she could graduate with her former classmates from Hawthorne Grammar School. We were all pleased to be home and settled back into the familiar L.A. life: shopping at our old market, reconnecting with our West Coast friends, especially Iva, Arlene, and Charlotte. I began to polish *All Under Heaven* for a go-round at the Ivar Theatre.

Steve Allen and Jayne Meadows, the sister of Audrey from *The Honeymooners,* came to the opening night. Jayne and Audrey were daughters of missionaries ("mish kids") and, like Pearl, were raised in China. It was wonderful to be playing this old landmark theater in the heart of Hollywood near the venerable restaurant Musso and Frank and all the historic movie palaces. In 1937, the film of *The Good Earth* premiered in this neighborhood. How gratifying that our "Pearl" project, which had started as Tony's idea and which we had both developed from the ground up, would be presented here at the Ivar Theatre. Great.

chapter
THIRTEEN

In 1999, during my final year of touring with *All Under Heaven,* Mary Tyler Moore and I began discussing bringing Mary Richards and Rhoda Morgenstern back to television. Nearly twenty years had passed since the finales of both *The Mary Tyler Moore Show* and *Rhoda,* and we thought that television audiences would be ready to see our characters once more.

As producer, Mary was considering different formats for the show—a half-hour comedy pilot or an hour-long show. Eventually, she sold a two-hour movie event to ABC, which would give us the chance to delve into and explore all the changes that two decades had brought for Mary and Rhoda. *Mary and Rhoda* would be a sort of back-door pilot. In other words, if the network liked the movie, they could order it as a series.

Mary and I had seen each other numerous times over the years. During my time in New York, she and I used to have lunch on the Upper East Side or in her beautiful Fifth Avenue apartment. She and her husband, Robert—both always so supportive of me—attended *Death Defying Acts* and *All Under Heaven*. But this was the first time we had been given the opportunity to work together—and bringing Mary Richards and Rhoda Morgenstern together after so many years of dormancy would be a true delight. Before we started working, she needed to confer with Jim and Allan. After all, Mary and Rhoda were their creations. Neither Jim nor Allan wanted to be involved in the script for *Mary and Rhoda*, which was written by Katie Ford, but they gave the project their blessing, and we were off to the races.

In twenty years, a lot had happened to Mary and Rhoda. When we meet them again, both women are single. Mary has recently lost her politician husband in a rock-climbing accident, while Rhoda has just divorced her second husband, an unfaithful Frenchman named Jean-Pierre. The women return to New York City, where they are reunited after two decades of estrangement. (Apparently, Mary never cared for Jean-Pierre, who made a pass at her at his and Rhoda's wedding.)

Each of them has a twenty-year-old daughter. Mary's daughter, Rose (after Rhoda), a student at NYU, is free-spirited and countercultural. Rhoda's more straitlaced daughter, Meredith (after Mary), is pre-med at Barnard. Mary has raised a Rhoda, and Rhoda has raised a Mary. Obviously, Mary and Rhoda really missed each other.

The moment Mary and I walked onto the set of *Mary and Rhoda*, it was as if no time had passed at all. We fell right back into the same lighthearted yet professional rapport we'd had on *The Mary Tyler Moore Show*. There was an immediate familial and nostalgic atmosphere to the set, as well as constant laughs.

Everything about working on the film felt instantly familiar. I loved being in the makeup chair beside Mary, kibitzing and gossiping. As thrilling as it was to be working at Mary's side, I was equally excited to revive Rhoda. Becoming Rhoda again was like falling off a log. I had internalized so many of her quirks that it was as if she'd been lying in wait inside me, biding her time before coming out to shine. She bubbled to the surface in an instant.

Shooting on location in New York was a pleasure and a challenge. Wherever we filmed, people were excited to see us. New Yorkers showed their enthusiasm loudly; the fans were incorrigible. The minute they glimpsed the two of us, they started laughing, clapping, waving, even screaming. "Look at you girls! Back together. This is so cool!"

Cops went out of their way to come say hello and surreptitiously confess they'd watched the show with their moms. In the middle of a take, passersby called out, "Hey, Rhoda. Hey, Mare. Long time." Their enthusiasm often interfered with shooting, forcing us to start a scene over from the beginning. Although our skillful director, Barnet Kellman, had his work cut out for him, Mary and I didn't mind the warm response from the public. Far from being forgotten, our alter egos were effusively welcomed back by New Yorkers of all shapes and sizes.

Rhoda had matured in the interceding twenty years. She was much more content with herself. For once, she didn't feel she needed a guy to make her life complete. Ha! Success! She had a beautiful daughter who was growing up to be the good Jewish doctor Rhoda never married. Fresh off a terrible divorce, she loved her new independence. Rhoda embraced her move to New York as the next in a series of adventures. She'd tried single in Minneapolis, married in Manhattan, married in Paris. Now she was back to her old stomping grounds on her own terms.

The fact that Mary and I had aged in tandem with our characters lent an important alchemy to the film. Rhoda and I were both mothers; like her, I had raised an intelligent, lovely, and independent daughter. Cristina, who was embarking on her own collegiate life, was roughly the same age as Meredith, my on-screen daughter. With Cristina, I had been through the requisite eye-rolling phase and the moments of minor rebellion. I'd also been through the wonderful experience of growing closer with her as she got older. Like Rhoda and Meredith, Cristina and I had learned that we would always need, respect, and rely on each other; our bond had deepened over time. It was easy to channel all of this into Rhoda.

Dressing like Rhoda once again was a blast. I knew that she would have kept her bohemian, eclectic tastes while evolving with the times. The modern-day Rhoda was the same woman as before, though now she had money. There would be no more cheap beads and feathers, no more thrift-store finds. Instead, her accessories would be souvenirs of her round-the-world travels with her ex-husband.

When we filmed the movie in 2000, Rhoda's original look— colorful scarves and gypsy-girl clothes—was very much in style with the younger set. Our eccentrically dapper costume designer, David Robinson, who sported an impressive handlebar mustache, knew that it would be easy to source clothes for Rhoda, but he wanted to update them to give her a more grown-up, sophisticated edge.

David found an absolutely gorgeous scarf from Etro in several fantastic shades of deep rust, ocher, and orange. At twelve hundred dollars, it was way out of the younger Rhoda Morgenstern's budget. Rhoda Morgenstern-Rousseau, however, might have splurged on such an item. David had two velvet jackets made for me, one in olive green and one in purple. We decided to hang up the head scarf, but in a nod to Rhoda's younger days, David found me some great hats, ones she might have picked up in a boutique in Paris.

On the first season of *Mary Tyler Moore,* Mary had been devoted to wearing clothes by Norman Todd, but then used several designers, including Michael Kors, over the course of the series. David thought that classy corporate-chic clothes were a perfect update to Mary's wardrobe because she looked great in anything. His only challenge in styling her for *Mary and Rhoda* was to find sophisticated vegan pumps—Mary, a devoted animal rights activist, no longer wore leather. When David and I were shopping for Rhoda's wardrobe in Saks or Bergdorf's,

I'd occasionally pick up a beautiful pump. "For Mary?" I'd ask David.

David would look at me and reply simply, "Moo."

Filming on location always poses difficulties and we shot all over one of the world's busiest cities from Harlem down to the East Village. As producer and star, Mary had a lot of responsibility on her shoulders. She never stopped working, even when the cameras weren't rolling.

One evening we were filming a dinner scene with our two daughters out on a terrace. I'd just arrived on-set; Mary had been shooting all day. Though it was quite late when we finished filming the scene, Barnet needed to shoot it again with the camera on me in a close-up. I saw that Mary was looking very tired as she patiently waited for the crew to adjust the lighting. She was going to do her part of the scene off-camera just to be helpful to me.

"Mary," I said, "they've got your footage. Why don't you go home?"

"No, Val. You're still working on our scene. I want to do the dialogue with you."

"Don't be silly," I told her. "You look exhausted. The script supervisor can read your lines."

"No, Val, it's not right. I can't leave." She was the soul of professional courtesy.

"Okay, Ms. Actress," I said. "But tell Ms. Producer that I won't continue if you stay."

After five more "Are you sure, Val?"s, she reluctantly left.

I felt so tender toward her in this moment that I almost teared up. Her steadfast assistant, Terry, hurried her off the set and home. And the audience never knew the difference. The magic of film!

The movie had some great moments that were reminiscent of the old *Mary Tyler Moore* days. Rhoda, always struggling to express herself artistically, gets a job as a photographer's assistant and tries to force the models to eat. Mary, desperate for work, takes a job that requires her to dance around in a pickle suit. Perhaps my favorite scene is one in which Mary and I go to see her daughter, Rose, do a stand-up routine in a downtown dive bar, filmed at the famed nightspot CBGB. Rose is bombing onstage, spewing one awful joke after another. Rhoda and Mary try to support her with overblown laughter. Here are these two middle-aged women, cackling and guffawing like crazy people in a roomful of silent, disaffected youth. It was monumentally awkward and true to life.

Mary was determined that *Mary and Rhoda* be current, interesting, and somewhat unconventional. In the second half of the movie, Mary Richards lands a job as a producer at ABC News and begins investigating a gang killing. As she gets deeper into the investigation, the film takes a darker contemporary turn while keeping comedic elements.

Stepping back into Rhoda's shoes was a pleasurable and effortless process—one that allowed me to reflect on all the changes that had happened in Rhoda's life since she first climbed through the window into Mary Richards's apartment on that cold

Minneapolis day in 1970. To commemorate our reunion, Mary, generous as usual, gifted me with a beautiful, enormous painting of two young women, one of them in a head scarf.

Over seventeen million people tuned in to the movie, which aired in March 2000. With such substantial numbers, it was surprising that ABC chose not to order a series. Nevertheless, it was great that Mary and Rhoda got to catch up with each other and the viewers after twenty years. Although I didn't get the chance to revive Rhoda in another series, she acted as an intermittent guardian angel, poking her head in now and then to influence my career. People loved Rhoda, so they embraced Valerie in different roles. Valerie has an association with Jewish cultural and humanitarian endeavors partly because Rhoda was Jewish.

One of the loveliest events I've ever been asked to be part of was a Hadassah presentation of the Los Angeles Jewish Symphony in June 2000. I did a reading along with opera singers and a full orchestra performing a cantata called *Women of Valor* by Andrea Clearfield.

The cantata *Women of Valor* is based in part on the *Eshet Chayil,* which is a long biblical poem honoring women's contributions to life. It has an acrostic arrangement in which the verses begin with the letters of the Hebrew alphabet in regular order. The poem describes the woman of valor as one who is energetic, righteous, and capable. The Jewish Symphony did a beautiful arrangement of the piece. They had opera singers performing the parts of Sarah, Ruth, Esther, and other female biblical figures; I was asked to read the English translation to accompany the singers and the music.

Rehearsing with the symphony was an incredibly uplifting experience, albeit terrifying. The conductor and artistic director, Dr. Noreen Green, a beautiful young blonde and a consummate professional, calmed my fear of missing a cue or jumping one. "If that happens," she said, "rest assured, we'll keep playing."

Although most of my reading was in English, I had to speak several phrases in Hebrew. My hairdressers at the time, two gorgeous redheaded Israeli sisters, Batia and Aleeza, coached me on pronunciation. So did Zvi, Penny's Israeli husband. At rehearsal, some of the committee ladies putting on the event questioned my Hebrew pronunciation. "So guttural. So Israeli," they said. They had expected me to sound like someone from Reseda on Shabbat, not like a person from the Holy Land. Or maybe they expected me to sound like Rhoda.

"You know what," I said, "Hebrew is not a dead language. A whole lot of folks in Israel speak it. I should sound like them, not a Valley Girl."

They agreed. My accent would be a reminder that correctly pronounced Hebrew lives on.

It was exhilarating, sitting on a stage surrounded by such exceptionally talented musicians and singers. After all my years struggling to become a dancer, I knew full well what it was like to devote yourself single-mindedly to an art. I was struck by the extent of the commitment and dedication of those around me. Hundreds of thousands of hours of practice went into forming these expert musicians, each individual honing his or her craft so that all of them could come together and produce such stupendous sound.

Around the time of the Jewish Symphony concert, our family was living above Sunset Strip in a house once owned by the famous game show creator and host Chuck Barris, Tony's former employer and pal. The house had a tiny secret room behind a false bookshelf where Chuck used to go when he wanted to disappear. I would have used it, but Tony and Cris would have known where to look.

Cristina was considering colleges, and Tony and I were unsure whether we wanted to settle permanently in Los Angeles or return to New York. *All Under Heaven* was booked for a two-month run at the Ivar Theatre in Hollywood. I continued to work steadily in television, doing guest spots and movies. I reunited with Paul Haggis for his television series *Family Law,* playing the mother of a high school mass murderer. I also played Debra Jo Rupp's more successful sister on *That '70s Show,* a cosmetics saleswoman who drove a pink Cadillac and wore hot pink from head to toe in every scene. Cristina had a small part and looked exactly like a teenage Grace Kelly. Debra Jo cautioned the boys in the cast about Cristina: "Don't even think about it! She's like my daughter." Mila Kunis was unbelievably sweet and welcoming to Cristina. The two of them bonded immediately. They hung out together, dancing wildly and tormenting their on-set tutor with their teenage antics.

I shot a very funny pilot about an Italian-American family called *The DeMarco Brothers* by John Levenstein. It was a really good script, and I was sorry that it didn't get picked up. But good doesn't always sell.

I had been spoiled by nine uninterrupted years on *Mary Tyler Moore* and *Rhoda,* and I was looking for steady work on-screen or onstage, something that would run for a solid period of time. Although pilot season was over, there was a chance I'd be called for a midseason replacement series. I wasn't sure if that would occur.

As often happens at the moment when you tell yourself you'll never work again, a call came from Manhattan Theatre Club, one of the nation's most acclaimed theater organizations. Under the leadership of artistic director Lynne Meadow and executive producer Barry Grove, this New York City company is committed to premiering new, innovative works and nurturing artists and audiences alike. They invited me to replace Linda Lavin (yes, again crossing paths!) in their hit production of *The Tale of the Allergist's Wife.* Stepping into the lead role in a successful Broadway comedy was extremely appealing, especially because the talented Lynne Meadow would direct the marvelous script by Charles Busch.

Marjorie Taub, the central character of *The Tale of the Allergist's Wife,* is an extraordinary role. Marjorie is originally working class from the Bronx but now lives in upscale comfort with her allergist husband, Dr. Ira Taub, on the Upper West Side. She spends her days struggling to shed her Bronx origins and improve herself by going to art openings, music recitals, and other cultural events. Despite her efforts, she becomes convinced that she will never be better than mediocre, which leads her to a have an emotional breakdown in the Disney Store, smashing many popular figurines. While recovering from this embarrassing outburst, Marjorie is visited by her childhood friend Lee Green, played by Michele Lee, whose flamboyance draws Marjorie out of her crisis.

The play was screamingly funny, insightful, and mysterious. Busch's terrific dialogue, full of intriguing literary and cultural references, tapped in to a particular New York neurosis that audiences adored. Marjorie was exactly the sort of woman whom Rhoda would have tormented in high school for her pretentious ways. No doubt Marjorie's elderly mother, played by eighty-year-old actress Shirl Bernheim, would have been a friend of Ida Morgenstern's. Her crass complaints, fixation on her bowel movements, and hilarious vulgarity brought the house down at every performance.

After Cristina's June graduation from Beverly Hills High and before starting college, she went with us to New York City to help me set up a place and have some fun. Cris and I haunted Bloomingdale's for towels, bedding, and dishes before she had to return to Los Angeles for college. We had to work fast because rehearsals began soon after for a July 28 Broadway opening. We rented an apartment on Central Park South with a lovely view of the park and a not so pleasant odor of horse dung from the passing hansom cabs. We kept the terrace doors closed in summer.

The actors—Tony Roberts, Michele, Shirl, and Anil Kumar, who played the doorman (again with the doorman!)—were all playing in *Allergist's Wife* when I arrived, so I rehearsed with the understudies. When you replace an actor in a running show, it's like jumping onto a fast-moving train. Coming into *Allergist's Wife* was not unlike when I replaced a dancer in *Abner,* although this time there were words—a lot of words—to learn.

My role required several very quick changes, from a robe to a pantsuit to a cocktail dress. Before my very first entrance, I stood in the wings, terrified that I'd get trapped in my clothes, flub my lines, or not be there for the other actors. Then I remembered Mary's advice to me the first night we filmed *The Mary Tyler Moore Show:* "Just take it one scene at a time, Val."

It worked. I calmed down and started to work through the play as it happened, not thinking ahead or worrying about what came next. Two hours later, I had gotten through my first performance. The toughest part was over. That night the Manhattan Theatre Club threw me a glamorous opening-night party on the top floor of the Marriott Hotel on Broadway.

At the party a large group of Japanese guests, all of whom were dressed in black tie, suddenly rushed over to Tony and started bowing to him. One by one they insisted on having their picture taken with my husband—dozens and dozens of pictures. Lynne Meadow saw what was going on and began to laugh hysterically. "Who do they think he is? De Niro or Pacino?"

"I don't know," I said. "Maybe they think all Italians look alike."

When Tony was free of his paparazzi, he joined us. "They're going to get back to Japan and proudly show these photos to their friends. And one of their friends is going to look at my picture and say, 'Who is this schmuck?'"

The Tale of the Allergist's Wife played at the Ethel Barrymore Theatre on Forty-seventh Street, just down the block from the Biltmore Theatre, a gorgeous old venue that had been sitting empty for fifteen years. Rats and bugs abounded. Rain coming through holes in the roof had damaged the interior, which had become a haven for the homeless.

The Manhattan Theatre Club had taken possession of the Biltmore with the intention of transforming it into a state-of-the-art Broadway theater. Lynne asked if I would accompany her and Barry Grove to Albany on my day off, to request financial support from the state legislature to help revitalize the Biltmore. I immediately agreed.

I drove up to Albany with Lynne and Barry. The first person we met with was the Democratic speaker of the assembly, Sheldon Silver. We explained the historical importance of the Biltmore and the goals of the Manhattan Theatre Club's restoration. MTC wasn't simply going to stage productions; they were going to transform the Biltmore into a vital community resource. "This will be a place for students from public schools all over the city to come and learn about theater," I said. "They will have educational programs and symposiums. We need state money to move it along." I went on to explain that the theater would provide a home for new American playwrights.

When the speaker heard from Lynne and Barry that Manhattan Theatre Club had already raised ten million dollars, he was impressed. He was accustomed to people coming to him hat in hand, with very little capital raised. The Republican head of the state senate, Joseph Bruno, and the governor's office each joined in and contributed a total of $800,000 to the effort.

With money from Albany and New York City added to the donations from the MTC board, major foundations, as well as corporations and private donors, the Manhattan Theatre Club was able to start on the renovation of the Biltmore, which became the restored yet modernized Samuel J. Friedman Theatre. Not long after they began to gut the theater, I started to notice a few creepy-crawlies backstage at the Barrymore. That didn't bother me; it was to be expected, with all the construction going on down the block.

One evening during a scene with Michele Lee, I noticed something moving along on her paisley-print shawl. A fat two-inch-long cockroach was slowly crawling up the folds of her scarf toward her neck. It was that unpleasant roach-y color, sewage brown, and had long, grotesquely intelligent-looking antennae. Though I was horrified, I managed to continue my lines, but I was transfixed as the bug crept closer to Michele's face.

She was oblivious to her little visitor. My mind was racing. I knew I had to get him off her and out of our scene. I waited for her to finish her line, then I swatted him, a monumental smack. The bug flew, and I heard it splat on the set behind us.

Michele was shocked by what I had just done. "I'm sorry, Lee," I said, staying in character. "I thought I saw something on you."

Right after our scene, when I explained to Michele what had really happened, she was deeply grateful. After the close encounter with that monstrous bug, we always made sure to shake out costumes during the quick changes in the wings.

Frantic costume changes aside, my role in *The Tale of the Allergist's Wife* involved a lot of screaming and yelling, which resulted in acute laryngitis. I went to a great vocal specialist, Dr. Scott Kessler, who diagnosed a blood blister on my vocal cord and prescribed complete and utter silence.

This was scary. I couldn't afford to lose my voice or damage my vocal cords, so I obeyed the doctor's order and scrawled notes to Tony instead of talking. On the Tuesday morning following my first appointment with Dr. Kessler, I was scheduled for a checkup. I was sitting alone in our living room when Tony ran in yelling, "Val, something terrible is happening at the World Trade Center!"

Like everyone else in the country—the world, even—we ran to our television and watched the tragedy unfold. As the towers fell, I furiously scribbled notes to Tony because I'd been ordered not to speak. Finally, neither of us could take our inactivity anymore. We flung on some clothes and ran to the nearest hospital to give blood. We were not the only New Yorkers with this idea. The sidewalk around the entire perimeter of Roosevelt Hospital was packed with people lined up like the audience at a Stones concert. In her dorm room in California, Cristina was wakened by a call from a classmate at six A.M. "Turn on the TV!" Half asleep, she saw what she thought was the Bill Pullman film *Independence Day*. Switching from channel to channel, she wondered why all the stations were playing the same movie. Turning up the sound, the horrible news hit her. She spent a panicky morning trying on three phones to get through to us.

Terrible news poured in throughout the day. "The Pride of Midtown" firehouse, located a block from the Ethel Barrymore Theatre, lost fifteen men on September 11, 2001. Michele Lee, who had gotten to know many of the firefighters and their families during her run in *Allergist's Wife,* was devastated. This disaster was a most shocking, horrific reality to confront.

Two days after 9/11, I got a call from the producers to come to the theater. The whole cast and crew assembled onstage, crying and comforting one another. Our show, like most on Broadway, was reopening that evening with a dimmed marquee.

Lynne was a rock. "I hate to have you guys go onstage," she told the cast. "If it were up to me, we'd stay closed all week. But we need to be here for people who've bought tickets and want to come."

We all agreed that was what we should do.

"But first," Lynne said, "we need to rework some sections of the play." I knew exactly what she meant.

There were several jokes referencing terrorism in *Allergist's Wife*. Three days earlier, these seemed both completely innocuous and very funny. Now they were totally unacceptable. Charles Busch, our brilliant playwright, was on hand to rewrite. He instituted changes throughout the play, transforming lines such as "Golda Meir was a terrorist?" into "Golda Meir was a spy?" It was a consolation to be together, working on the script with our theater family during this time of unspeakable sorrow.

I knew that we owed it to our audience to perform, but like everyone else in New York, I was severely rattled by the events of

9/11. I was afraid that the audience might not be ready to laugh and that I wouldn't be able to deliver what they needed so soon after the terrorist attacks.

"Remember," Tony said, "the Taubs and the other characters in this play haven't experienced 9/11 as we have. They are living in a New York City with the Twin Towers."

My wise husband! My character, Marjorie Taub, was a citizen of a New York that existed a week earlier—a time when it was possible to lose yourself in theater and art. I needed to remind the audience of that time, and I needed to suggest that it would return. Tony even made an offer to the producers that I would take no salary until business picked up. They were very appreciative, but declined.

The Ethel Barrymore seats over a thousand people. On September 13, roughly two hundred seats were filled. Before the curtain, the stage manager invited everyone to come down as close to the stage as possible and fill the orchestra seats. Given the fear in the city, it was a wonder anyone showed up.

Before the show started, I peeked out at the audience and was inspired by what I saw—a brave little group of individuals sitting there because they believed in the theater. Anil, who played Mohammad (of all names!), hugged me before we went out for the opening scene. "Come on, Val. Let's do this," he said. And we did.

Charles had written a short curtain speech for me to deliver at the end of the show, thanking the audience for their extraordinary courage in being able to set aside their fears of another attack, and for coming out in support of us, New York City, and the country.

The next night there were four hundred people in the audience. The next night, five hundred. As time went by, the crowd continued to grow, and my speech got cut off earlier each night with grateful applause. Soon the show was selling out once again. People would wait outside the stage door and tell me how far they'd traveled to New York to support the city and the theater. Two pretty thirtysomethings had flown in from Houston. A group of seniors said that, despite their fears of traveling through a possible target like the Lincoln Tunnel, they'd all come in on a bus from Union City, New Jersey.

Post-9/11 was an emotional and thrilling time to be on Broadway. The entire theater community banded together. There are so many ancillary businesses dependent on Broadway that the city needed audiences to come back. Besides my own cast, lots of stars in New York at the time—Helen Mirren, Kristin Chenoweth, Joel Grey, Brooke Shields, Harvey Fierstein, Glenn Close, Brian Stokes Mitchell, Susan Lucci, Alan Alda, Nathan Lane, Bernadette Peters, B. D. Wong, Matthew Broderick, and many more—did extensive outreach: talk shows, press conferences, public service announcements, whatever we could to urge audiences to come back to Broadway.

One afternoon virtually the entire cast of every Broadway show congregated in Times Square and sang "New York, New York." We had prerecorded the song earlier that week, grouped in fours around microphones. My group included Patti LuPone,

Bebe Neuwirth, and Michele Lee, all of whom have powerhouse voices. I've never sounded so good!

Rosie O'Donnell also had me on her show with Christine Ebersole, who played my neighbor back on the *Valerie* NBC show, and Mario Cantone from *Sex and the City*. When she introduced the three of us, Rosie explained that we were the three comforting pals she wanted around at this terrible time. Meanwhile, Ms. O'Donnell was spreading around plenty of comfort on her own. Rosie also lightened the mood by revealing that she had gone to audition for a part in a play years before. After hearing her thick New York accent, the creepy guy running the auditions yells out, "Thank you, thank you, but the part of Rhoda Morgenstern has already been cast." How mean! How dumb about talent!

I shared some excruciating moments with Michele at our local Broadway firehouse. It was "The Pride of Manhattan," "Never Missed a Performance," Engine 54, Ladder 4, Battalion 9, fifteen good men gone. The two of us tried to provide some comfort, but mostly we encountered bravery. We met a terrific woman named Rosemarie Foti, a mother of two firemen, Joseph from this firehouse and Robert of Engine 16, Ladder 7 on East Twenty-ninth Street, who died at the Towers. We chatted with the families, bought Beanie Babies for the kids, held some fund-raisers, attended funerals, cried a lot, and laughed, too. Many months later, when Michele hosted the unveiling of a memorial to the fallen men on West Forty-eighth Street and Eighth Avenue, just around the corner from the firehouse, I sat with Rosemarie Foti.

Sometimes people asked me how I was able to perform in

the face of so much tragedy. This is what I told them: "I can do it because of people like Rose Foti. She lost one son, and the other son is down at Ground Zero digging every day to see if he can find his brother. He and his colleagues are doing their jobs with tears streaming down their faces. The least I can do is get my butt on a Broadway stage and try to make people laugh."

It was that simple. Whatever your job is, you keep going. If you can make people laugh during tough times, you do it. Over the years, I've heard from a multitude of fans how much joy Rhoda Morgenstern brought into their lives even during their toughest times. I thought that Marjorie Taub could do the same. I know she did.

chapter

FOURTEEN

In 2005 Tony received a phone call from David Fishelson, the lead producer of the Broadway smash *Golda's Balcony*. The play, which had recently become the longest-running one-woman show on the Great White Way, was written by the inimitable playwright William Gibson, author of *The Miracle Worker*. Tovah Feldshuh had received a Tony nomination for her portrayal of Israel's first female prime minister. A national tour of the play was planned because it was clear that there was a whole country waiting to see *Golda's Balcony*. I was asked to step into Golda's shoes.

How could I not jump at the chance to play Golda Meir, one of the towering figures of the twentieth century? Her strength, unshakable resolve, and pioneering spirit were heroic. And a hero she was, not just to the Jewish people but to women and people of conscience everywhere.

Coming off of *All Under Heaven,* I felt completely prepared to carry another one-woman show. I knew the play, and I knew how much work was involved. But I welcomed the challenge. As coproducer of the tour, Tony began dealing with the business side of things, while I dove into preparations for the role. Not yet fully conversant with the Internet, I went to the Santa Monica Public Library and plunged myself into Golda's life, checking out an armload of books, including her autobiography, *My Life*. I was with Nicole and her then husband, Lowell, at a jammed Madison Square Garden in June 1967. The whole world thought Nasser's Egyptian Army would push the Jewish state into the sea. We all sat holding candles and our collective breath and literally prayed. As a result of the highly coordinated, surprise bombing of the Egyptian airfields, the Israelis won a stunning, rapid victory in the Six-Day War.

In the 1960s and 1970s, during my involvement with the feminist movement and the Equal Rights Amendment, I had often seen Golda in the media or in New York, at a TV press conference or a fund-raiser for Israel. She was an icon, a champion. During those years, she had been voted the Most Admired Woman in America by the Gallup Poll in 1971, 1973, and 1974. Hanging in the offices of many women's organizations was a poster of Golda's unmistakable face with the sardonic caption: "But Can She Type?"

Golda was a diminutive but sturdy woman. With her frizzy gray hair in a bun, thick stockings, and trademark orthopedic shoes, this powerful international leader looked like a granny—dowdy, homely, though tough as nails. I discussed Golda's hair with my phenomenal British stylist, Heather Lloyd—she and her daughter Francesca Windsor, a superb colorist, have both worked diligently to take years off my appearance. I suggested that I let my hair go gray with its natural kink so that I wouldn't even need a Golda wig. Heather didn't say a word. She stared at me speechless, as if she'd turned to stone. I dropped that idea as fast as I'd expressed it.

Besides Golda's look, there was the way she sounded. I had heard Golda speak, and I knew that I could re-create her accent. The trick would be to capture her inner strength and her single-minded dedication to the Jewish people and the state of Israel. I had to explore and discover what gave her so much conviction and determination—in essence, what made Golda Golda.

Becoming Golda Meir presented much more of a challenge than I'd faced with becoming Pearl Buck. Pearl was known to the public more through her writing than through her appearance and personality. Golda was world-famous, iconic. In the 1970s she was ubiquitous: People knew her; they'd met her; they'd seen her speak in person or on television. Thousands of Americans had stories of meeting Golda, of what she was like. On her endless fund-raising tours across the country, she had stayed in private homes, sleeping on couches or wherever people could accommodate her. She made an impression on everyone she met. I had to honor these memories of *Golda Shelanu,* Hebrew for "Our Golda."

One of the interesting aspects for me in playing Golda was to reach inside myself and find a sense of stillness. By nature, I am an active, in-motion kind of person. But to play Golda, I had to slow down and find inner calm in order to channel her singularly focused mind.

Golda was born in Russia, where she grew up speaking Yiddish. When she was eight, she moved to Milwaukee and learned to speak English like a midwesterner. Listening to tapes of her speeches and interviews, I could hear the blend of these influences. My friends Iva and Penny offered their husbands to coach me, Ron Rifkin for Yiddish and Zvi Almog for Hebrew. Better, more committed teachers I couldn't have.

Golda's voice was quite deep. After some practice, I was able to capture her register. The only difficulty that posed was when I had to create male characters such as Moshe Dayan and Menachem Begin. Then I'd have to lower my voice even further. (David Ben Gurion was no problem, as he had a high, piercing voice.) The play called for over thirty distinct characters, which made it really challenging but great fun to work on.

In order to prepare for *Golda's Balcony*, I did something I'd never done before: I learned my lines before I started rehearsal. Normally, I would stay on book, gradually discovering the performance. But with limited rehearsal time, the mother lode of memorization, and the directors blessing, I decided to learn the text before making any decisions about how I was going to play it.

Every day that I sat down to learn *Golda's Balcony*, I grew more and more thankful that I had a project like *All Under Heaven* under my belt. Even on my darkest, most difficult days, when I simply couldn't make it through more than several pages, I knew that I'd be able to accomplish it.

Unlike *All Under Heaven,* a two-act play, *Golda's Balcony* ran for an uninterrupted ninety minutes, which takes stamina but was great in another way. You're on. You go for it. You're off.

While I was watching DVDs of Golda, studying Jewish history and practicing accents, preparations were being made for the national tour. Right before I flew to New York to film the commercial promoting *Golda's Balcony,* the lead producer, David Fishelson, called to discuss my costume.

"Val," he said, "Golda, as you know, has a prominent . . . very large nose. Tovah's nose is very small, so we had a false nose made for her. But what I'm thinking is that since people know you as Rhoda, maybe you shouldn't use the nose."

"David," I said, "have you seen my face? My nose is smaller than small. That's not something I can act." Never mind the fact that people were coming to see Golda, not Rhoda, though I refrained from pointing that out to David. I recognized the impulse, if not the logic, of his thinking. People like having Rhoda around—she's certainly been great company to me over the years.

A false nose wasn't the only prosthetic I needed. For the first time onstage, I actually wore padding to beef up my figure. What a change! Instead of worrying that I was too big for a role, I was too small for Golda. This time there would be no corrective underwear, no Spanx, no constricting girdles, no sucking in and pinching. I wore a padded undergarment that made me stocky and gave me ample breasts. I could gain weight on the tour—something that tends to happen—and it wouldn't matter at all. Until later.

After the costume fitting, nose sculpting, wig styling, filming the commercial, and shooting promotional material, rehearsals began. I knew my lines—thank God—and I was ready to go. Scott Schwartz, who had directed the Broadway production, worked long and hard to get me comfortable with the role without ever suggesting I do it "the way we did it before."

Much appreciated, Scott!

Our first preview was on a Thursday in Fort Lauderdale, Florida, at the Parker Playhouse. The theater critic from the local paper was scheduled to come in on Sunday, when I'd have a couple of performances under my belt.

For a few days, the National Weather Service had been issuing warnings about the impending hurricane, Wilma. What nobody told me was that in order to avoid the hurricane, the critic came to one of the first shows, when I was still finding my way. I didn't learn that he had come early until his tepid review came out. Aaarrgh.

On Sunday, the day I expected the press to show, Tony and I relocated from our beach hotel to a smaller place inland, where Erin Roth, my makeup and wardrobe assistant, was staying. Wilma hit Fort Lauderdale with full force, and our rooms were plunged into darkness, so we fumbled our way down to the lobby, which was floor-to-ceiling windows.

"Guys," said Erin, our dry-wit voice of reason, "I don't think being surrounded by glass is our best choice."

Just outside the lobby was the pool, which was blanketed in whitecaps from the strong winds. I had never in my life seen whitecaps in a pool! The sound of the wind was deafening, and power lines came down. It was eerie and surreal.

In the morning we saw that the damage was extensive. The city was flooded. There was no electricity so the elevators were out of service, and we had to trek up and down stairs to fill wastebaskets full of water from the pool so we could flush our toilets.

We needed to stay in Florida until we knew if our show would reopen, so we drove north to Orlando and found rooms there that had electricity. Yaaay! Now the problem was gas. We waited in line for six hours along with everyone else, so it was kind of an adventure!

Since the theater was flooded and inoperable, it was decided that we all head home, and then reconvene in Detroit in a few weeks as scheduled. Shut down by a hurricane! This was a new one.

Tony and I returned to Los Angeles, and in preparation for Detroit, I rearranged all the furniture in our living room and ran through *Golda's Balcony* every day from start to finish, as if I were performing. Well, it worked for me when I practiced ballet in my parents' house as a kid!

We opened in the Fisher Theater in Detroit in early November. We had a three-week run that really allowed me to develop my performance. I'd remembered Tony Roberts, my costar in *Allergist's Wife,* once telling me, "You don't fully have your performance until twelve weeks after your Broadway opening night." Wise Mr. Roberts.

The reviews in Detroit were excellent and set the tone for the rest of our midwestern tour—Milwaukee (Golda's hometown), Cleveland, Cincinnati, and Columbus. Wherever we performed, I was greeted by Israeli consuls general, delegates, members of Jewish organizations, and, most touchingly, Holocaust survivors. I was taken to local Jewish museums and given tours of memorials. In every city we visited, people came up to me and said, "We knew her. It was like seeing her again. Thank you!"

The reviews got better and better as the tour went on. However, one critic—only one—said, "There's a bit of Rhoda in Golda." I wanted to scream. Yes, Rhoda and Golda are both Jewish-American women who shrug and say funny things. (Golda had a sharp, natural wit. "I can understand that the Arabs want us dead. But do they really expect us to cooperate?" she once famously said.) Humor aside, you have to be a fool to go see a play about the amazing Golda Meir and look for Rhoda Morgenstern onstage, especially with me in my Golda drag. Talk about inability to suspend disbelief. Sometimes critics have their review written before they enter the theater.

The tour of *Golda's Balcony* lasted just about a year. Sometimes there would be enough time between shows to return to Los Angeles; other times we'd stay out on the road for months at a time. When there was a break in the tour, Scott Schwartz would fly to Los Angeles or whatever city we were in to help me refresh the show.

As satisfying as it was to play Golda and to see how her story inspired and delighted audiences, the play exhausted me. From time to time, I felt like some sort of indentured servant. No matter how tired or, heaven forbid, sick I was feeling, I could not miss a show. There was no understudy. Most matinee days, I ate alone in my dressing room and made myself not talk, lie down, and try to nap. (I took my mom's advice: Even if you can't sleep, just lie there and rest.)

The tour concluded with terrific runs in Washington, D.C., Philadelphia, and Hartford, where Penny came to the show with her husband, Zvi, my very proud Hebrew coach and Israeli history tutor. We also returned to Florida, where we played to sold-out audiences who had missed their chance to see *Golda's Balcony* on account of Hurricane Wilma. Happily, along the way we won the Touring Broadway Tony Award of 2006.

When I was first contacted about taking on the role of Golda for the national tour, Tony negotiated a deal for me to also star in the movie version of *Golda's Balcony,* which he secured the rights to produce with David Steiner of Steiner Studios New York City.

The movie was filmed at the conclusion of the tour. Our director, Jeremy Kagan, who had directed me in an episode of *Columbo* in 1971—you see, if you stay in show business long enough, you'll encounter everyone at least twice—did a masterful job of adapting this one-woman play for the screen. We shot for five days in Calabasas. It was very much a family event—Tony produced, and Cristina was hired as a production assistant but was quickly promoted to production coordinator. She was absolutely indispensible given our super-short shooting schedule. (I'm speaking as an actor, by the way, not a mom!)

It was a strange transition from stage to screen. I was used to running through ninety minutes of text without a break. Because I knew the material so well, I was doing two to three pages without stopping. After one very long take, the cameraman said jokingly to Jeremy, "Doesn't this broad ever take a break?"

What works in the theater doesn't always work on film, especially in the case of a one-person show. Rather than shooting the play as it would have been presented on a stage, Jeremy had me do all the scenes in front of a green screen, which allowed him to show whatever background he desired in post-production. Jeremy used archival footage, original artwork, and photographs to underscore Golda's memories. He also helped me tremendously in modulating my performance for the camera.

The film opened at the Quad Cinema in Greenwich Village, then played a range of theaters around the nation. Beyond providing a record of William Gibson's play in performance, the DVD of *Golda's Balcony* was used as an educational and fund-raising tool for Jewish organizations in numerous cities. It seemed a fitting end point to my portrayal of Golda—traveling the country just as she had, sharing her magnificent life to raise money for the very causes she championed.

Golda's Balcony had been a thrilling and challenging experience. The tour was exhausting, but each performance was rewarding. Coming off of *Golda*'s long run onstage, and then the subsequent film adaptation, I had no idea what to expect next. Golda was a tough act to follow. Besides, some badly needed R and R, Iva and I quite impulsively jumped on a plane together to surprise Nicole in New York for her milestone birthday celebration. We left our respective husbands, screamed with laughter on the plane, and stayed in Iva and Ron's exquisite Soho apartment. What a great trip! We were eighteen again but in a vastly improved space; with great patina on the friendship.

In 2008 Tony received a call out of the blue from Matthew Lombardo, who had written a play called *Looped,* based on an actual recording or "looping" session during which the divine Tallulah Bankhead had to redub lines of dialogue for her film *Die! Die! My Darling!*

I was fascinated by the thought of playing Tallulah. Back in my days of acting class in New York, my pals and I had done impressions of her. An attractive aspect of *Looped* was that it had three characters—Tallulah, the sound editor, and the studio tech—which meant less pressure on me than in my previous two productions.

The play was very funny. In the first act, Tallulah arrives at the recording studio divinely high, somewhere between unwilling and unable to work. She may be looped, but quickly sizes up Danny, the editor, as a closeted gay and begins to draw him out and break him down, revealing intimate details about both of their lives in the process. Although the second act needed work, *Looped* seemed like it could be a lot of fun.

Tony and I got in touch with Matthew, who offered to send us a tape from the studio session that had inspired *Looped.* The tape was a riot but also quite touching and extremely valuable to me in capturing this flamboyant, larger-than-life woman. Here was the real Tallulah, unaware that the tape was running between takes, behaving and sounding as she did in life rather than in a performance.

I was drawn to Tallulah, a singularly vibrant personality and one who could not have been more different from Golda Meir. Tallulah was extravagant, self-involved, and committed primarily to having a good time. She was also indulgently crazy, shockingly brash, and hilarious. Tallulah, a great talent, once was serious about the theater and acting, but by the time of *Looped,* she had dwindled to a faded and filthy-mouthed old glamour-puss. I wanted the part.

Tony and I called Rob Ruggiero, our director from *All Under Heaven,* to see if he might be interested in directing *Looped.* By one of those unexpected coincidences, he and Matthew Lombardo both lived in Hartford, Connecticut, and knew each other. Rob gladly came on board.

Preparing for Tallulah presented some different challenges. Like Golda, Tallulah was a chain-smoker, so I dusted off my old trick for passing as a lifelong smoker onstage. I couldn't inhale (I'd cough), and I certainly didn't want to learn. I drew the smoke into my mouth, raised my chest as if inhaling, and then exhaled without letting the smoke touch my lungs. Smoking was one of Tallulah's lesser vices. During her recording session, she drank Scotch and took cocaine. I had to learn to fake scooping out a little of the (fake) powder on my pinkie nail and lift it to my nose like an experienced addict.

Creating Tallulah's distinctive gravelly voice was one of the biggest challenges. My voice is moderately pitched. Tallulah's voice wasn't just low, it was in the basement. Every time I thought I had achieved it, Rob would call out, "Lower, Val. Lower!"

Then Matthew would chime in with a deep baritone: "Dahling," and Tony would pile on by emphatically pointing toward the floor. And then I would scream in frustration, "Ruggiero, Lombardo, Cacciotti—what is this, the voice mafia?!" We all laughed but these three guys helped get me "low down."

With Rob directing and Tony producing, we were set to open *Looped* in the Pasadena Playhouse where Matthew had a commitment for a production. Everything fell into place so quickly that I had little time to prepare before the opening. Since the commute between Pasadena and the beach where we live would cost me three hours a day that I could spend learning the part, I checked in to the Pasadena Marriott in order to study, stay rested, and get ready to become Tallulah.

After only seventeen days of rehearsal, we previewed at the Pasadena Playhouse. With so little lead time, *Looped* was still a work in progress. Nevertheless, we did tremendously: *Looped* played to nearly sold-out houses for five weeks. Even with an older, conservative audience, the raunchy humor elicited enormous laughs.

In theater, it's a great gift to be supported by friends and family. Cristina and Sue Cameron were there opening night and my Second City Story Theatre compatriots came in a group. Iva and Ron, Arlene, Wendy, Nicole (who flew in from New York), plus my *Mary Tyler Moore* buddies Ed and Gavin, all came during the run. Betty was out of town but stepped up in another way. When Cristina saved a tiny black kitten stuck in the fountain pipes in the restaurant where she was working, it was Betty, animal lover extraordinaire, who got my daughter to a no-kill shelter. Vigilant Ms. White also warned us to be especially careful with black kitties around October because of the danger of Halloween abuse at the hands of disgusting people. I love Betty and have so much respect for her.

Our next stop was West Palm Beach, Florida, where we could do extensive rewrites and work on the show for two months. We all stayed in an offbeat but charming bed-and-breakfast and worked on the play. We even celebrated a whimsical Floridian Christmas together.

Because *Looped* was such a wild ride from start to finish, reaction from the seats was often sidesplitting. The theaters in Pasadena and Florida were midsized, and the audience sat close to the stage, which I guess made them feel as if they were part of the production. Sometimes people would talk back to us as we performed. The sexually explicit jokes brought the house down. When I delivered them, I could hear young guys howl, "Oh no!" as if watching someone miss the ball at a game.

During one show in Pasadena, when Tallulah begins questioning Danny about his closeted homosexual past, she asks, "Who was he?"

A man in the second row spoke out louder than he realized: "Who was *he*?" He obviously thought I'd misspoken and meant to say *she*.

I glanced at Chad Allen, who played Danny. He was struggling to keep his composure. I knew that every inch of him wanted to burst into laughter. Finally, he pulled himself together and continued the scene. "Just a guy," he said.

"A guy?" the same man asked, incredulous. The poor thing couldn't get with the program. Later Michael Orenstein, who played Steve, the unseen studio tech (another Carlton in my life!), was afraid he had shaken the darkened sound booth from laughing.

In Florida, the audience was even closer to the action than they had been in Pasadena, so close that they felt comfortable propping their feet up or resting a purse on the stage. They commented on the production as we rolled along, not realizing we could hear them. At intermission, one lady asked our stage manager, "Can you move this chair so I can see better?" "No!" snapped our stage manager, "the actors need to sit on it." There was loud lozenge unwrapping and the occasional, annoying cell phone tune, but by and large, whether they knew Miss Bankhead or not, they unanimously loved the show.

Looped opened with Tallulah blustering into the sound studio, belligerent because there was traffic on the freeway. I often struggled to speak my opening line without being muffled by entrance applause. The line was "Fuck Los Angeles!"

One night in Florida, Matthew watched an older man turn to his friend and ask, "What did she say?"

"Uhhhh. . . . 'I'm fabulous!'" his friend replied. That is priceless.

At the end of the first act, Tallulah suffers a cataclysmic breakdown from all of the substance abuse, and one suntanned matron whispered to her friend, "I don't know what's going on."

"Tallulah doesn't know where she is," her friend confided. "It's the drugs."

After we finished the run in Florida, we regrouped in Los Angeles and reworked the play further. We were headed to the illustrious Arena Stage in Washington, D.C., a larger venue. We improved our sets, lighting, and sound. We were able to get William Ivey Long, the famous Broadway costume designer, to style the most unbelievably fabulous blue silk charmeuse dress for me to slink around in.

Before heading to D.C., I decided to have some surgery. My wrist had been giving me trouble for over a year. I'd done my best to ignore it, but it had become so painful that I was having difficulty holding my glass of booze onstage. My magic healer of a chiropractor, Joe Horrigan, discovered the problem and recommended a surgeon. There was a tiny, broken bone in my wrist that needed to be repaired before we continued with the play. Tallulah could not drop her glass at the wrong moment.

I was scheduled for surgery in Los Angeles with Dr. John Knight, a genius hand and wrist specialist, but I needed a routine chest X-ray before going under the knife. Tony and I were in New York for Jane Fonda's Broadway opening of 33 *Variations,* so my doctor told me to have the X-ray done on the East Coast so that I would be ready for surgery when I returned home.

I went over to Roosevelt Hospital to take care of the X-ray and asked the radiologists to send it directly to my longtime physician, Dr. Arman Hekmati, in Los Angeles, as I was late for lunch with my good friend Nicole. I hustled down the street to Joe Allen and thought nothing more of my brief trip to the hospital.

chapter
FIFTEEN

Nicole Barth, my close friend ever since we both danced in *Take Me Along* in 1959, and I were sitting at Joe Allen in the heart of the theater district, busily catching up on each other's news when my phone rang. It was Dr. Hekmati.

"Valerie, I've got to tell you something. Don't be nervous. I want you to go back to the hospital and get another X-ray. The doctors in New York think they've spotted something on your lung. It could be nothing—scar tissue, an infection—but I want you to get it checked out immediately."

My heart started racing. I'd left the hospital half an hour earlier after a simple chest X-ray, and now I was headed back. Nicole and I canceled our lunch order and dashed into a cab and went straight back to Roosevelt.

The doctors and radiologists ushered me into a darkened room. Nicole went with me. They hung my X-ray on the light box for me to see. And there it was, high up on the right side, a little shining dime, a tiny gleaming moon.

My God, I thought, *look at that. What the hell is that doing there?*

Nicole stayed with me all afternoon. I didn't panic, because she and Dr. Hekmati wouldn't allow me to. During several calls from the West Coast, my great doctor, who has always been there for me and mine at all hours, held my hand transcontinentally. "Nothing is certain yet, Valerie, so take it one step at a time. First let's get you in for more tests in New York."

The next morning I went in for a PET scan, during which I had to drink a glucose shake to determine if the "something" on my lung was metabolically active, meaning growing. I was hoping for scar tissue or an infection. But no such luck. When the glucose reached the dime-shaped spot, the spot wiggled. Just like me, it was fond of sugar. Still, there was a chance it was nothing more than a benign tumor, living but not cancerous. Hope springs eternal.

Nicole met me after the PET scan and told me that she was going to get a chest X-ray herself, since she'd had an annoying cough for months. "Run, don't walk, dear friend," I urged.

The minute the spot on my lung was determined to be growing and possibly cancerous, Dr. Hemakti ordered me back to Los Angeles.

"Will a few days matter?" I asked. "I agreed to attend Jane Fonda's Broadway debut." Tony and I had promised Molly Smith, the artistic director of the Arena Stage in Washington, D.C., where we were going to open *Looped,* that we would attend this play that had originated in her theater.

"Okay," Dr. Hekmati said. "Just get back here as soon as you can. I have a specialist I want you to see."

I wanted to enjoy Jane's play before the monumental worrying set in. So, like Scarlett O'Hara in *Gone with the Wind*, I determined I'd "think about it tomorrow." I did my best to have fun at the theater that evening. *33 Variations* was fascinating, and Jane was terrific in such a demanding role. There was a gala after the show, and miraculously, I managed to have a wonderful time. My Scarlett act really did the trick.

The morning after Jane's play, Tony and I flew back to Los Angeles. We rushed to Cedars-Sinai for an appointment with Dr. Robert McKenna, the surgeon recommended by Dr. Hekmati. I was terrified. Tony was terrified. I had lost three mothers to lung disease: Mom, Angela, and Nancy Walker, my TV mom, Ida. On the way to the hospital, my mind started to go crazy—what had I done to bring this on myself? I didn't drink. I'd never smoked. Maybe it was from doing Golda and Tallulah? Could that even be possible? Could *pretending* to smoke have created the spot on my lung?

Dr. McKenna's office was exceptionally busy. Nevertheless, his wonderful wife, Kathy, who works with him, greeted us warmly. Dr. McKenna reminded me of a young Wilford Brimley, with beautiful blue eyes and a lush mustache. He had a reassuringly calm manner, serious but with a twinkle. I trusted him on sight.

"Listen, Valerie," he said. "No matter what it is, this spot needs to come out."

"Do you think it's cancer?" I asked.

"Yes," Dr. McKenna said. Stab in my heart.

"Why?" I managed to croak.

"The shape," he said. "But it's contained, which is great."

"But I've never smoked," I said, trying to disqualify myself.

"Twenty percent of women with lung cancer don't smoke or have never smoked," he said.

"Oh, great," I said. "I'm back in the running."

"Well, let's find out what it is first."

Dr. McKenna explained how we'd find out. He was going to remove the tumor from the lung using a procedure called VATS—video-assisted thoracoscopic surgery. He pioneered this minimally invasive surgical procedure for lung disease in 1992. While I was still on the operating table, the tumor would be biopsied in an adjacent room. If it was benign, it was already out of my body, and that would be that. If it was malignant, Dr. McKenna would remove the top right lobe of my lung, where the little visitor had set up house, ensuring that all the cancer cells would be gone.

This amazing operation was performed through several inch-long incisions using a tiny video camera, special instruments, and a whole truckload of skill. It was like arthroscopic knee surgery, but in the lung. Fantastic.

I was worried about having a lobe taken out. When I discussed my concern with Dr. Hekmati, he said, "You won't even miss it. The remaining lung will fill up the chest space." That sounded good, but I was praying the tumor would be benign and the lobe would stay put.

To put my mind at ease, I kept reminding myself that Dr. McKenna was a premier specialist in the field and that he and his team had performed VATS for nearly three thousand lung cancer patients. This surgeon developed the procedure and has had more experience performing it than anyone in the world. What was more, my surgery was scheduled for St. Patrick's Day, and my doctor was Irish-American. Perhaps luck would be on my side.

During the days leading up to my surgery, there wasn't much sleep or peace of mind in the Cacciotti house. A few hours before my operation, I called Cristina, who was studying for midterms at Emerson College in Boston.

"Cristi," I said, "I have something to tell you, but please don't be alarmed. I'm going in to surgery shortly for a very small tumor on my lung. It could be cancerous. It could be nothing. I just wanted you to know what's happening and that I love you. Please do not breathe a word about this to anyone. I'm here in the hospital as Valerie McConnell, Grandma's maiden name. Dad will call you the minute it's over."

"I'm coming, Mom," Cristina said with her customary determination.

"No," I said. "It'll all be over before you arrive. And don't tell a soul. This is just in our family. Tu capiche?"

"Capiche. I love you," Cristina said.

Keeping up a brave front, Tony had driven me to Cedars-Sinai. My darling husband tried valiantly to mask the fear in his eyes with forced joviality. Just seeing how much he was suffering prevented me from feeling sorry for myself.

"Why you, Val?" he said, stroking my forehead.

A good question. But I had an answer. "Why me? Why not me?" I have the finest doctor in the world, health insurance from my performers' union, plus Medicare, and the most wonderful husband God ever put breath into. Better me than someone without resources. As I lay in the hospital bed preparing for my surgery, the concept of affordable health care for all never felt more urgent to me, more necessary. Everyone deserved the same chance I had to get well.

Early in the morning Dr. McKenna came to my hospital room. "Okay, Valerie," he said, "we're good to go." Yikes!

As the gurney was wheeled down the hall, Tony walked alongside me, holding my hand as long as he could. When we parted, he gave me the biggest, most encouraging smile and two thumbs-up. And then the doors swung closed.

The room I was wheeled into looked like a high-tech military control room—they could have used it in *Mission: Impossible*. The anesthesiologist was a really affable guy, and joking that "video-assisted" would be right up my alley. Just what I needed— a comic! Really, he was great. He administered the anesthetic and told me to count backward from ten. The next thing I knew, I was looking into my husband's smiling face.

"Was it cancer?" I whispered.

"Yes, but it was tiny, and it's out," he said.

Okay, I thought, *it's over, and I'm still here.*

The good news was that the surgery went perfectly. There were no stray cancer cells hanging around. The great news was that there was no need for chemo or radiation. I was cancer-free. As my genius doctor said with a beaming smile, "This is the best possible outcome." I was a very lucky girl. Happy St. Patrick's Day!

I couldn't believe that the top lobe of my lung had been slipped out of a minute incision on my side. I thought of my mom's surgery for a similar type of cancer back in the 1970s. She, also a nonsmoker, had suffered through an extremely invasive operation. This was pre-VATS, and her incision ran from her breastbone all the way around her side to the middle of her back. It's incredible how far medicine has progressed since then.

With cancer on the rise, especially among women, I cannot stress enough the importance of early detection. More women are dying of lung cancer these days than breast, ovarian, and colon cancer combined. Yet, ten times more money is spent on research for breast cancer than for lung cancer. The overall cure rate for the disease is only fifteen percent. To change that grim statistic, we need more funding, more research, and much earlier diagnosis.

My friend Nicole, also a lifelong nonsmoker, got checked for her cough, as she'd promised. While I was at home convalescing from my surgery, she called with the results from her checkup. "You won't believe this, Val, but I have lung cancer, too."

I couldn't believe it. I didn't want to believe it. We started crying on the phone together, three thousand miles apart but never closer. I had to put aside my shock and fear and comfort my dear, sweet friend of fifty-three years.

While we discussed Nicole's next steps—a referral from Dr. McKenna, figuring out her insurance coverage—she kept interjecting questions about my health and convalescence. Glorious Nicole, thinking about me at a time like this. When we hung up, I locked myself in the bathroom and screamed in anger until my throat hurt. Good thing I was alone in the house.

When I told Iva about Nicole's diagnosis, she was heartbroken and beside herself. "Oh no, no, no, no, no," she cried, "not another girlfriend. I smoked. I smoked in our twenties. Why you two?"

Nicole and I talked every day, sometimes multiple times. She was being treated at our old standby, Roosevelt Hospital. We discussed each test and each result. In my 2009 datebook, I kept thorough records of Nicole's progress. Unfortunately, VATS wasn't an option for her, but she responded beautifully to chemo and radiation.

Except for a few close friends and family, I didn't tell anyone about my own cancer diagnosis. *Looped* was scheduled to open at the Arena Stage in Washington, D.C. I didn't want the audience to know that I'd been sick, especially with something as serious as lung cancer. I didn't want the word *cancer* to overshadow the play. We were trying to do comedy, for God's sake! Most important, I was out of the woods—I'd even received permission from Dr. Hekmati and Dr. McKenna to "smoke" for the role. There was no reason for my health to be a topic of discussion. I didn't want to talk about my cancer; I didn't want to be pitied; I wanted to move on.

Tony and I decided to spend a couple of weeks rehearsing in Hartford, where both our director, Rob, and playwright, Matthew, lived. Then we headed to Washington for a tremendously interesting three-month run. We played at the historic Lincoln Theatre—where the Arena Stage was in residence during the construction of their own new theater complex—which had seen the likes of Duke Ellington and Ella Fitzgerald among other great stars. *Looped* was gaining momentum. We had reworked the play, given it more of a structure and a clearer story and we had a different Danny—a terrific actor, Jay Goede. When I wasn't performing, I spent my free time lobbying Capitol Hill and met with many well-known lawmakers on behalf of RESULTS and RESULTS Educational Fund, a volunteer lobbying organization that takes action to end poverty and hunger. I know the founder, Sam Daley-Harris, and the current executive director, Joanne Carter, extremely well and love them very much! We have been working together on these issues for decades. People like them will save the world. They're in the process of doing so now.

When our time in Washington was over, we came home to Los Angeles and waited for a Broadway theater to become available. Tony, Rob, Matthew, and I retrenched and rewrote and just before Thanksgiving thanks to Joe Horrigan my chiropractor I had partial knee replacement surgery by superb Dr. Andrew Yun. Looking back, three surgeries in one year. Holy smoke! Thank goodness for Ana Miriam Jimenez, my fantastic, longtime housekeeper, who cared for me like a mom. When I grumbled about taking three trips to the operating room she reminded me in her El Salvadorian accent: "Joo didn't take four." *Sí, Miriam!*

Come December, we headed to New York to cast for the Broadway production of *Looped*. Brian Hutchison joined us as Danny, and Michael Mulheren, as Irish as Paddy's pig, took on the role of Steve, the sound booth tech. It was exciting and gratifying to prepare for the Great White Way presentation. The play was truly Tony's baby. My husband had nurtured and financed and maneuvered all four productions of *Looped* into being. We'd covered a lot of ground in a year and a half. Now we were ready for Broadway. That New Year's Eve (2009-2010), Tony and I left our hotel to go out and watch the ball drop. It was freezing cold, we kissed and celebrated. I realized the last time I'd been in Times Square for New Year's was with Barbara Monte and a pack of high school friends in 1955. New York City keeps on rollin' along!

When we went to New York to rehearse, an extraordinary and beautiful thing happened. I had instantly bonded with Artie Siccardi, our technical director, who has since received a Lifetime Achievement Tony Award for his consistently spectacular work on Broadway shows. One day I mentioned that my friend Nicole Barth had sent him her regards. Artie, a very tall, attractive, genuine New Yorker and a guy Rhoda really would have gone for, smiled the sweetest smile and said, "Oh, Nicole! I remember her. She's married, in real estate sales, and lives on Long Island."

"No," I said. "She's single, in theater ticket sales, and lives in Manhattan."

"No kidding," Artie said. "Give me her number."

Artie and Nicole had worked on a show together forty years earlier. That day Artie called Nicole, and they met for drinks. They've been together ever since. I love stuff like this!

On Sunday, March 14, 2010, *Looped* opened in New York City at the Lyceum Theatre, a gorgeous Beaux Arts building on West Forty-fifth Street. Declared a landmark theater, the Lyceum, built in 1903—the year after Tallulah was born—is the oldest continually operating legitimate theater on Broadway, small but elegant, with elaborate marble staircases and a charming history. The impresario who built the theater had a peephole installed so he could watch the actors onstage and wave a handkerchief at his actress wife if she was overacting. Maybe Tony should do that! The Lyceum's vintage glamour was perfect for Tallulah. The only trouble was the location, rather sequestered, east of Broadway close to Sixth Avenue, away from the madness, the excitement, and the foot traffic that was the heart of the theater district.

My dear pal Iva and her husband, Ron Rifkin, flew in from Los Angeles for opening night, as did Wendy, my darling stepdaughter, who had time off from her long-running TV series *American Dad*, in which she plays the wife, Francine. Tony's friend of nearly forty years, agent Larry Becsey, and his wife, Devra, traveled from the coast to attend. Although she had the flu, Cristina came down from Boston. Even my old friend C. Robert, who'd cast me in *The American Nightmare,* where I'd been seen by Ethel Winant from CBS, flew in from New Orleans. Gorgeous flowers overran my dressing room, dozens of peach roses from Bob Boyett (from the *Valerie* show), glorious white peonies and hydrangeas from Rosie O'Donnell, orchids and bouquets from so many dear pals and loved ones. This'll make you feel like a star! After the show, there was an opening night party at Sardi's, where Jackie Gleason had thrown away the offending velvet rope during the cast party for *Take Me Along* fifty years earlier. Nicole had been with me at that opening, too!

The reviews were mixed, some very good—as they were everywhere we played. Critics seemed to prefer the performances to the play itself. Audiences shrieked with laughter and friends and family (over twelve years old only!) came in droves. Ginger had to leave James, ten, and Angela, six, home but my little sister led an entire New Jersey contingent of family and PTA ladies across the river to the show. Penny, who had recently lost her husband, Zvi, came with three of her kids: Danit, the beautiful assistant district attorney, Sharon, the gorgeous teacher, and dashing Michael, the PhD, who dubbed me "Vallulah"! Unfortunately, early in the run, a key investor backed out, leaving us with a shortfall that made it impossible to continue. So we closed. *Looped* was such a fun ride, and I was disappointed when it was over. But at least I didn't have to fake-smoke anymore.

I was happy to come home. Though I'd wished *Looped* had gone on longer, some things are not in the cards. About two weeks after we closed, I received a phone call from Jackie Green, a crackerjack publicist and a terrific friend whom I'd worked with on many New York shows.

"You know, Val," she said, "they're announcing the Tony Awards this week. You guys should fly in. There's an immediate press junket that happens the second the nominations are announced."

Tony and I hadn't been seriously considering going to New York for the nominations. But I would be shooting an independent film called *Certainty*, directed by Peter Askin, in early June, and I'd received some terrific reviews as Tallulah. But a Tony nod? That was asking too much. Still, at Jackie's urging, we packed our bags and went to New York early. I told myself not to expect anything, to go along for the ride. Plus, I'd have the opportunity to spend time with Nicole.

Tony and I checked into an apartment we often rent near Times Square. The morning the nominations were announced, we discovered that our television was broken. Frantically, we called Cristina, our resident technology expert. A patient daughter, she explained to her technologically backward parents how to use a computer to watch the nominations.

Tony and I huddled in front of the computer. Jeff Daniels read the names. "In the category of Best Actress in a Play: Viola Davis." He was going alphabetically. "Valerie Harper." Tony and I leaped out of our chairs. We couldn't stop jumping and running around. We kissed and hugged and even shrieked. I couldn't believe it. My portrayal of Tallulah had come all the way from Pasadena, by way of West Palm Beach and Washington, D.C., to the Big Apple. And now I'd been nominated for a Tony. This was a thrill beyond all imagining. Later that same day was the Times Square bombing attempt near our hotel that was thwarted by an alert Muslim vendor reporting the car to the police. Thank heaven for the outcome and it didn't dampen our Tony spirits one bit.

I was immediately hurled into a swirl of events—luncheons, cocktail parties, and press meet and greets. It was dynamite. One afternoon all the Tony nominees gathered for a group photo on the steps of the Plaza Hotel and then went upstairs and had a sumptuous lunch. I sat next to Christopher Walken, and boy, was that fun. I remembered him as a little kid, a few years behind me at a different professional children's school in New York. I told him that I'd seen him in *The Visit* on Broadway. "No, that was my brother, Kenny," Chris said.

"Oh yes, I remember Kenny, too. I danced with him at a party at Sal Mineo's brother's house," I said. "He asked me if anything was going to happen between us. I told him no. He said, 'Okay,' and walked away. But you know, I loved his honesty."

"Oh yeah," Chris replied, "my brother was quite a player."

The Tony Awards were held at Radio City Music Hall. I wore a gorgeous cobalt-blue chiffon gown by Pamella Roland. It was raining slightly—misting, really. What I wouldn't give for Heather Lloyd and her flat iron! Luckily, I chose a slightly wavy style for my hair, so the humidity didn't ruin it. I held my husband's hand as we walked down the carpet and into the theater. "This is incredible," I whispered. "I was working here in 1956 as a dancer. And now in 2010, as an actress, I'm nominated for a Tony and, more important, I'm *with* my Tony." Corny but true!

We were seated near Liev Schreiber and Alfred Molina, two actors I respect tremendously. All around me were wonderful artists who were seriously committed to theater. I felt that I belonged among them. I was proud of myself for my accomplishments in *Looped*, but also for the path my career had taken. I wanted to ask my fellow actors, "Did any of you dance on your toes on that stage? I did! I'm probably the only one here who was on pointe up there."

Although I didn't expect to win, I had a speech prepared about how I started right on this very stage, how a starry-eyed sixteen-year-old girl was so proud to be a dancing gold nugget in the Corps de Ballet.

I didn't get to make my speech because Viola Davis won in the category for her exquisite performance in Langston Hughes's *Fences*. I blew her a kiss as she ascended to the stage in her gorgeous chartreuse gown. I couldn't help but reflect on the change that had occurred from the time I started on Broadway, when it was a struggle for an African-American or other minority to get cast in a show. And now here was lovely Viola, a black American woman, being duly recognized for her excellence. About time!

At Radio City—especially at the Tonys—there's a ghost that hangs in the air, making you aware of all the people who have passed through before you, all the luminaries of stage and screen and all the chorus dancers and singers hoping for their big break, all the hours of practice and repetition that have gone into all the performances that have taken place on that magnificent stage, all the performers who've been honored there.

As I sat in the audience, watching so many of my friends and acquaintances accept awards or present them, I couldn't help remembering my first years working in the business, classes at Ballet Arts and Luigi's, high school at Quintano's. When I look back, those years seem like a movie, something Michael Bennett might have written a musical about—a young girl living alone in the big city, hoping to make it as a dancer and, later, as an actress.

When I was starting out in the theater, so much of my life *did* seem like the movies—the first time I entered through a stage door, the first time I stood in the wings of a Broadway theater, my cross-country train trip with the cast of *Abner,* my first Hollywood studio, the first time I drove onto the lot and saw my name on a parking space. I've never taken these simple offstage moments for granted. They're the experiences that give resonance and meaning to any of my accomplishments. It's the journey, not the destination.

Despite all the incredible times I've had onstage and in front of the camera—all the wonderful people I've worked with, all the fantastic characters I've played—I have always rejected that old saying "Show business is my life." It isn't. Only my life is my life. My life is Tony and Cristina, my family, friends, and sister-friends Leah and Ginger (shades of Rhoda and Brenda!). The engrossing activities that are most important to me are also my life. And every day I find something to say "thank you" for.

Show business can be a perfect workplace to engender powerful relationships. The theater has provided me with a tight-knit circle of friends, girls I met not long after my debut at Radio City: Iva, of course; Arlene and Nicole, the vanilla and strawberry to my chocolate; Penny Ann, Norma, and my male "girlfriend," dear Gene. Television brought Mary, Cloris, Charlotte, Sue, Mimi, and Carol into my life as bosom buddies. I was lucky enough to work in a business where I met wonderful people—many men as well as women—and cultivated remarkable friendships that have lasted over half a century. Can that be true? How lucky can a person be?

These friendships, which have withstood a roller coaster of life experiences, are perhaps one of the most vital influences on my portrayal of Rhoda Morgenstern—for Rhoda, above and beyond all else, is a paragon of friendship, whether to Mary or to Brenda or to the millions who rooted for her week after week.

Rhoda and all the other women I've played have brought such joy and happiness into my life. They've allowed me, in different guises, to share the qualities I value most in people—the abilities to laugh, to care, to be committed, to have fun, to contribute, to love. Pearl, Golda, and Tallulah (to name a few), but particularly Rhoda, have kept me busy, kept me working, and they have given that little girl who never stopped moving an outlet for her overflowing energy and enthusiasm. They have given her an excuse to overdo.

EPILOGUE

After twenty-five years of enjoying, appreciating, and laughing at Julie Kavner and her supremely talented compatriots on *The Simpsons*, co-developed by Jim Brooks, I finally did an episode in April 2012. I hadn't spent time with Julie in ages—maybe twenty years—but we were in touch through our mutual loving pal, Mimi. Then suddenly, there was Ms. Kavner, looking wonderful. She bounced into the studio to take her place at the microphone. Her hair was short and very, very curly.

"A perm?" I asked.

"No, menopause. I don't know why or what happened, it just curled up," she said in that voice like no other.

We hugged, we kissed, and we quickly exchanged news. This was in the middle of a recording session, with the other actors and the whole *Simpsons* team patiently, kindly letting this reunion occur. Julie's body was tiny and in fabulous condition in her pencil jeans. When she said how great I looked, I told her that besides having a terrific dermatologist, Dr. Douglas Hamilton, I'd had veneers put on my six front teeth when I'd turned seventy. As my British hairdresser, Heather, says, "When one hits a certain age, darling, what's really important is hair and teeth." Don't tell the plastic surgeons!

"Speaking of teeth . . ." Julie said as she flipped out onto her tongue a small plastic apparatus with three fake teeth attached to it, revealing a dark space where her front teeth should have been. I laughed so hard—this was my fantastic Julie, grinning at me like an adorable jack-o'-lantern. "I'm going to the dentist soon for the permanents, but these have been so much fun!"

I resumed my place at the mic to continue the recording session when it hit me. What a path we'd taken together so many years ago, and now here we were, right back on it, in an instant! I found my eyes welling up with tears and my heart seemed to rise up out of my chest. I turned to Dan Castellaneta, the brilliantly talented man who voices Homer Simpson and a myriad of other characters, at the microphone right next to me, trying to get my emotions under control. He smiled sweetly, understanding—and then, on we went. It was really great to be a part of this wonderful group of actors bringing Simpsonland to life, especially with my former "little sister."

You *can* go home again.

AFTERWORD

There is often, if not always, more to the story. The "more" in my story came as a huge and frightening revelation—one that occurred days before *I, Rhoda* was first published and, unfortunately, contradicts a statement I made in the final chapter of this book . . .

There I was in New York City just after Christmastime, preparing to do publicity for the release of my memoir and rehearsing the role of outrageous actress Tallulah Bankhead for a stage tour of the comedy *Looped* that my husband, Tony, was producing. These were exciting and wonderful times. During a scene with Brian Hutchison, my excellent co-star in the Broadway production, I experienced a severe headache and had difficulty remembering my lines. Suddenly, my lower-right jaw went numb as if I'd had a shot of Novocain. Fearing a stroke, Tony rushed me to Roosevelt Hospital, where, after extensive testing, he was told the dreadful news. I was diagnosed with a rare and incurable cancer located in the lining of the brain: leptomeningeal carcinomatosis. It was estimated that I had three months or so to live, maybe less, and they could do nothing for me.

What!!! Life, it's what happens on the way to your plans.

While keeping this prognosis from me, Tony was devastated and infuriated at the same time; he refused to accept that we must surrender to this illness without a fight. I was pretty much out of it from the medication I'd been given, but my sister Ginger had rushed over from New Jersey to be with us. Then a day or two later, when I was wheeled back to my room after one of many tests, a whole bunch of loved ones had gathered in my hospital room—Tony and Cristina, Iva with her husband, Ron, Nicole with a large teddy bear decorated with bright red felt hearts. They all had forced smiles on their faces, including the bear, and I sensed something was up.

Back at our hotel I pressed Cristina for information. With her beautiful green eyes wide open in disbelief, she asked, "Hasn't Dad told you yet?" Terrified, but hiding it, I said, "You tell me . . . please." And she did, bless her courageous little heart. Being told I had cancer was one thing—I'd had lung cancer in 2009 and had been in remission for four years, and there are plenty of folks living with it, fighting it, and surviving. But hearing the words "three months or so to live" is a ticking time bomb. A death sentence.

Shocked, scared, and deeply saddened, I was still grateful to Cristi for letting me know the doctor's full analysis of my condition. The grim finality of that concise word—"incurable"—hit me like a sledgehammer; I was terrified. My poor husband, in complete denial, refusing to believe there was "nothing to be done," had been unable to repeat the diagnosis to me. At warp speed, Tony sought a second opinion.

Thankfully, my "niece" Sharon (Penny's youngest) was able to arrange an immediate consultation with noted neurologist Dr. Lisa DeAngelis at Memorial Sloan-Kettering Cancer Center. She concurred with Roosevelt Hospital that it appeared I had "lepto" (the disease's cute abbreviated nickname), but that more testing was required to identify the cancer cells and their source so as to determine the best course of treatment.

Talk about a detour! I'd hit a big one. I had been easin' on down the road and *bam*—my way was blocked, my priorities turned upside down. I felt so terrible having to drop out of the book tour after all the hard work and commitment the Simon & Schuster folks had put into publishing *I, Rhoda*. And to have to leave the play, Tony's production with actors and staff who I loved, was so disappointing. But the hands of the clock were moving—time was short. As our plane took off, Tony and I looked out over the glorious panorama of New York City, which for decades had meant so much to both of us, and wondered: After so many marvelous trips here together, would this one be our last?

Back home in Los Angeles, we immediately went to Cedars-Sinai Medical Center and there they were, my team—the dynamic duo, Dr. Ronald Natale, medical director of the clinical lung cancer program, and neurooncologist Dr. Jeremy Rudnick—standing ready and willing to maintain hope in what seemed to be a hopeless situation. Always truthful, sometimes painfully so, these two were vitally engaged in fighting these sneaky, rotten little devils that had crept into the lining of my brain to insidiously, quietly grow.

Back in 2009 when I'd had surgery on my lung, Dr. Robert McKenna, my genius surgeon from Cedars, had asked if I would donate my tumor for future research. "Sure, of course!" was my response. That lung tumor was still frozen, stored away in beeswax, and was now available for testing with respect to my current disease. What luck! Who knew that four years later that intrusive little blob from my lung would turn out to be useful in identifying what was going on in my brain. *CSI* time!

Turns out, I had lung cancer in the lining of my brain—not brain cancer—and was put on an oral medication called Tarceva, which I named: To Aggressively Remove Cancer Everywhere Val Announces. One terrible side effect of the medication that first week was a facial breakout of multitudes of tiny pimples. Waves of them. They made me look like the Elephant Man! Dr. Natale was pleased, however, reassuring me that a breakout may signify that the Tarceva was working. *Okay!* I thought. *I'll just stay in the house!*

Through Cristi, we found Dr. Hua-Bing Wen, an acupuncturist and practitioner of both Western and Chinese medicine. With both of my oncologists' approval, I drink special herbal tea daily and have regular acupuncture treatments. Approximately half of Dr. Wen's practice consists of cancer patients and he works to support their other treatments. We've consulted with a vibrant, inspiring woman, Kim Norris, who lost her husband thirteen years ago to lung cancer. As a result of her personal tragedy, she cofounded and is now president of the Lung Cancer Foundation of America (LCFA). This devastating illness remains the nation's leading cause of cancer deaths for both women and men, and is quite misunderstood with regard to smoking—sixty percent of new lung cancer cases are found in nonsmokers! "Like you, Val," Kim reminds me. In the field of oncology, there has been a transformation in the manner of fighting the many forms of cancer and also the development of many promising new options on the horizon. Kim Norris is one of the heroes who is spreading the word about these improvements and raising funds for sorely needed research.

So far, there has been a positive response to the Tarceva and acupuncture treatments according to the periodic brain scans. By no means am I "out of the woods"—this is, after all, an incurable condition. "*So far* incurable!" Tony insists. "Let's extend your time, Val, because a cure may be right around the corner." It's impossible to be negative or resigned around Tony—although I have my moments and his response is to hug me until they pass. He's right, though. I have a fighting chance until I'm gone, so I try to focus on being here *now*. I wish everyone had a Tony, or someone like him in their life, to ease their way. His support, strength, courage, and love—indescribable!

Tony faced his own almost insurmountable hurdle and went with me to make the necessary arrangements with the lawyer and the cemetery. We, like so many others, had avoided these end-of-life directives—me out of laziness, Tony out of foreboding. We have since discovered a terrific new, online free resource called MyDirectives.com. I have joined their advisory board because you can't make these decisions too early, but you can be too late.

As we walked around the beautiful Hollywood Forever cemetery replete with flowering plants, tame peacocks, and many a famous resident, our guide showed us plots that had "a great view of the Hollywood sign." So wonderfully funny! We made our pick, and now our kids aren't burdened with that decision.

Cancer makes real what we try to obscure from ourselves. Death. The disease reminds me of a very bad but tenacious performer who, although no one wants to see, insists on doing an encore, having a return engagement, making a comeback, and worst of all, going on tour. In my case, at the moment it seems to be staying put in the meninges (the fluid-filled membrane surrounding the brain) and has surprisingly not been detected anywhere else in my body. Dr. Natale says he hasn't seen a case like mine in more than thirty years as an oncologist. (By the way, his name means "Christmas" in Italian—perfect, because he, Dr. Rudnick, and their staff have certainly been gifts in my life.) So I am taking everything one day at a time, which I think is the best way to live anyway!

At first, I hesitated about going public with the truth about my situation. But instead of allowing lies and misinformation to dribble out over the Internet, not to mention the fact that I, Rhoda had just been released and in it I'd written that I was cancer free in 2009, which was no longer true, I felt compelled to set the record straight. Most important, I've been in the public eye for more than forty years and have been so warmly embraced by so many folks; people feel they are my pals, girlfriends, and family because of their love for Rhoda. And they deserve to be treated like family and hear the news from me and not through the grapevine.

When *People* magazine ran a cover story about my battle with cancer in March 2013, two months after my initial diagnosis, and I appeared on a plethora of television and radio talk shows, the news of my illness reached a lot of people. And it seemed as though most of them sent me cards, notes, letters, flowers, gifts, books (over forty of them!), treatment and religious guidance, talismans, artwork, hand-knitted shawls, angel figurines, lucky coins, hundreds of phone calls, and, of course, cake and chocolate. I received the most touching, sometimes humorous, and completely loving messages of thanks, concern, hope, encouragement, and good wishes. I'm so grateful for all of them!

The interest in my situation was unexpected and overwhelming. I received a lot of great suggestions. A dear actor friend of mine, George Coe, sent me a book entitled *Healing Visualizations: Creating Health through Imagery* by Gerald Epstein, MD. George, battling his own cancer, said, "Val, we're actors—imagery and visualizing is our business!" I've been creating my own cancer-fighting imagery using the book as a guide. At the urging of Mimi, my former assistant, and others, I've been drinking vegetable juices ("green drinks") and avoiding sugar and salt. Tony encourages me to walk every day and to exercise, which is crucial in supporting health. Having received this disastrous diagnosis, I was provided with a wonderful opportunity to share a reality that most of us refuse to face out of fear. We are all terminal—none of us is getting out of this life alive. But there's no point going to the funeral until the day of the funeral. We must do our best to stop fearing death; it is out there ahead of each and every one of us, inevitably. So there's not a moment to lose. We must live life fully and with as much energy, attention, appreciation, love, and joy as we can muster. And if fear, grief, terror, remorse, or regret move in on me—which they do—I let the emotions in. I experience the feeling until it dissipates and then I concentrate on being here right now and being grateful for this very moment.

I joke that I am well past my expiration date already, but I don't take a second of it for granted. In the months since my illness was diagnosed, I've been around for some unbelievably happy moments—beginning on April Fool's Day when the female cast of *The Mary Tyler Moore Show* was reunited. Mary, Cloris, Georgia, and I joined Betty on her television comedy *Hot in Cleveland*. It was so marvelous to go home again. And on April 17, my friend Muhammad Yunus was honored in Washington, D.C., with the Congressional Medal of Honor. There I was with Tony in the magnificent rotunda of the Capitol Building to witness this wonderful, inspiring citizen of the world, Yunus, receive this well-deserved recognition of his life's work. The same day we took the Acela Amtrak train to New York to attend a Broadway opening that my dear friend Lynne Meadow directed. And in early May, we attended the Kentucky Derby festivities (our pick, Orb, won the race!) and then flew back to New York, where my career began in the 1950s, to shoot material for a prime-time NBC special of my personal journey. Tony was keeping me too busy to be sick!

Then came Mother's Day, and I spent it in my garden planting flowers with Cristina. She'd brought a hanging fuchsia plant for me. Every plant Cristina has ever given me lasts forever. A little ficus plant about eight inches tall, which she had given me when she was seven, stands in our backyard to this day—and is now over nine feet tall, and thick with shiny, dark green leaves. So much to be grateful for!

In early June, my brain scan displayed some promising news. Both Dr. Natale and Dr. Rudnick were quite pleased, and said they never expected to be sitting talking with me in such condition. So far, so good. One day at a time.

Then came the most thrilling gift from more than ninety of my colleagues whom I'd worked with over the years in the hunger-ending effort. Some of these folks were with me at the launch of the Hunger Project in 1977 or on a fact-finding mission to East Africa in the 1980s. Others were from the End Hunger Network, LIFE, Results, and many other organizations that I've been lucky enough to be working with in the trenches. Charlie Deull (whom I've known and worked with since he was a teenager) and his wife, Laurel Dutcher, Joan Holmes, Joanna Ryder, and others initiated a creation of the Valerie Harper Women Leaders Fund. Oh my goodness, I have a foundation named after me! What an honor, and from these people whom I respect and love so much.

The funds they so generously provided will be administered by the Hunger Project to empower women in the developing world, who, against all odds, are expressing their personal leadership. This is an issue that has been close to my heart for the past forty years. What I experienced, by having this foundation established in my name, was a beautiful memorial while I was still alive. How many folks get to have that? I feel very honored and lucky.

What will tomorrow bring? Who knows! But right this instant, I am happy. I am at peace. I am filled with love.

Thank you for reading *I, Rhoda,* for being in Rhoda's life, and being there for Valerie's. Please know that I've had the most beautiful time in this world. And I'm so glad to have had you each be a part of it.

GREAT THINGS PEOPLE HAVE SAID

Nicole Barth, on the original three
female *Mary Tyler Moore* characters:
"Mary is who you wish you were.
Rhoda is who you probably are.
And Phyllis is who you're afraid you'll become."

Iva March Rifkin, on the unavoidable fact of aging:
"I don't mind getting old, I just don't want to look it."

Penny Almog, on dealing with the death of Zvi, her husband:
"I concentrate on his presence, not on his absence."

Arlene Golonka, on a banking problem:
"My check bounced because of insignificant funds."

Loren Lester, on stars' behavior toward others:
"Either you remember where you came from or you do not."

Gene Varrone, on what to do with
my four Emmy Awards:
**"Put a thick piece of glass on them
and you've got a coffee table."**

Cristina Cacciotti, on punctuality:
"If you are exactly on time, you're already late."

Howard Donald Harper, on avoiding
being late for appointments:
**"Make yourself leave your home
and don't do that 'one more thing.'"**

Angela Harper, on an action movie star
she didn't appreciate:
**"He doesn't act—what does he do?!?
He jumps off a bridge and blows himself up!"**

Virginia "Ginger" Harper, on intelligence:
**"Physical fitness is great but how about
a little mental fitness. Read a book!"**

Dr. Arman Hekmati, on health:
"Today, you can live a full life with cancer in check."

I, RHODA

Regarding a person who never seems to have all the facts:

Hazel Catmull: "'Tis a pity she's a shingle short."

John Amos:

"The thing is . . . she ain't wrapped tight."

Charlotte Brown:

"Yes, well . . . she owns property in Oz."

Victor Matosich, my nephew,

at eleven, on cursing:

**"Profanity is the attempt of a lazy
and feeble mind to express itself forcefully."**

Leah Matosich, my big sister,

on covering for me:

**"I won't tell Mom and Dad you broke my front tooth.
I'll say I fell."**

Eva Schaal, Dick's German grandma,

on dealing with a yelling husband:

**"When Herman gets angry and starts shouting,
I just say 'woof woof' and walk away!"**

AFTERWORD

Federico García Lorca,
on ending world hunger:
**"The day that hunger is eradicated from the earth,
there will be the greatest spiritual explosion
the world has ever known. Humanity cannot
imagine the joy that will burst into the world
on the day of that great revolution."**

Iva McConnell Harper,
on how to keep your balance:
**"It's not what happens to you in life
but how you handle it."**

Tony Cacciotti, on relationships:
"I love you, Val."

ACKNOWLEDGMENTS

At an awards ceremony, one of my favorite actors, Maureen Stapleton, said in her acceptance speech, "I'd like to thank everyone I have ever met in my life." Love Maureen! I think she expressed a certain existential truth—but there are certain people that I want to specifically single out and acknowledge, so here goes:

Tricia Boczkowski, my editor and spectacular support system, for her warm encouragement, excellent advice, skillful guidance, and avid appreciation of Rhoda Morgenstern.

Dan Strone, my literary agent, CEO of Trident Media Group, who assembled the necessary elements, including a title, for this book. Kseniya Zaslavskaya, Dan's industrious assistant, and Rick Hersh of Celebrity Consultants, who introduced me to Dan.

Ivy Pochoda, for her talent, time, and effort in providing a road map through seven decades of memories, and her diligent transcriber, Andrea Gallo.

ACKNOWLEDGMENTS

Louise Burke, my publisher at Simon & Schuster's Gallery Books, and her expert associates:

Jen Bergstrom, editor-in-chief

Alexandra Lewis, editorial assistant

Jen Robinson, publicity director

Carly Sommerstein, production editor

E. Beth Thomas, copy editor

For helping to resurrect Rhoda Morgenstern for the great cover, thank you:

Christopher Sergio, art director

Blake Little, cover photographer

Simon Tuke, stylist

Heather Currie, makeup artist

Heather Lloyd, my hairstylist, and Francesca Windsor, my hair colorist—dear friends both—of Lloyd-Windsor for Hair (LloydWindsor.com).

Dr. Andrew Frank, DDS, and Joseph Whaley, master ceramist, for brightening my smile.

Tony Cacciotti, for encouraging fitness, health, and proper eating all these years.

Thank you also to:

Michael Anthony Cacciotti, Tony's eldest and one of the finest, kindest, and most generous people I have ever known.

Feliza Vanderbilt Plowe, for your friendship, and for being a wonderful neighbor.

ACKNOWLEDGMENTS

Mimi Kirk, my superlative assistant, "Rhoda Look" source, seeker of truth-fun-love, and inspired vegan cookbook author of *Live Raw*; www.youngonrawfood.com.

Audrey Harris, for keeping me sane, laughing, and supported all through the *Rhoda* years.

Vera Hinic Deacon, for your expert, loving care of our family, especially Cristina and Mom.

Ana Miriam Jimenez, for all the remarkable, unending assistance you've given me and your sunny, ebullient spirit.

Bob Thomas, for all of your help, especially through the daunting terrain of cyberspace.

My siblings—Leah, Don, and Ginger—for living life with me.

My nieces and nephews—Victor, Anton, Tanya, Valerie, Russell, James Howard Harper, Angela Marie—darlings, all!

Tony's sons—Ronald, John, and "Little" Michael—three terrific guys!

Cristina Harper Cacciotti, my beautiful daughter, who I love and of whom I am endlessly proud.

Tony Cacciotti, again, for being the best partner imaginable in life, business, love, in everything in every way.

With gratitude for your inspiring work:

Joan Holmes, John Coonrod, Joanna Ryder, John Denver, Raul Julia, and Lynne Twist of the Hunger Project, committed to ending world hunger.

Sam Daley Harris, founder of RESULTS, and Joanne Carter,

executive director of RESULTS Educational Fund and for citizen efforts for the eradication of global poverty.

Dennis Weaver, Gerry Weaver, and Tony Cacciotti, founders, and Sandy Mullins, executive director, of LIFE (Love Is Feeding Everyone), a volunteer food distribution program for hungry Los Angelenos.

César Chávez and Dolores Huerta, founders of United Farm Workers, supporting justice in the fields and a safe food supply.

Gail Abarbanel, founder of the Rape Treatment Center of Santa Monica–UCLA Medical Center, supporting victims of rape.

Zane Buzby, founder of Survivor Mitzvah, aiding elderly, impoverished, and forgotten Jewish Holocaust survivors.

My Screen Actors Guild heroes:

Presidents: Ed Asner, William Daniels, and Alan Rosenberg

National officers: Kent McCord, Sumi Haru, Elliott Gould, Anne-Marie Johnson, and Connie Stevens

Board members: David Joliffe, Frances Fisher, George Coe, Joe D'Angerio, Tom Bower, Gary Epps, Jane Austin, Nancy Sinatra, Michael Bell, Renée Taylor, Joe Bologna, Lainie Kazan, Diane Ladd, Jane Austin, France Nuyen, Scott Wilson, Renee Aubry, Loren Lester, Ed Harris, Martin Sheen, Clancy Brown, Esai Morales, Bob Carlson, Russell McConnell, Bonnie Bartlett, Jeff Austin, Justine Bateman, Scott Bakula, and any other actor on or off the board who fought for our union.

James L. Brooks and Allan Burns, thank you for creating RHODA MORGENSTERN.

PHOTO CREDITS

PHOTO CREDITS